HEALTH AND SAFETY – ARE YOU AT RISK?

HEALTH AND SAFETY

ARE YOU AT RISK?

Martin W. Hopkins
Partner in Eversheds Wells & Hind, Birmingham

Martin H. Warren
Partner in Eversheds Phillips & Buck, Cardiff

CCH Editions Limited
TAX, BUSINESS AND LAW PUBLISHERS

Published by CCH Editions Limited
Telford Road, Bicester, Oxfordshire OX6 0XD
Tel. (0869) 253300. Facsimile (0869) 245814.
DX: 83750 Bicester 2.

USA	Commerce Clearing House, Inc., Chicago, Illinois.
CANADA	CCH Canadian Limited, Toronto, Ontario.
AUSTRALIA	CCH Australia Limited, North Ryde, NSW.
NEW ZEALAND	CCH New Zealand Limited, Auckland.
SINGAPORE	CCH Asia Limited.
JAPAN	CCH Japan Limited, Tokyo.

This publication is designed to provide accurate and authoritative information in regard to the subject-matter covered. It is sold with the understanding that the publisher is not engaged in rendering legal or other professional services. If legal advice or other expert assistance is required, the services of a competent professional person should be sought.

The publisher advises that the legislation in this publication is not the authorised official version. In its preparation, however, the greatest care has been taken to ensure exact conformity with the law as enacted.

While copyright in all the legislation resides in the Crown, copyright in indexes and annotations relating to the legislation is vested in the publisher.

Ownership of Trade Marks

The Trade Marks

CCH ACCESS, COMPUTAX and COMMERCE CLEARING HOUSE, INC.

are the property of Commerce Clearing House, Incorporated, Chicago, Illinois, USA

British Library Cataloguing in Publication Data.
A catalogue record for this book is available from the British Library.

ISBN 0 86325 317 2

© **1993 CCH Editions Limited**
All rights reserved. No part of this work covered by the publisher's copyright may be reproduced or copied in any form or by any means (graphic, electronic or mechanical, including photocopying, recording, recording taping, or information and retrieval systems) without the written permission of the publisher.

Typeset in Great Britain by ROM-Data Corporation Ltd, Falmouth, Cornwall.
Printed and bound in Great Britain by The Eastern Press Limited, Reading.

Preface

Our sympathy for the large number of professional advisers and business people who endeavour to understand and comply with the constant flow of new health and safety legislation has prompted us to provide a practical and no nonsense guide to the new health and safety regulations introduced on 1 January 1993.

We are keenly aware from our experience that many textbooks only make things worse by adding to the level of detail to be grappled with rather than simplifying it. This book does not fall into that trap because it has not been designed to be a full discussion of every point of detail which these regulations cover. Instead it gives an overview of each of the new regulations and highlights what we see as the most important features of each, giving practical guidance drawn from our own experience along the way.

The book is not intended to be a replacement for a detailed examination of the regulations themselves, and the guidance notes and approved codes of practice published by the HSE, if any or all of them have a direct impact upon your business. It will, however, help you to establish quickly whether any of the regulations are likely to have such an impact so that you only have to undertake that detailed examination when it is absolutely necessary.

We should like to thank our colleagues Therese Embley, Rachel Kidley and Sarah Winter for their invaluable help in all aspects of the research for and preparation of this book.

The law is stated as at 1 January 1993.

Martin Hopkins
Martin Warren
Eversheds

About the Publisher

CCH Editions Limited is part of a world-wide group of companies that specialises in tax, business and law publishing. The group produces a wide range of books and reporting services for the accounting, business and legal professions. The Oxfordshire premises are the centre for all UK and European operations.

All CCH publications are designed to be practical and authoritative and are written by CCH's own highly qualified and experienced editorial team and specialist outside authors.

In the UK CCH Editions currently produces a comprehensive series of reporting services on UK and international tax, business and law, and many books covering specific areas of interest for accountants, lawyers and business managers. Irrespective of the subject matter being discussed or the depth and scope of its treatment, the material is always dealt with in the same clear and concise manner.

CCH is committed to you and your information needs, and this commitment is reflected in the constant updating and development of our reporting services and the growth and expansion of our range of publications.

If you would like to know more about our books or loose-leaf services telephone (0869) 253300.

About the Author

Eversheds is one of Europe's largest law practices and has over 200 partners, 1,700 staff and 36 specialist teams covering almost any business law requirement. Eversheds has offices in London and 11 other commercial centres across the UK.

The principle contributors are:

Martin Hopkins, a partner, who heads up the Birmingham office employment law unit and has specialised in employment, and health and safety law for 11 years. Martin also lectures regularly on these topics throughout the country.

Martin Warren, a partner in the Cardiff office, who specialises in employment and environmental law advising companies, corporations, and the public sector. He is a director of Principle Training Ltd and a part-time lecturer on environmental law at the University of Wales College of Cardiff.

Acknowledgement

The statutory instruments set out in Part II of this book are Crown Copyright and are reproduced with the kind permission of the Controller of Her Majesty's Stationery Office.

The EC directives set out in Part III of this book are reproduced with the kind permission of the Office for Official Publications of the European Communities.

Contents

	Page
Preface	v
About the Publisher	vi
About the Author	vii
Acknowledgement	viii
Glossary	xiii

Part I – Lawyer's Opinion

1 Introduction   3

¶101	What regulations?	3
¶102	Existing health and safety legislation	4
¶103	What does 'so far as reasonably practicable' mean?	5
¶104	The consequence of non-compliance with the regulations	5
¶105	Approved codes of practice and guidance notes issued by the HSC/HSE	6
¶106	Construction sites	6
¶107	Beware scaremongers	6

2 The Management of Health and Safety at Work Regulations 1992 (The Framework Regulations)   7

¶201	What is the purpose of the Framework Regulations and why are they needed?	7
¶202	Should I be concerned about the Framework Regulations?	7
¶203	What are the essential features of the Framework Regulations upon which I should concentrate?	8
¶204	Risk assessment (reg. 3)	8
¶205	Arrangements for protective and preventative measures	10
¶206	Appointment of competent people to assist with protective and preventative measures (reg. 6)	16
¶207	Complying with the Framework Regulations – is it worth it?	17

Health and Safety – Are You at Risk?

	Page

3 The Personal Protective Equipment at Work Regulations 1992 (The PPE Regulations) — 18

¶301 What is the purpose of the PPE Regulations and why are they needed? — 18
¶302 Should I be concerned about the PPE Regulations? — 19
¶303 What are the essential features of the PPE Regulations upon which I should concentrate? — 20
¶304 Complying with the PPE Regulations – is it worth it? — 24

4 The Provision and Use of Work Equipment Regulations 1992 (The Work Equipment Regulations) — 25

¶401 What is the purpose of the Work Equipment Regulations and why are they needed? — 25
¶402 Relationship with existing health and safety legislation — 25
¶403 Relationship with other new health and safety legislation — 25
¶404 Essential features of the Work Equipment Regulations — 26
¶405 Do the Work Equipment Regulations apply to me? — 26
¶406 What do the Work Equipment Regulations say? — 27

5 The Health and Safety (Display Screen Equipment) Regulations 1992 (The VDU Regulations) — 33

¶501 What is the purpose of the VDU Regulations and why are they needed? — 33
¶502 Should I be concerned about the VDU Regulations? — 33
¶503 The scope of the VDU Regulations — 33
¶504 What are the essential features of the VDU Regulations upon which I should concentrate? — 35
¶505 Risk assessment (reg. 2) — 36
¶506 Workstation requirements (reg. 3) — 38
¶507 Work routines (reg. 4) — 39
¶508 Eye and eyesight tests (reg. 5) — 39
¶509 Provision of training and information (regs. 6 and 7) — 40
¶510 Complying with the VDU Regulations – is it worth it? — 41

6 The Manual Handling Operations Regulations 1992 (The Manual Handling Regulations) — 43

¶601 What is the purpose of the Manual Handling Regulations and why are they needed? — 43
¶602 Should I be concerned about the Manual Handling Regulations? — 43

Contents

		Page
¶603	What are the essential features of the Manual Handling Regulations upon which I should concentrate?	44
¶604	Complying with the Manual Handling Regulations – is it worth it?	50

7 The Workplace (Health, Safety and Welfare) Regulations 1992 (The Workplace Regulations) — 52

¶701	What is the purpose of the Workplace Regulations and why are they needed?	52
¶702	Should I be concerned about the Workplace Regulations?	53
¶703	What are the essential features of the Workplace Regulations upon which I should concentrate?	54
¶704	Maintenance (reg. 5)	54
¶705	Ventilation (reg. 6)	55
¶706	Temperature (reg. 7)	55
¶707	Lighting (reg. 8)	55
¶708	Cleanliness and waste materials (reg. 9)	56
¶709	Room dimensions and space (reg. 10)	56
¶710	Workstations and seating (reg. 11)	56
¶711	Traffic routes (reg. 12)	56
¶712	Falls or falling objects (reg. 13)	57
¶713	Windows, transparent or translucent doors, gates and walls (reg. 14)	58
¶714	Windows, skylights and ventilators (reg. 15)	58
¶715	Ability to clean windows, etc. safely (reg. 16)	58
¶716	Organisation, etc. of traffic routes (reg. 17)	59
¶717	Doors and gates (reg. 18)	59
¶718	Escalators and moving walkways (reg. 19)	60
¶719	Sanitary conveniences (reg. 20)	60
¶720	Washing facilities (reg. 21)	60
¶721	Drinking water (reg. 22)	61
¶722	Accommodation for clothing (reg. 23)	61
¶723	Facilities for changing clothing (reg. 24)	61
¶724	Facilities for rest and to eat meals (reg. 25)	62
¶725	Complying with the Workplace Regulations – is it worth it?	62

Part II – Regulations

The Management of Health and Safety at Work Regulations 1992 (SI 1992/2051) — 65

The Personal Protective Equipment at Work Regulations 1992 (SI 1992/2966) — 77

	Page
The Provision and Use of Work Equipment Regulations 1992 (SI 1992/2932)	90
The Health and Safety (Display Screen Equipment) Regulations 1992 (SI 1992/2792)	105
The Manual Handling Operations Regulations 1992 (SI 1992/2793)	113
The Workplace (Health, Safety and Welfare) Regulations 1992 (SI 1992/3004)	119

Part III – EC Directives

Council Directive 89/391 (12 June 1989) on the introduction of measures to encourage improvements in the safety and health of workers at work	137
Council Directive 89/656 (30 November 1989) on the minimum health and safety requirements for the use by workers of personal protective equipment at the workplace (third individual directive within the meaning of Article 16(1) of Directive 89/391/EEC)	148
Council Directive 89/655 (30 November 1989) concerning the minimum safety and health requirements for the use of work equipment by workers at work (second individual directive within the meaning of Article 16(1) of Directive 89/391/EEC)	160
Council Directive 90/270 (29 May 1990) on the minimum safety and health requirements for work with display screen equipment (fifth individual directive within the meaning of Article 16(1) of Directive 87/391/EEC)	167
Council Directive 90/269 (29 May 1990) on the minimum health and safety requirements for the manual handling of loads where there is a risk particularly of back injury to workers (fourth individual directive within the meaning of Article 16(1) of Directive 89/391/EEC)	173
Council Directive 89/654 (30 November 1989) concerning the minimum safety and health requirements for the workplace (first individual directive within the meaning of Article 16(1) of Directive 89/391/EEC)	178
Index	191

Glossary

The following terms are used in this book:

ACOP	Approved Code of Practice
COSHH	The Control of Substances Hazardous to Health Regulations 1988 (SI 1988/1657)
The Framework Regulations	The Management of Health and Safety at Work Regulations 1992 (SI 1992/2051)
HSC	The Health and Safety Commission
HSE	The Health and Safety Executive
The Manual Handling Regulations	The Manual Handling Operations Regulations 1992 (SI 1992/2793)
OSRPA	The Offices, Shops and Railway Premises Act 1963
The PPE Regulations	The Personal Protective Equipment at Work Regulations 1992 (SI 1992/2966)
The VDU Regulations	The Health and Safety (Display Screen Equipment) Regulations 1992 (SI 1992/2792)
The Work Equipment Regulations	The Provision and Use of Work Equipment Regulations 1992 (SI 1992/2932)
The Workplace Regulations	The Workplace (Health, Safety and Welfare) Regulations 1992 (SI 1992/3004)
The 1961 Act	The Factories Act 1961
The 1974 Act	The Health and Safety at Work etc. Act 1974

PART I
LAWYER'S OPINION

1 Introduction

¶101 What regulations?

The year 1993 is one of dramatic change for UK health and safety law. It has long been a goal of the European Community to harmonise and heighten health and safety at work standards throughout the Community. In 1989 it started to make that goal a reality by adopting what has become known as the 'Framework' or 'Mother' Directive which identifies in one document the general duties to be imposed on employers so as to protect the health and safety of their employees and others. The first five of a theoretically never-ending series of 'daughter' directives followed covering specific health and safety risks associated with:

(1) the manual handling of loads;

(2) display screen equipment;

(3) the workplace;

(4) the use of work equipment; and

(5) the use of personal protective equipment at work.

All member states were under a duty to adopt these six directives into their own national law by the end of 1992. Hence the following regulations were introduced into UK law with effect from 1 January 1993:

(1) the Framework Regulations (implementing the 'Framework' Directive);

(2) the Manual Handling Regulations;

(3) the VDU Regulations;

(4) the Workplace Regulations;

(5) the Work Equipment Regulations; and

(6) the PPE Regulations.

These regulations not only cover all types of work activity but, in certain cases, duties are imposed on the self-employed and are owed to non-employees (such as the general public) who may be at risk from certain working activities.

Employers are required to comply with the standards set down by each of the six regulations from 1 January 1993.

¶102 Existing health and safety legislation

It should be remembered that certain work activities may not only be subject to the new regulations but also to existing legislation. Whenever this occurs it will be the higher of the two standards which must be satisfied.

A brief refresher course on existing health and safety law is therefore worthwhile. The common law imposes a duty on employers to take reasonable care to protect their employees' health and safety. Additionally, certain more specific obligations are imposed by statute such as:

(1) The 1974 Act

Under the 1974 Act an employer (in respect of their employees) is obliged, so far as is reasonably practicable, to:

- provide and maintain a safe working environment and safe systems of work;
- make arrangements to ensure safety and the absence of health risks connected with the use, handling, storage and transport of articles and substances;
- provide information, instruction, training and supervision to ensure the health and safety of employees;
- maintain the workplace (and access to and exit from it) in a condition that is safe and without risks; and
- provide and maintain a safe working environment free from health risks and provide adequate welfare facilities.

Both employers and the self-employed are under a duty to carry out their work, so far as is reasonably practicable, as to ensure that persons not in their employment, but who may be affected by their working activity, are not exposed to risks to their health and safety.

An employer employing five or more employees must draw up and, where appropriate, revise, a written statement of their health and safety policy and bring it to the notice of all employees.

An employer must recognise safety representatives appointed by a recognised trade union and consult with them about measures to be taken to ensure the health and safety of employees.

(2) COSHH; the Noise at Work Regulations 1989

These regulations impose a duty on employers to carry out risk assessments. It may be that if you have already carried out a risk assessment pursuant to COSHH then you will not have to repeat the task in order to comply with the six new regulations, but merely review that assessment, in the light of the more specific duties of the new regulations.

(3) The 1961 Act and OSRPA

The new regulations seek to eliminate the distinction between shops, offices, etc. and factories by introducing a common standard of health, safety and welfare for every workplace. There is a considerable overlap between the provisions of the 1961 Act and OSRPA and the obligations imposed, in particular, by the Workplace Regulations, to protect the health and safety of everyone in the workplace and to ensure that certain minimum welfare facilities are provided.

¶103 What does 'so far as reasonably practicable' mean?

These words have always been common in UK legislation and are scattered liberally throughout the new regulations. They are, however, frustratingly imprecise and their use, in any context, does not help the employer to know how far they are obliged to go.

The best guidance which we feel that we can give is to point out that in deciding whether something is 'reasonably practicable' you need to carry out a balancing exercise to weigh the risk to health and safety against the sacrifice (in terms of time, trouble and money) of implementing any measures needed to avoid it. It is only if the sacrifice is grossly disproportionate to the risk that you may consider the measures not to be 'reasonably practicable'.

¶104 The consequence of non-compliance with the regulations

The new regulations do not bring any new types of penalty with them, but a summary of existing penalties will do no harm.

Inspectors appointed by the HSE and local authorities are responsible for enforcement of all health and safety legislation. They have wide-ranging powers enabling them, for example, to enter premises and take copies of records, photographs or samples of substances found.

If the inspector feels that a statutory provision has been contravened then he may serve either an improvement notice (requiring the contravention to be remedied within a certain time period) or, if he feels that there is an imminent risk of personal injury, a prohibition notice (requiring that the activity in question not be carried out until the contravention is remedied).

Further, s. 33 of the 1974 Act makes it a criminal offence for a person to contravene health and safety legislation, the penalties include fines and/or imprisonment. Most importantly, directors, managers and other similar officers can be prosecuted personally where it is shown that they have consented to, or connived at, the commission of any offence or where an offence has been caused by neglect on their part.

A breach of, or non-compliance with, health and safety legislation can also form the basis of a civil action, normally when the alleged breach or non-compliance has resulted in personal injury. It can also be seen as a breach of individual contracts of employment entitling the employee to resign and claim that he has been unfairly dismissed.

¶105 Approved codes of practice and guidance notes issued by the HSC/HSE

The Framework Regulations and the Workplace Regulations are supported by an ACOP which has been produced by the HSC. Although failure to comply with the code is not in itself an offence, it may be taken as proof that a person has contravened the relevant regulation. It would, however, be open to the individual to prove that they had complied with the regulation in some other way.

The HSE have produced guidance notes on the remaining four new regulations.

¶106 Construction sites

It is worth mentioning one set of regulations not yet available, remembering that we have pointed out earlier that the flow of directives from Europe on very specific issues is going to be fairly constant. New regulations are being developed in the UK in order to implement the Temporary and Mobile Construction Sites Directive adopted on 24 June 1992 regarding construction site management. It is envisaged that these regulations will come into force in January 1994 and that they will be accompanied by a new approved code supplementing the code published in connection with the Framework Regulations. Therefore, if you are involved with the construction industry, look out for these new regulations and the new code of practice.

¶107 Beware scaremongers

It is very important to keep everything in perspective. Although these new regulations are wide-ranging, their objective is mainly to supplement and clarify existing duties set out in existing legislation. You should also remember that many of the duties expressly set out in the new regulations are actually implicit in the 1974 Act and so if you have a good existing health and safety record then you should also find that compliance with the new regulations is not that onerous a task.

2 The Management of Health and Safety at Work Regulations 1992
(The Framework Regulations)

¶201 What is the purpose of the Framework Regulations and why are they needed?

The EC's main desire is to introduce minimum basic health and safety standards throughout the Community. The first step is to require all member states to introduce a general framework of health and safety law such as the one which we have been working to in the UK since 1974 and which is contained in the 1974 Act. This is therefore the purpose of these regulations which came into force on 1 January 1993, and which run alongside the 1974 Act.

Because the 1974 Act is fairly comprehensive, this particular set of regulations is not going to have such a major effect as some of the other legislation that came into force on the same date, which is designed to put flesh on the bones of the general framework, and which will be discussed later on in this book. Such effect as these regulations will have upon the framework created by the 1974 Act will be highlighted below.

¶202 Should I be concerned about the Framework Regulations?

Undoubtedly, the answer to this question must be yes. They apply to almost all working activities excepting those specifically referred to in the regulations as being excluded such as seamen. They apply to all businesses regardless of size, although the nature, extent and cost of the measures which will need to be taken to ensure compliance will vary depending on the nature of the health and safety hazards and level of risks associated with different industries.

Certain duties are imposed not only on employers but also on the self-employed, while others are owed not only to employees but also to non-employees who may be affected by the work activity, for example the general public, visitors, contract cleaners or security guards.

¶203 What are the essential features of the Framework Regulations upon which I should concentrate?

The three key areas of the new regulations concern:

(1) risk assessments (reg. 3);

(2) arrangements for protective and preventative measures (reg. 4); and

(3) the appointment of competent people to assist with protective and preventative measures (reg. 6).

These key areas are looked at in more detail below.

¶204 Risk assessment (reg. 3)

In many ways, risk assessment is the key to these regulations because it requires people to examine their own working environment so as to identify what specific steps need to be taken to ensure that all other health and safety obligations (whether in these new regulations or anywhere else) are being complied with. It requires you to be your own gamekeeper.

Risk assessment has four central features:

(1) The identification of hazards. This will probably be the most difficult part of the whole process and the one where it is most likely that you will need outside help, either from professionals, employers' associations, trade press, company or supplier manuals or from the HSE itself.

(2) The quantification of the likelihood of each hazard occurring. You are only expected to cater for hazards which are reasonably foreseeable; you need not cover every eventuality. However, in assessing the likelihood of something going wrong you must work from the working practices which *are* followed rather than those which *should* be followed.

(3) You should note that the ACOP published with these regulations makes it clear that you will be expected to have read any relevant material such as HSE guidance notes, trade publications, and company or supplier manuals in order to familiarise yourself with hazards and risks associated with your work activity.

(4) The evaluation of the consequences of each hazard occurring. How many people might be affected and what sort of injuries might be caused.

There are three additional obligations which follow on from the completed risk assessment as follows:

(1) To identify and implement protective or preventative measures which are needed to minimise or eliminate the hazards which have been identified. For example, should outdated equipment be replaced, should protective equipment

be purchased or should training be given? This particular issue will be examined in a little more detail in ¶205 below.

(2) To review and revise the risk assessment on a regular basis. In reality, assessment has to be an ongoing process if it is to have any real value. The hazards themselves can change, equipment can become ineffective and people can get out of good and safe working habits which they need to be reminded of. We would advise that it is essential to carry out a review after any accidents occur.

(3) To record the results of the risk assessment. This is only an obligation for employers employing more than four people, although we would strongly recommend that anybody making a risk assessment should keep a record of it. The record should be in writing or on computer disc or tape and should cover the main findings of the assessment, details of steps taken to reduce risks which have been found and to identify any individuals felt to be especially at risk. Details of the points considered will help to establish that the assessment carried out was 'suitable'.

The ACOP provides that trivial risks, or risks arising from routine activities associated with life in general, can be ignored unless the work activity compounds that risk or unless it is especially relevant to the particular work activity. However, we would advise that unless it would be an excessively onerous task, you should play safe and, if any risk exists, assess it.

The duty to carry out a risk assessment falls on both employers and the self-employed and must cover the risks not only to employees (and in the case of the self-employed, his/herself) but also to *anyone* who might be affected by their working activities, such as visitors to, or contractors on, the premises.

The question of how extensive a risk assessment needs to be depends largely upon the nature of your individual business and the number of hazardous activities which it involves. It will often, but not always, be the case that the larger the business the more extensive the risk assessment will need to be.

Example

Hack & Sons is a small firm of solicitors. It employs four solicitors, an office manager, five secretaries and an office junior.

The senior partner asks the office manager to read, in detail, the new health and safety regulations. The office manager must then carry out a risk assessment of all work activities in the firm.

In addition, all members of staff are asked to spend one hour in the afternoon considering the risks and health hazards which they have identified as being associated with their own particular work activities. They are asked to record this self-assessment in writing and to give it to the office manager by the end of the week.

¶204

The office manager is told that once he has prepared a written record of the risk assessment and the protective or preventative measures needed, he must prepare a summary of the report and circulate it to all employees. This report must also include details of all information required to be given to employees by virtue of reg. 8 (see ¶205(4)).

This memo should also make it clear to the employees what is expected of them as regards health and safety in the workplace.

The memo should stipulate that if any employee is found, for example, not to be using equipment in accordance with health and safety training given to them then this will be treated as an act of misconduct and the disciplinary procedure will be brought into effect.

Similarly if it is evident that an employee was aware of the serious danger to health and safety in the office and did not inform his/her employer of this then this will be treated as an act of misconduct.

¶205 Arrangements for protective and preventative measures

As mentioned at ¶204 above, the key to the new regulations is the risk assessment. The natural follow on to that is the obligation mentioned briefly above to identify and implement protective and preventative measures needed to minimise or eliminate the hazards identified through the risk assessment. It is worth examining that obligation in more detail.

(1) Health and safety arrangements

Regulation 4 imposes a duty on an employer to draw up and implement a health and safety scheme which, like the risk assessment, must be recorded if more than four employees are employed, and should cover the following four points:

(1) Planning, i.e. it should set the objectives and priorities seen as the keys to reducing or minimising risks and identify how it is intended to achieve these objectives.

(2) Organisation, i.e. it should state how and when protective and preventative measures will be introduced in order to ensure that there is a progressive improvement in health and safety.

(3) Control, i.e. it should provide for a system that will ensure that the protective and preventative measures will actually be implemented and not just remain as plans.

(4) Monitoring and review, i.e. it should stipulate how and when the protective and preventative measures will be monitored as to their effectiveness and how they will be adapted if necessary.

Parts of the new regulations give more specific guidance as to the type of protective and/or preventative measures which should be taken.

The Management of Health and Safety at Work Regulations 1992 11

(2) Health surveillance
Regulation 5 provides that appropriate health surveillance must be provided by an employer where risks to health and safety have been identified by the risk assessment. For example, employer A runs a factory where nickel is produced by a particular work activity. A medical specialist who assisted with the risk assessment has advised that lung cancer is a disease believed to be associated with this process.

One of the measures which employer A should therefore take is to set up individual health records for each worker involved in this process. Clinical examinations should also be arranged at set intervals and the specialist's advice should be taken as to who should carry out the examination and how often it should happen.

(3) Emergency procedures
Regulation 7 requires employers, as part of the health and safety scheme, referred to in ¶205(1) above, to establish and implement procedures to be followed in the event that *any person at work* (i.e. not just employees) is exposed to serious and imminent danger, such as fire (relevant to all types of environment), or the escape of poisonous gases. The procedure should be notified to all employees and, as before, should be recorded where more than four employees are employed. The procedure should:

- inform people of the nature of the hazard and the steps being taken to protect them;
- enable them (by giving clear guidance so that action can be taken without further instruction) to stop work and go to a place of safety if they are exposed to serious and imminent danger; and
- save in exceptional circumstances (e.g. emergency service workers) require them not to resume work until the danger has passed.

The employer must also nominate and identify in the procedure a competent person(s) (this definition is dealt with later at ¶206) to deal with evacuation of the premises, for example, a fire officer.

Remember that the duties imposed by reg. 7 require you to inform 'any persons at work' exposed to dangers of the nature of the hazard and the steps being taken to protect them.

Consider also the visitors who come to your premises. Are they all made aware of the hazards involved with your work activity? Do you explain your fire evacuation procedures to all of them?

Example
Jane Smith has just started work at her local railway station as a ticket salesperson/inspector. On her first day she is given various health and safety leaflets issued by her employer including one headed 'bomb alerts'. The document sets out:

¶205

(1) what she should do if she sees an unaccompanied box or parcel in the station and who she should report the matter to (Mr Thompson);
(2) what steps Mr Thompson will take on receiving this information;
(3) when she hears the station alarm bell she must leave the premises immediately, without waiting for instruction, and proceed to a place of safety (this place is identified in the leaflet) and, when she gets there, report to Mr Thompson;
(4) that she must not return to the station until advised to do so by Mr Thompson.

Jane is told by other members of staff that practices of this procedure take place from time to time.

(4) Information for employees

Regulation 8 obliges an employer to give his employees (including temporary staff) full information presented in an easy to understand way about:

- the hazards identified by the risk assessment;
- the preventative and protective measures being taken;
- any 'serious and imminent danger' procedures including the identity of the 'competent person' nominated in respect of them; and
- any information which the employer may have received from another employer who shares the workplace regarding risks arising out of that second employer's business.

Although there is no stipulation that this information needs to be provided in writing it has to be sensible to do so.

Example

An employer runs a small business and employs a large number of Asian and Chinese workers, some of whom either do not speak English or are not completely fluent in English.

The employer is aware of his obligations, under reg. 8, to provide information on all risks, preventative measures and procedures, etc. to his staff. The employer therefore:

- Arranges for a staff memo (incorporating all of the relevant information listed in reg. 8) to be translated into the appropriate languages which his employees will fully understand.
- Makes sure that those who have problems reading (the employer also employs some people with learning difficulties) are spoken to about the relevant information and that this information is clearly communicated and explained to them. The employer has also had drawn up several notices which

The Management of Health and Safety at Work Regulations 1992   13

are placed in conspicuous areas of the workplace. These notices have symbols and diagrams which clearly indicate, for example, health hazards around the workplace, fire exits, etc.

(5) Capabilities and training

Regulation 11 provides that an employer must take into account, when giving employees tasks to do, their capabilities (including their understanding of the hazards associated with the particular tasks) so that the demands of the tasks are not such that they exceed the employees capability and as a result place themselves or others at risk.

The same regulation requires employers to provide periodic adequate health and safety training (at the recruitment stage and periodically afterwards) which should be adapted on an ongoing basis to reflect any changes to the risks associated with the work activity and also any changes in duties.

(6) Outside workers

Regulation 10 imposes obligations on employers and the self-employed in relation to a category of people referred to as 'outside workers'. In simple terms, these are employees of other employers who are working on your premises. The employees of a subcontractor on a building site would be a classic example.

Regulation 10 requires that the employer of the 'outside worker' (e.g. the subcontractor in the example used above) is given comprehensive information about:

- the hazards arising out of the work activity; and
- the protective and preventative measures being taken in relation to those 'outside workers'.

The employer of the outside workers must be given enough information to be able to identify the 'competent person' nominated in respect of the 'serious and imminent danger procedures', and must take all reasonable steps to ensure that the outside workers themselves actually receive sufficient information to identify that 'competent person'.

Example

Bill runs a small tool manufacturing company. His accountants have informed him that they are going to send a member of staff to his premises in order to audit the year end accounts.

Bill writes to the partner of the firm of accountants and states:

(1) the risks of injury to which the auditor may be exposed and which are associated with the manufacturing processes that take place on his premises;

(2) the measures that he intends to take to ensure that the auditor will not be exposed to these risks;

(3) the fact that Mr Stevenson (the works supervisor) is the person who will implement evacuation procedures in the case of an emergency.

¶205

Bill then writes to the auditor and notifies him of the possible risks to his health and safety. He also provides comprehensible information and instructions regarding those risks.

On the day the auditor arrives he is introduced to Mr Stevenson the works supervisor and told that he deals with evacuation of the premises in cases of emergencies.

(7) Temporary workers

Regulation 13 imposes duties in respect of 'temporary workers', which term includes employees on fixed-term contracts and employment agency staff.

Every employer must give to a person employed on a fixed-term contract, before they commence employment, full information about:

- any specific qualifications or skills which they need to carry out their work safely; and
- any health surveillance that is to be provided for them.

Example

Matthew Johnson is about to start work at a private nursing home as a physiotherapist. He is employed on a fixed-term contract for six months whilst the existing physiotherapist is on maternity leave.

A week before he is due to start work he is asked to attend the nursing home so that he can be shown around. At that meeting he is told:

(1) to carry out his work safely he will need to have a degree (or diploma) in physiotherapy;

(2) at certain intervals in the six month period he will be asked to meet with the nursing home's medical officer to discuss (and if necessary undergo an examination) regarding back or muscle strain resulting from the lifting and turning of patients;

(3) when he starts work he will be given a pamphlet called 'Your Health & Safety'. This will provide him with comprehensive information about the risks of the workplace, precautions taken and evacuation procedures set up as a result of a risk assessment carried out (see reg. 8 at ¶205(4) above).

After the meeting Matthew is given a letter confirming these points in writing.

Every employer and self-employed person must give an employment agency worker the information referred to above. They must also provide the staff agency employer with details of any specific qualifications or skills needed to carry out the work solely and details of any special features of the job that might affect health and safety. The staff agency employer is then under a duty to pass this information on to their employees.

¶205

Example

Gail Townsend works for a nursing agency. Her agency have entered into a contract with the nursing home for her to work two evening shifts a week.

When Gail arrives to start work she is spoken to by the nursing home manager. She is told that she needs to have been on a training course regarding manual handling in order to carry out her work safely, if she has not, one must be arranged immediately. She too will be asked to discuss with the medical officer any strains she might experience in helping to lift or turn patients. She is also provided with information and instructions regarding all risks to health and safety associated with the working of the nursing home and sufficient information for her to identify the person responsible for emergency evacuation (see reg. 10 at ¶205(6) above). She is also given details of all information required to be given to employees pursuant to reg. 8 (see ¶205(4) above). All of this is confirmed to her in writing.

The nursing home manager has already spoken and written to the owner of the nursing agency and told her that:

(1) Gail needs to have received training in respect of manual handling in order to do her job safely;

(2) in view of the fact that many of the residents are very old and infirm, she will be asked to assist with a great deal of lifting and turning of patients. Hence there is a risk of personal injury, and this information needs to be passed on to Gail.

The nursing home manager also sets out all other additional information required to be given to an 'outside worker's' employer by virtue of reg. 10 (see ¶205(6) above) such as details of the preventative and protective measures being taken in relation to the risks identified and sufficient information for the employer to identify the 'competent person' in charge of evacuation procedures.

(8) Co-operation and co-ordination

Regulation 9 provides that when two or more employers (including the self-employed who themselves have employees) share a workplace, on a temporary or permanent basis, each must:

- co-operate with the other to ensure that their respective obligations under all health and safety legislation are met;
- take all reasonable steps to co-ordinate the measures that they are each taking in order to comply with all health and safety legislation; and
- exchange information with the other about the risks to the other's employees which arise out of or in connection with their own work activities.

In practical terms, it will also be necessary in such a situation for the two risk assessments and 'serious and imminent danger procedures' of employers sharing a work site to be co-ordinated.

(9) Employees' duties

Regulation 12 creates obligations on employees in relation to their own health and safety. For example, they are obliged to make proper use (in accordance with training and instruction they have received) of machinery and equipment, dangerous substances, transport equipment, means of production and safety devices. They are also under a duty to inform their employer, or their employer's representative, of anything they think may be a serious danger or a shortcoming in the employer's arrangements for health and safety.

We would advise that in order to prevent your employees from ignoring any health and safety instructions given to them or neglecting to use any protective equipment supplied to them, you make it clear (either in contracts of employment or your disciplinary procedure) that a failure to comply with the duties placed on employees by virtue of reg. 12 will be considered to be misconduct and will be treated accordingly as a disciplinary offence. Remember, if you do find that someone is ignoring your health and safety standards you must implement the disciplinary procedure (e.g. by giving the employee a warning) so that you protect your own position and are seen to be effectively implementing the measures identified by the risk assessment.

¶206 Appointment of competent people to assist with protective and preventative measures (reg. 6)

Regulation 6 requires every employer (other than sole traders and partnerships) to appoint one or more 'competent persons' to help implement the measures needed to comply with all obligations under all health and safety legislation. Additionally, the employer must ensure:

- that where more than one person has been appointed that there is adequate co-operation between them;
- that the number of persons appointed, the time available to them in order to fulfil their function and the means available to them are adequate having regard to the size of the undertaking, and the level and nature of risks involved;
- that any 'competent person' not in the employer's employment is told of all factors, known to, or suspected by, the employer which have the potential to affect the health and safety of anyone coming into contact with the business; and
- that the 'competent person' is told which people working for the employer are temporary (i.e. employed on a fixed-term contract) and which are agency employed staff.

Sadly, however, the new regulations do not give a precise definition of a 'competent person' but only vague guidance. They refer to somebody with 'sufficient training and experience or knowledge and other qualities'. This does not necessarily mean that the person has to be a specialist, or qualified in any way, or even engaged full time in health and safety work.

At the end of the day different levels of 'competence' will be required in different environments. In an extreme case, such as a large chemical plant, a team of full time, fully trained, health and safety specialists will be needed. At the other extreme in a small business, where there are few or minimal risks, a 'competent person' might be a particular employee who has a good knowledge of the working activity and the hazards associated with that work activity, knows their own limitations, and is willing and able to expand upon their own health and safety knowledge and experience.

The HSC ACOP gives some very useful tips about what an employer should consider in deciding whether a person is 'competent'.

The rules do not apply to a sole trader who is personally 'competent' to undertake any necessary measures. Similarly in a partnership, where one partner can be described as 'competent', there is no need to seek the assistance of others, so long as that partner ensures that the other partners co-operate in taking the necessary measures.

¶207 Complying with the Framework Regulations – is it worth it?

The consequences of non-compliance with the regulations are detailed at ¶104 above and will hopefully convince employers that it is worth complying with the regulations.

There is, however, a more positive aspect to all this, because anything which reduces the risk of suffering to employees or others and/or which reduces absenteeism thereby saving money has to be worthwhile.

3 The Personal Protective Equipment at Work Regulations 1992
(The PPE Regulations)

¶301 What is the purpose of the PPE Regulations and why are they needed?

As an employer you will already be aware of your general obligations under the 1974 Act, and more recently under the Framework Regulations, to identify and deal with the risks to which your employees are exposed during the course of their employment. The PPE Regulations are designed to focus attention on one specific way of reducing any risks to the health and safety of your employees, by ensuring that you provide adequate protective clothing and equipment for all of them.

Hazardous occupations, for example those involving work in the nuclear or chemical industries, are already well regulated and employees coming into regular contact with radioactive, carcinogenic or other noxious substances can be assured that risks to their health and safety have already been, and will continue to be, assessed and regulated to ensure that they are minimised. The PPE Regulations are not intended to replace the detailed provisions already in place to protect such workers, but are designed to impose an obligation on employers to assess and deal with those less obvious risks which are not already well-regulated. Their purpose is to make each and every individual worker as safe as they can be by issuing them with suitable equipment with which to protect themselves.

It is worthy of note that the risks covered by the PPE Regulations extend, for example, to the damage to health caused by being exposed for long periods to rain and wind, imposing a duty to provide appropriate weatherproof clothing.

A prudent employer will therefore take some time to think further about the PPE Regulations to see if there are any employees not already adequately provided for to whom they may apply, and also to ensure that the standard of protection afforded to employees, for whom legislation is already in place, is still sufficient, in view of the more onerous obligations now laid down.

¶302 Should I be concerned about the PPE Regulations?

All employers need to take a few moments to consider the PPE Regulations and the impact they will have on their business.

The very largest employers in the industrial sector will have sophisticated and well-defined health and safety procedures already in place under the 1974 Act. They will therefore in the first instance only need to ensure that any additional obligations set out in the framework regulations do not catch them out.

However, having done this, there is also now a duty on the employer to consider specifically whether personal protective equipment (PPE) should be provided, and if it should how this will affect their employees' ability to perform their jobs. This duty is owed to all employees and not just to those in obviously hazardous occupations such as the handling of chemicals. The obligations are now more onerous than ever, for example it is necessary to carry out a detailed assessment of the suitability of all PPE and of course this obligation is a continuing one.

If you fall into this category of employer, in assessing your existing procedures you will frequently find that you already comply with most, if not all, of the PPE Regulations. Nevertheless, the specific tasks set out in the regulations, such as the PPE assessment prior to selection of equipment, must also now be undertaken and documented where appropriate. At this stage it might be helpful to remember that the equipment provided to you by all manufacturers will now have to comply with specified standards which is to your considerable advantage as a quality control mechanism.

Medium-sized and smaller employers in non-specific risk businesses will need to look at the PPE Regulations equally carefully.

You will need to assess the risks to which your employees are subjected which cannot be alleviated in any way other than by providing PPE. You must assess the criteria that the particular item of PPE must have in order to eradicate, or if this is not possible, substantially reduce, the risk in question, and then compare the different types of PPE on the market to see which fulfil these criteria. If more than one make or design is available the relevant merits and drawbacks of each will then have to be assessed.

This is not such an onerous task as it may at first glance seem to be as the additional duties imposed on manufacturers will mean that they are keen to provide detailed explanations of their equipment and available support services so as to increase their market share. You may therefore find that the selection of PPE is rather easier than it was before.

Employers with only a handful of employees and also the self-employed must be equally mindful of the PPE Regulations and carry out similar assessments of any PPE required. Although the assessments you will need to undertake will inevitably be less complicated they are just as important. If you are self-employed you should be aware that the PPE Regulations stress throughout their applicability to you and all other self-employed persons.

¶303 What are the essential features of the PPE Regulations upon which I should concentrate?

(1) The duty to provide suitable PPE (reg. 4)

Regulation 4 imposes a duty on every employer to ensure that suitable PPE is provided to such of their employees as may be exposed to one or more risks to their health or safety while at work, except to the extent that any risk has been adequately controlled by some other means.

You will already have carried out a comprehensive risk analysis exercise under the Framework Regulations and having done this you should remember as a basic principle that it is always better to reduce or eliminate a risk at source. For example, in a number of industries employees on the production line will be working directly under overhead conveyors, which may have heavy objects suspended from them. If a safety mesh is built around the conveyor to catch any objects which may accidentally fall from it, then it is not necessary for the employees at risk to wear hard hats, which would only offer them limited protection in any event. Only if it is not possible to eliminate a risk by some other means should you resort to protecting your employees by the use of PPE.

You should also be aware that it is not sufficient just to issue PPE to employees exposed to risk on a daily or regular basis. The PPE Regulations are designed to safeguard employees who may be exposed to a risk at any time. For example an industrial engineer carrying out a work study will be exposed to some, if not all, of the risks to which those employees he is observing are exposed. You will therefore need to assess his need for PPE as well.

It is important not to forget that the PPE Regulations extend to the self-employed, and impose the same obligations on them as they do on employers.

The equipment provided in accordance with reg. 4 must be suitable. Clearly, employees at risk from chemical splashes on their hands must be provided with gloves, but how does an employer go about assessing the suitability of a particular pair of gloves and whether any other PPE is required in addition?

The PPE Regulations themselves set out in detail the factors to be taken into account when assessing PPE for suitability.

Set out below is a non-exhaustive list of the sort of questions you as an employer should ask yourself:

(1) *What risks are there in doing this particular job?*

   For example, suppose Mr Smith works in a plant which dyes fabrics. You will need to consider whether the chemicals used will stain his hands temporarily or permanently, whether they are also corrosive and will therefore cause burning or blistering of the skin, whether they are harmful if accidentally ingested, i.e. if food is handled immediately after contact with the dye stuffs, and whether the dye stuffs are also volatile thereby causing an additional risk of an entirely different nature.

(2) *Where do these risks occur?*

For example, is the risk only at one particular stage of a multi-stage process operated by one employee?

(3) *Will one piece of PPE inhibit an employee from carrying out another task forming an integral part of his job?*

For example, will gloves prevent an employee from operating a sensitive weighing machine or other apparatus? If the answer to this question is yes then you will need to consider whether the problem can be solved by supplying gloves which are readily removable or perhaps a pair of gloves offering greater sensitivity is the solution. Ultimately, of course, the safety considerations are paramount even if this means an employee is slower in performing his job.

(4) *Do any of your employees suffer from any health problems which may be aggravated by the wearing of PPE?*

For example, do any of your employees who have to wear protective gloves suffer from eczema or dermatitis which will make the wearing of PPE uncomfortable for them? Perhaps this could be alleviated by inserting sterile cotton linings into the gloves before use.

(5) *Should you provide each employee with their own PPE or can they share?*

The answer to this question will almost invariably be that for hygiene reasons each employee should have their own equipment, whatever the PPE under consideration, and whether or not more than one employee needs to use the PPE at any one time.

(6) *If PPE is interchangeable amongst employees what sizes will you need to have available to ensure that all your employees are properly protected and can still perform the tasks required of them unimpaired?*

For example, gloves which are three sizes too big could cause unnecessary spillages that are not only wasteful but also potentially hazardous.

(7) *Where an individual employee is subject to more than one risk will the PPE used to eliminate one increase the likelihood of injury as a result of another?*

For example, suppose Mr Jones has to lift heavy machined components prior to deburring. Obviously he has to wear gloves to prevent cutting his hands on the sharp edges of the components. However, in wearing such gloves he will inevitably suffer some loss of grip making it more likely that he will drop the component, thereby increasing the risk of injury to his feet and lower legs.

(8) *Alternatively, will the PPE worn to eliminate the first risk increase the chances of injury as a result of the exposure to a second risk, by reducing the effectiveness of a second piece of PPE required?*

¶303

For example, in a steelworks an employee may have to wear ear defenders because of the noisy environment and a hard hat. The wearing of the hat may impair the effectiveness of the ear defenders and you will therefore need to revise your requirements for PPE and provide hard hats with integral ear protection.

(2) The duty to carry out an assessment of PPE to be provided (reg. 6)

Before an employer can properly identify what type of PPE should be provided and to whom, a careful and methodical assessment of the tasks of all of the at risk employees will need to be carried out.

This is specifically provided for in reg. 6 which states that before choosing PPE an employer must carry out an assessment to ensure the suitability of the proposed PPE. This assessment must include:

- An assessment of the risks to health or safety not avoided by other means. In practice, this will form part of the all embracing review carried out under the Framework Regulations and the information can simply be lifted from that as the starting point for this particular assessment.
- A list of characteristics which the PPE must have in order to protect against the identified risks, taking account of any risks the equipment itself may create. For example, will protective footwear slip on a wet floor?
- A comparison of the available PPE in order to identify the most suitable product.

The obligation to carry out an assessment of this type extends to a review of any such assessment which has been carried out in accordance with the PPE Regulations as and when necessary. You cannot therefore afford to relax once the initial assessment has taken place. For example, if you change the solvent used for a particular part of the manufacturing process you will need to review your assessment to ensure that any gloves currently in use will not perish when they come into contact with the new solvent.

As we have already pointed out, this assessment, although quite distinct from the risk assessment which must be carried out in accordance with the Framework Regulations, is not an entirely separate exercise. The basic risk assessment exercise will therefore stand you in good stead for the first part of this assessment, and it therefore follows that if you already undertake careful and thorough health and safety reviews the additional obligations imposed by the PPE Regulations will not constitute too much of an additional burden on your resources in terms of either management time or direct cost.

(3) The duty to instruct and train employees in the use of PPE (reg. 9)

Once the correct PPE has been identified and purchased the PPE Regulations impose a rigorous obligation on employers to provide instruction and training in its use. This obligation is set out in detail in reg. 9.

¶303

It is not sufficient just to show an employee how to wear a piece of PPE correctly, your obligations as an employer mean that it will be necessary for you, in addition, to explain the following:

- The risks which use of the PPE will avoid.
- The purpose of the PPE in terms of how it reduces/eliminates those risks and how to use the PPE properly.

  Should you be wondering at this stage whether this is a worthwhile process, it is, of course, human nature that those employees who understand thoroughly why they are being asked to wear, for example a hard hat, are more likely to remember to do so and to do so willingly.

- Any steps the employer needs to take to ensure that the PPE remains in good working order.

  Once again, if employees are aware of the risks that the PPE is trying to protect them from they will be more willing to take a few moments to ensure that it is working properly.

You should note that if any of your employees have difficulty in understanding English, there is an express duty on you as their employer to provide this training in the appropriate language so as to ensure that the training is properly understood.

(4) Continuing obligations (reg. 10)

An employer's obligations will not stop once suitable PPE has been identified and issued to employees who are properly trained in its use and maintenance. Regulation 10 imposes an obligation on employers to take all reasonable steps to ensure any PPE provided is properly used.

At first glance this has the potential for causing employers considerable difficulty, especially in a large scale manufacturing environment. Is it really practical to police and enforce the use of PPE? The answer to this question will invariably be yes via existing supervisory structures.

In addition, the PPE Regulations do, in fact, also impose an obligation on every employee to use any PPE provided and a further obligation to use it in accordance with any instructions and/or training they have received. However, this is not enough and you must put in place systems of monitoring employees to ensure that they are using the PPE provided. It is, after all, in your interests to do so as it reduces the prospect of having to defend a personal injury claim.

On a practical note, a prudent employer will also make misuse of PPE and failure to use it in accordance with instructions given, a disciplinary offence. This will enable you to deal effectively and properly with persistent offenders.

Finally, reg. 11 imposes an obligation on an employee to report any loss of or obvious defect in his PPE to the employer. Employers will therefore need to put in place a reporting system and maintenance programme. PPE will have to be repaired

¶303

or replaced immediately. Therefore if production is not to be unduly affected you will need to consider your ability to store spare equipment on site and also the optimum size or range of sizes for this spare equipment.

You may take some comfort from the knowledge that manufacturers will almost certainly offer a comprehensive repair and maintenance service themselves, and it may be that this is the most cost effective way of complying with this aspect of the regulations.

¶304 Complying with the PPE Regulations – is it worth it?

At first glance the additional administrative and cost burden in complying with these and other regulations will seem enormous, particularly to smaller employers and the self-employed. However, you should remember that to a large extent the regulations merely add extra detail to the obligations under the 1974 Act with which you have already been complying for nearly 20 years. In addition, effective health and safety procedures are, of course, an essential part of good business management and in the medium to long-term will reap enormous rewards in terms of reducing legal costs, compensation payments and lost production time resulting from accidents in the workplace.

4 The Provision and Use of Work Equipment Regulations 1992
(The Work Equipment Regulations)

¶401 What is the purpose of the Work Equipment Regulations and why are they needed?

The Work Equipment Regulations take effect in two stages. Some regulations came into force on 1 January 1993 and others are due to come into force on 1 January 1997. They apply to all employees and the self-employed, subject to limited exceptions.

The Work Equipment Regulations impose duties on employers, persons in control of certain premises and the self-employed to ensure that suitable equipment, proper maintenance, training, information and instruction is provided. They also set out details of the equipment required to control selected hazards such as dangerous machine parts, and risks, such as fire.

¶402 Relationship with existing health and safety legislation

There is already an array of legislation on the subject and the work equipment regulations amplify existing duties to provide safe plant and equipment and a safe system of work. They therefore consolidate existing law and 'best practice', to be applied across all sectors.

¶403 Relationship with other new health and safety legislation

Some of the other sets of new regulations covered in this book will operate alongside the Work Equipment Regulations, particularly the Framework Regulations. They require a *risk assessment* to be carried out in respect of the health and safety of workers and any others who may be affected by the work which is being carried out. The purpose is to identify and implement measures that prevent and minimise safety hazards associated with the workplace and its contents.

Where the Work Equipment Regulations overlap with other legislation, compliance with the more specific or onerous obligation will normally be sufficient.

¶404 Essential features of the Work Equipment Regulations

(1) What is 'work equipment'?
This is defined extremely broadly, and includes things as wide-ranging as portable hand tools, blast-furnaces and combine harvesters. In contrast, the Work Equipment Regulations state that livestock, certain substances (e.g. cement, acids) and parts of structures such as walls, stairs and roofs do not constitute 'work equipment'.

(2) What equipment is covered?
All equipment falls into one of two categories:

(1) '*New equipment*' introduced on or after 1 January 1993 must meet the requirements of all the Work Equipment Regulations immediately.

(2) '*Existing equipment*' which is 'first provided for use' before 1 January 1993 is *immediately* subject to regs. 1–10 but will *not* be subject to regs. 11–24 inclusive, and reg. 27 and Sch. 2 until 1 January 1997.

The phrase 'first provided for use' has a special meaning. It does *not* mean the first time it was actually used, but simply the date on which it was first *supplied* in the 'premises or undertaking'.

'Premises or undertaking' is also broadly defined and includes, for example, offshore installations, mines, office blocks and individual plants.

Certain premises may be part of a larger undertaking such as a chain of shops. Where, for example, work equipment was 'first provided for use' at one shop *before* 1 January 1993, and is then transferred to another shop in the same chain on or after that date, it is to be treated as 'existing equipment', and has until 1 January 1997 to comply.

(3) What about second-hand equipment?
If the purchaser buys second-hand equipment from another company and brings it into use on or after 1 January 1993 it falls within the definition of 'new equipment'. It must therefore comply with all the regulations (including regs. 11–24) *before* it is put into use.

(4) What if I hire or lease equipment?
Such equipment is treated in the same way as second-hand equipment and therefore if introduced on or after 1 January 1993, must comply with all the regulations immediately.

¶405 Do the Work Equipment Regulations apply to me?

If you are an *employer* who provides work equipment to employees, or allows employees to provide their own work equipment then the answer is *yes*. On multi-contractor sites, employers must arrange between themselves who is responsible for equipment in common use.

The *self-employed* must also comply with the same duties in respect of 'work equipment' that they use at work.

Persons *in control* of non-domestic premises (such as the owner of a building under multi-occupation), who provide items of work equipment will have a responsibility to ensure that it complies with the Work Equipment Regulations.

The Work Equipment Regulations will not apply to seagoing ships in respect of 'normal' shipboard activities.

¶406 What do the Work Equipment Regulations say?

(1) Work equipment must be suitable (reg. 5)

Equipment must be suitable not only by design, but also by construction or adaption for the actual work it is provided to do. Regard must be had to its inherent *suitability* for the task, the *place* where it will be used, and the *purpose* for which it will be used.

It should therefore have been produced for the task which is to be undertaken, and used in accordance with manufacturers' specifications and instructions. Any in-house adaptions must not reduce the suitability of the equipment for the particular task.

Initial suitability will include the consideration of things such as protective devices and guards. The employer is required to assess the suitability of the *location* in which it is to be used. He should address risks which can be reasonably foreseen, and must account for risks which may be location-related. For example, the use of electrical equipment in a damp atmosphere would not be suitable, nor should a petrol generator be used in a confined space where fumes could be dangerous.

It must be suitable for the *particular process* for which it is used, and manufacturers' specifications, such as load bearing limits, should always be adhered to.

Example
John is employed as a gardener at a residential home for the elderly. He uses a hover mower to cut the grass but was seen by the manager using the hover mower to trim the hedge at the end of the garden as well. Such equipment is clearly not suitable to trim a hedge and John should be informed of this and advised that if he continues to use the hover mower in such a manner he may be subject to disciplinary action.

(2) Work equipment should be appropriately maintained (reg. 6)

Equipment design should enable maintenance to be carried out without risk to health and safety (reg. 22), and it should be maintained in an 'efficient' state so that its condition does not affect health and safety. For example, a failure to lubricate regularly might lead to danger because of seized parts or overheating.

Other equipment such as safety guards will have to be maintained in a functional state at all times. The extent and complexity of maintenance and the frequency of checks needed will vary tremendously with the nature of the equipment involved. Only adequately informed, trained and instructed persons should undertake maintenance activities, which should include any and all manufacturers' recommendations.

Planned preventative maintenance encourages the replacement of parts before they reach the end of their active lives. Such a formal system of planned maintenance may be necessary where devices are likely to fail in a dangerous way.

Where machinery has a maintenance log, it must be kept up to date.

(3) Specific risks should be identified (reg. 7)

Where use of work equipment may involve a specific risk to health and safety, the employer must ensure that the use and maintenance of such equipment is restricted only to designated and properly trained persons. The provision of that training is also the responsibility of the employer.

(4) Availability of information and instructions (reg. 8)

Employers have a duty to make relevant health and safety information available to their work-force together with written instructions on the use of work equipment. Instructions should be clear and easily accessible.

The employer should take into account the degree of skill of relevant employees, together with their experience and training and the amount of supervision in the context of the complexity or otherwise of that particular job.

Such information should also be available to supervisors and managers. The amount of information that will need to be immediately available will vary depending on circumstances, but it is important that supervisors and managers know the extent of the information that is available and where it can be found.

The instructions should also cover foreseeable but abnormal situations which would affect health and safety if they arose and set out the appropriate action to be taken. In order that the information is comprehensible to all, it may be necessary to provide it in more than one language. Special arrangements may be required for employees with learning difficulties or physical disabilities so as to ensure that they understand the information they are being provided with. The Work Equipment Regulations allow for the information to be provided verbally but we always recommend that it be provided, or confirmed, in writing if possible.

(5) Appropriate training (reg. 9)

Persons who use work equipment and those who supervise or manage them must be adequately trained to do so. Existing legislation may already require training to be carried out; this should be supplemented with more specific training on the use of work equipment. Of course, the amount of training needed will vary according to the circumstances. For example, a higher level of training may be appropriate for someone

¶406

who is to work unsupervised, and young people may be singled out for special attention because of their relative unfamiliarity with the working environment. Induction training is of particular importance. We recommend that the essential features of any training are also confirmed in writing so that the employee in question can keep a written record of what is expected of them.

(6) Comply with EC requirements (reg. 10)

The 1974 Act places general duties on designers, manufacturers, importers and suppliers to ensure that work equipment is safe, as far as this is reasonably practicable. Those same duties apply equally to employers who buy such equipment and who put it to use.

Those duties have recently been broadened because employers must also now ensure that work equipment, which is first provided for use in the workplace after 31 December 1992, meets any relevant minimum safety standards set down by the EC in product directives which are designed to harmonise technical standards and to assist the free movement of goods in the Community. As at 1 January 1993 not all work equipment is covered by existing product directives.

New or existing work equipment which complies with any relevant product directive is exempt from the provisions of regs. 11–24. You can tell whether a piece of work equipment complies with any relevant product directive by seeing if it bears a 'CE Mark'.

(7) Dangerous machine parts (reg. 11)

This regulation covers risks arising from most mechanical hazards.

The principal duty is to take effective measures to prevent contact with dangerous parts of machinery. This can be discharged either by preventing access to or by stopping the movement of, the particular part before a person can reach it. There are many ways to achieve this result such as fitting enclosing guards, or providing protection appliances to eliminate direct physical contact.

As always, it is important to provide your employees with clear written warnings about the dangers associated with particular machine parts (or the machines themselves if possible), to train them how to avoid those dangers and to supervise them adequately so as to keep the dangers to a minimum.

The hazards will be identified as part of the risk assessment required by the Framework Regulations and it is quite possible that a combination of measures will sometimes be needed as one particular machine may present a range of different mechanical hazards all of which need to be provided for.

The risk assessment should cover the machine not only in operating mode, but also during times of repair, cleaning and maintenance.

Protective devices should be suitable for their purpose, well-made and maintained properly. The devices should also be designed in such a way that it is difficult for them to be ignored or bypassed even by an employee who is determined to do so. Their

¶406

design should also not obstruct the operator's view if such an obstruction would in itself create or heighten a safety hazard.

(8) Specified hazards (reg. 12)
Special provision is made for 'specified hazards', such as materials falling from equipment (e.g. molten metal spilling from a ladle), material which is unexpectedly ejected from equipment, the breaking of a mechanical part which is subsequently ejected, overheating or explosion, which are identified by the risk assessment which everybody will have to carry out in order to comply with the Framework Regulations.

(9) Temperature extremes (reg. 13)
Protection should be provided to prevent burning, scalding or searing injuries caused by any work equipment which is subject to extreme temperatures such as gas cookers and cold stores. Risks from contact may be reduced by insulation or barricading and splashing may be prevented by the provision of deflection systems or covers.

(10) Controls and control systems (regs. 14–18)
These regulations specify that controls and/or control systems must be provided where 'appropriate', i.e. where their absence could have health and safety implications. Start/stop and emergency stop controls will be required where machine powered moving parts are involved and where the risk of injury is more than negligible.

Most, but not all, types of work equipment to which these regulations apply will have moving parts. Good examples of pieces of work equipment which will need to be provided with controls or control systems even though they have no moving parts, are ovens and lasers.

In practice, most individual items of equipment are likely to be supplied with the appropriate controls, but for complex systems comprising more than one individual piece of equipment a more detailed assessment of the risks may be required and more sophisticated controls may be needed.

In general terms, these regulations require the provision of the following controls or control systems:

- One to start a piece of equipment or make a significant change in operating conditions – such as controlling speed.
- Stop controls which should be easily accessible and should bring the equipment to a halt in a safe manner.
- Emergency stop controls should be provided where other safeguards are not adequate to prevent risks when an irregular event occurs. They should be designed to bring the equipment under control in such a way as not to create an additional hazard.

¶406

The Provision and Use of Work Equipment Regulations 1992

These regulations also provide that controls must be clearly visible and, where necessary, distinguishable by touch. They should also be positioned at a point where operators can see everybody who is at risk. It may be that mirrors or cameras are required to achieve this.

Example
Bill is an operative on moulding machinery which is designed with the control panel on one side of the machine and the access for maintenance on the other side of the machine. Mirrors have therefore been carefully placed so that Bill can clearly see that no one will be put at risk when he starts the machinery. Additionally, an override button is situated on the access side of the machine so that anyone carrying out maintenance on the machine can prevent it from being started from the control panel.

The regulations also require that the control systems are designed so that any failure within them leads automatically to a 'failsafe' condition which does not impede the operation of the stop controls.

(11) Isolation of energy sources (reg. 19)
The Work Equipment Regulations provide that suitable means of isolating work equipment from all sources of energy must be provided and that they should also be clearly identifiable and easily accessible.

In some instances simply removing an electrical plug may be sufficient for these purposes. In others, a multiple locking device may be required so that several persons must physically act to ensure that the equipment can be isolated from its power source.

(12) Stability and lighting (regs. 20 and 21)
The Work Equipment Regulations require that precautions should be taken to affix or stabilise potentially unstable work equipment. For example, scaffolding used in windy conditions should be strengthened correspondingly.

The Work Equipment Regulations also require that lighting sufficient to remove or minimise any hazard which would otherwise exist be provided.

(13) Maintenance work (reg. 22)
The Work Equipment Regulations also require that the construction of work equipment should take account of risks associated with the maintenance of it. This may have been considered and provided for at the design or manufacture stage or it may need to be incorporated subsequently. For example, lubrication points should be located where they may be used safely when the machine is in motion. Further safeguards might include the use of temporary guards, limited movement controls or a crawl speed governor.

(14) Marking and warnings (regs. 23 and 24)
Inherently dangerous work equipment should be marked with warnings accordingly.

¶406

For example, gas cylinders should identify their contents by a notice or colour coding, and a lifting beam should have its maximum load clearly marked on it. There may also be a need for portable warnings to be used during temporary operations. Warning devices can be audible (e.g. the reversing alarms on vehicles) or visible, such as a warning light on a control panel. Whatever their form, they must be easily perceived and unambiguous. It must also be possible to distinguish the warnings from separate warning devices.

Example
David works on a production line in a factory where parts are fed by means of a conveyor. An alarm sounds whenever there is a blockage on the conveyor, but David has also been trained to make a visual check of the control panel where a light shows if a blockage has occurred. It is not satisfactory simply to rely upon the audible signal as the environment is noisy and David may not always be able to distinguish the warning sound.

Example
Bob Smith runs the Model Carpet Company. He recently ordered a new machine and stipulated to the supplier that it should comply with any applicable EC product directive. He knows that this equipment will constitute 'new equipment' under the Work Equipment Regulations.

As a result of the risk assessment which he carried out several months ago with the assistance of the HSE, he has also specified the following:

(1) that the lubrication points on the machine be situated further away from any moving parts and, wherever possible, be accessible from ground level;

(2) that where this is not practicable, that locking protective guards should be installed so that the maintenance operative is physically prevented from being able to touch moving parts;

(3) that the machine can be set at idling speed and the controls padlocked in that mode by the maintenance operatives, to be released by them only when the maintenance work is completed;

(4) that mirrors be positioned on the machine so that the operator can see all parts of the process from his control panel; and

(5) that the emergency stop controls are finished in fluorescent colours for easy location.

Bob has also ensured that his maintenance operatives are familiar with the specification of the new machine, and has arranged a full briefing before it is installed. He has also made it clear to his work-force that only appropriately trained operatives should work on the new equipment, and that persons failing to observe this rule may be subject to disciplinary action.

¶406

5 The Health and Safety (Display Screen Equipment) Regulations 1992
(The VDU Regulations)

¶501 What is the purpose of the VDU Regulations and why are they needed?

The VDU Regulations relate to an area of work activity which prior to 1 January 1993 was not covered by specific legislation.

Although work with display screen equipment is generally regarded as not being high risk, physical problems, visual fatigue and mental stress can result. They are not unique to display screen work nor are they inevitable consequences of it. Such problems can, however, be overcome by good ergonomic design of equipment, furniture, the working environment and the tasks performed.

¶502 Should I be concerned about the VDU Regulations?

The short answer is yes. The impact of these regulations is profound and it is an area where many employers will have to amend their current practices.

Potentially, every member of staff who has a computer on or near their desk may be covered by the new provisions. Care must also be taken because the VDU Regulations do not only apply to employees; employers also owe duties towards self-employed individuals using display screen equipment in their businesses.

¶503 The scope of the VDU Regulations

The scope of the VDU Regulations is limited by definitions and the first requirement must of course be to establish what equipment and which people will be covered by the legislation.

(1) Display screen equipment

The definition of 'display screen equipment' is contained in reg. 1 where it is defined as 'any alphanumeric or graphic display screen, regardless of the display process involved'.

With a few exceptions, notable ones being portable computers not in prolonged use, and typewriters described as 'window typewriters', the VDU Regulations apply to virtually every form of computer which may be found in the office. In addition to the typical visual display units, process control screens and microfiche are included in the definition.

It is not safe to assume that merely because display screen equipment is not covered by the VDU Regulations that the use of it is not subject to any restrictions at all. The provisions of the 1974 Act must be complied with in any event to ensure that risks to those using any display screen equipment are reduced to the lowest extent reasonably practicable. Furthermore, the risk assessments required by the Framework Regulations and the assessment of risks and measures taken to control the use of display screens not covered by the VDU Regulations should take account of ergonomic factors applicable to display screen work.

(2) Workstation

Duties imposed by reg. 2, 3, 6 and 7 refer in part to workstations. The definition of 'workstation' is in reg. 1 and you may be surprised by what is covered. The HSE's guidance notes published to accompany the VDU Regulations interprets 'workstation' in a wide sense, extending not only to the display screen equipment, and optional accessories, but also to the work surface, the document holder, the work chair, work desk and the immediate working environment around the display screen equipment.

(3) Users and operators

The VDU Regulations apply to:

(1) All employees, even if they work at home or at another employer's workstation, provided that they habitually use display screen equipment for the purposes of an employers undertaking as a significant part of their normal work. Such employees caught by the VDU Regulations, whether employed by the employer or another employer, are referred to in the VDU Regulations as '*users*'.

(2) Self-employed persons who habitually use display screen equipment as a significant part of their normal work. Such individuals are referred to in the VDU Regulations as '*operators*'.

The distinction is made because not all of the provisions of the VDU Regulations have been extended to '*operators*'.

Unfortunately, it is not possible to lay down rigid rules determining who should be classified as a '*user*' or '*operator*'. In some instances, for example secretaries, typists or journalists, it is obvious that the individuals are caught by the VDU Regulations as their work mainly involves working with display screen equipment and such use could be described as more or less continuous on most days. The difficulty arises where the use of display screen equipment is less continuous or frequent. You have to assess the

¶503

The Health and Safety (Display Screen Equipment) Regulations 1992

relative importance of different aspects of the work and the HSE's guidance notes advise that where use is less frequent, a person would generally be a '*user*' or '*operator*' if most or all of the following criteria are satisfied:

- carrying out the job depends on display screen equipment;
- there is no discretion as to the use of the display screen equipment;
- significant training and/or particular skills in the use of display screen equipment to do the job are needed;
- use of the display screen equipment is in continuous spells of an hour or more at a time;
- use is more or less daily;
- there is fast transfer of information between the user and screen and this is an important requirement of the job;
- the work is intensive with high levels of attention and concentration by the user.

Example
Sally is a receptionist for a fairly large firm of solicitors. Her job entails checking and entering visitor details and allocating car parking facilities and conference room facilities using display screen equipment. Visitors may also request information which Sally gleans from the display screen equipment. It is a busy firm with many visitors and she spends regular and long periods of time working at the display screen. When compared to the amount of face to face contact and telephone calls that Sally deals with, the majority of her work is spent using her display screen. It is likely that Sally is classified as a '*user*'.

¶504 What are the essential features of the VDU Regulations upon which I should concentrate?

The specific duties laid down in the VDU Regulations can be broken down into six key areas:

(1) risk assessment (reg. 2);

(2) workstation requirements (reg. 3);

(3) work routines (reg. 4);

(4) eye and eyesight tests (reg. 5);

(5) provision of training (reg. 6);

(6) provision of information (reg. 7).

These key areas are looked at in more detail below.

¶505 Risk assessment (reg. 2)

The major requirement is that every employer must make a suitable and sufficient assessment of the health and safety implications of workstations, which include the immediate working environment. Employers must analyse workstations used for the purpose of the undertaking by '*users*', whether such '*users*' be their own or someone else's employees, for example, temporary staff employed by an employment agent. Additionally, if employers require their employees to use workstations at home, these too will need to be assessed, even where that furniture and equipment is the personal property of the '*user*'. Individual workstations used by '*operators*' where the workstation is provided by the employer will also need to be analysed and the risks assessed.

If there is doubt as to whether an individual is a '*user*' or '*operator*', the best approach undoubtedly will be to carry out an assessment which should assist in reaching, what can be, a difficult decision.

Paragraphs (1)–(4) below provide some practical suggestions which may be of assistance to an employer seeking to comply with their obligations under reg. 2.

(1) Plan the assessment

The assessment should be systematic, comprehensive and appropriate to the likely degree of risk. The structured approach is probably the best option and the risk assessment should:

- Identify the hazards – what could potentially cause harm? This could cover factors such as the job, workplace and individual factors.
- Quantify the likelihood of it occurring. The likely degree of risk will depend largely on the duration, intensity or difficulty of the work undertaken. Therefore, make sure that you know exactly what practices are adopted by the work-force as opposed to those that should be adopted.
- Evaluate the consequences of the risk occurring. Consider the number of people that might be affected and the extent and severity of the consequences for them.

(2) Who should do the assessment

The person who carries out the assessment must be familiar with the VDU Regulations and should have the ability to assess risks that arise from the workstation. They should be able to draw valid and reliable conclusions from the assessment and be able to communicate the findings to those who are required to take action. Assessments could be carried out by health and safety personnel or mainstream managers who are familiar with health and safety issues in general and the contents of the VDU Regulations in particular. It is important that those carrying out the assessment recognise their own limitations so that further expertise can be called upon if necessary. For example, outside assistance may be needed where the display screen equipment design is faulty or unusually complex.

It may be that you have many small branch offices located throughout the country and therefore it may be totally impractical for one particular person to carry out an assessment for all branches. In such situations it may be appropriate to delegate the responsibility to managers at the particular branch offices provided they are familiar with the VDU Regulations and the HSE's guidance notes and know their own limitations.

Example
Richard is responsible for health and safety within a company with many small branch offices located throughout the country. He considers that it would be totally impractical for him to carry out a risk assessment of workstations in all the branches. Richard has therefore decided to delegate the responsibility to carry out these risk assessments to managers at the particular branch offices, and has arranged for each of them to attend a training course which he will undertake to ensure that they are familiar with the VDU Regulations and the HSE guidance notes and that they each know their own limitations as to the risk assessment. Each manager will then report and discuss their findings with Richard.

It must be remembered that the views of the individual '*users*' about their workstations are an invaluable part of the risk assessment. Users should therefore be consulted during the risk assessment process and some form of self-assessment is essential to ensure a satisfactory result. Perhaps consider categorising your workers according to particular types of equipment, because some aspects of a workstation can be assessed generically such as chair adjustability or keyboard characteristics. You should always remember, however, that issues relating to subjective things such as comfort, will still need to be assessed individually. Perhaps a checklist distributed to all employees together with comprehensive instructions on how to use it would be a good method of obtaining this information. You may also wish to consider whether it would be appropriate to give training to employees before they carry out the self-assessment exercise so that they can understand how to complete it. As an alternative approach, staff with greater knowledge of health and safety issues could complete the assessments in consultation with the '*user*'.

Remember that the VDU Regulations apply to employees, whether on or off site and employees working from home and also to workers working on your site who are not your own employees.

(3) Written record
It is advisable for a record of the risk assessment to be kept in written form, or some other retrievable form. This would assist in ensuring continuity and accuracy of knowledge amongst those who need to know. This is particularly important as there is the requirement to review the risk assessment if you suspect that the last one is no longer valid or where there has been a significant change of equipment, such as new hardware, software or furniture or personnel since the last risk assessment.

¶505

The risk assessment must obviously be kept up to date and must be readily available to enable information to be updated.

(4) Risks identified

Once a risk assessment has taken place and risks identified, action must be taken to reduce any such risks identified to the lowest extent reasonably practicable as quickly as possible. Some may be removed by straightforward remedial action. For example, postural problems may be overcome by the simple adjustment of a chair and by training the employee to use equipment correctly. Visual problems may also be tackled simply by repositioning the screen and ensuring it is kept clean, or perhaps by providing more appropriate lighting.

It is very important to note that the transitional period allowed in respect of existing workstations (see ¶506 below) does not apply to the requirement to reduce the risk. Any risks identified in the risk assessment must be remedied as quickly as possible.

¶506 Workstation requirements (reg. 3)

The Schedule to the VDU Regulations sets out minimum requirements for display screen workstations which cover not only the display screen equipment itself, the keyboard, desk and chair, but also the working environment. There is no substitute for reading and familiarising yourself with those requirements which are, in the main, self-explanatory and supported in any event by the HSE's guidance notes.

The requirements are however applicable only in so far as the components referred to are present at the workstation concerned. For instance, whilst there is reference to a document holder in the VDU Regulations, this should not be interpreted as a requirement that all workstations should have one – the device is only necessary where the risk assessment suggests that the provision of one would be beneficial to the worker.

It is important to note that compliance with the minimum requirements is in two stages:

(1) workstations, whether or not they are new, which are first put into service on or after 1 January 1993 must comply with the minimum requirements immediately; and

(2) workstations which existed prior to that date have to comply by no later than 31 December 1996.

However, you must not be led into a false sense of security by thinking that action is not required in the interim. As previously explained, risk assessments of workstations must be carried out now and any risks uncovered by such assessments should be dealt with as quickly as possible and certainly not left until the 1996 deadline.

Furthermore, the reference to workstations first put into service on or after 1 January 1993 includes workstations which were in use prior to that date but which have been substantially modified after that date, and also those which have been rearranged or relocated after that date, such as may occur when an office move takes place. It is important to note that if new display screen equipment is introduced at an existing workstation, then the whole workstation concerned should be regarded as new and brought into compliance with the Schedule immediately. However, if any other part of an existing workstation is changed, only the new component need comply with the Schedule straight away, and the remainder of the workstation need not comply until 31 December 1996.

¶507 Work routines (reg. 4)

Every employer is required to plan the activities of display screen equipment '*users*' so that there are breaks or changes of activity. There is no specified maximum time for a period of work with display screen equipment, nor is there a requirement for fixed breaks. It is important to note that this part of the VDU Regulations only relates to employees working at the employer's undertaking. It should also be understood that these breaks from screen work do not mean enforced idleness. Most '*users*' spend only a portion of their day working at a display screen and the time they spend in other normal activities will be sufficient to break up the day. However, for those employed *exclusively* as VDU operators, there may be no opportunity to introduce changes of activity and in such a situation the most prudent approach will be to introduce short breaks at frequent intervals. The timing of the break is more important than its length with short frequent breaks being more satisfactory than occasional longer breaks.

You may find that some employees have to be encouraged to adopt sensible work routines; factors such as the pressure of deadlines, enthusiasm and heavy workloads may result in breaks not being taken and a structured approach by the employer will be needed to help overcome such reluctance to take time away from the screen. You may also need to educate the people who produce the work for the '*user*' to encourage them to take breaks.

Example
Mary is a secretary to a partner in a firm of accountants and regularly receives lengthy documents which need to be produced within short deadlines. In order that Mary can have a change of activity away from her display screen, she agrees with the partner that she will receive such lengthy documents piecemeal, rather than when the partner has completed the entire document.

¶508 Eye and eyesight tests (reg. 5)

Only employees are entitled to free eye and eyesight tests. They are entitled to appropriate eye and/or eyesight tests on request in the following circumstances:

(1) before becoming a '*user*';
(2) at regular intervals after commencing display screen equipment work;

(3) where the '*user*' experiences visual difficulties which may reasonably be considered to be caused by work on display screen equipment.

Employees are entitled, but not obliged, to undergo an eye and eyesight test. There is no duty to provide eye and eyesight tests for non-employees such as applicants for jobs. However, if you recruit an employee who will be a '*user*' then they must be given an eye or eyesight test (if they want one) before they do sufficient display screen work for it to be regarded as a significant part of their normal activity.

Further follow up tests should be given at regular intervals if the employee wishes. The employer should be guided by the clinical judgment of the optometrist or doctor in each case as to the frequency of testing and it is a good idea to ask the person carrying out the initial test to indicate a time-scale for a repeat test. It is also a good idea to design a form which the employee signs confirming their consent for information to be given to the employer by the optometrist or doctor regarding the recommended frequency of further tests (see Appendix A at p. 42).

Any special corrective appliances (usually glasses) identified by the tests as being necessary for working at a display screen must be provided at the cost of the employer. The employer is liable for a basic appliance of a type and quality adequate for its functions. If an employee elects to buy a more expensive pair of glasses (for example with designer frames) the employer is not obliged to pay for it. The employer can either provide the basic appliance, or agree to contribute an amount equivalent to the cost of the basic appliance, and it is sensible for an employer to establish and publish a clear policy on such issues.

Example
Andrew is a journalist with a local newspaper and spends a substantial amount of time using display screen equipment. He already wears glasses and has recently had an eyesight test, which his employer has paid for. The eyesight tests revealed that he does need to wear glasses when working with his display screen but that the glasses which he already has are adequate for this purpose. Andrew has wanted to replace his glasses for some time and is unhappy when he is advised by his employer that they are not prepared to supply additional glasses because his existing glasses are adequate for working with his display screen equipment.

¶509 Provision of training and information (regs. 6 and 7)

Employers have duties to provide information and training for display screen equipment '*users*' and to a lesser extent, '*operators*'. Training must be provided to existing '*users*' and to employees before they become '*users*' or after any substantial modification to the workstation. The training which should, if possible, be carried out in such a way as to enable employees to pass on their experience and knowledge should cover things such as:

- the '*users*' role in detecting and recognising hazards and risks;
- a simple explanation of the causes of risk, such as poor posture;
- actions to be taken and procedures to be followed by the individual which will bring risks under control and/or reduce them to acceptable levels, such as the adjustment of work chairs;
- how to bring symptoms or problems with the workstation to the attention of management;
- general information on the VDU Regulations;
- the importance of the '*users*' contribution to risk assessments.

Use of a checklist will assist in ensuring that all appropriate training has been undertaken and a written record of all training should be kept.

The provision of information relates to '*users*' employed by the undertaking, '*users*' employed by other employers and '*operators*' in the undertaking. In addition the employer is required to tell '*operators*' and '*users*' what they have done to discharge their obligations under the VDU Regulations. Further, '*users*' who work in the undertaking must be provided with information about the measures taken concerning their daily work routine and '*users*' actually employed by the employer must be advised of the steps taken to ensure compliance with the eye and eyesight requirements and in relation to initial training.

Ideally this information should reinforce any training provided by the employer and serve as a reminder.

The HSE guidance notes make it clear that there is a general requirement under the Framework Regulations for employers to provide information on risks to health and safety to all their own employees as well as to employers of other employees on site, to visiting employees, and to the self-employed.

¶510 Complying with the VDU Regulations – is it worth it?

Conformance with the requirements of the VDU Regulations may both avoid the incidence of injuries and also provide employers with the opportunity to defend themselves should injuries occur and should legal proceedings follow. Furthermore, the employer should benefit from a gain in output if the level of sickness absence for reasons related to the use of display screen equipment work is reduced.

Appendix A

PRIVATE & CONFIDENTIAL
Optometrist/General Practitioner

SAMPLE LETTER

Dear Doctor [Name]

RE: [NAME OF EMPLOYEE]

[Name] is employed by us as a [job title]. His/her employment requires him/her to operate word processing equipment for a substantial part of his/her working day.

At [name]'s request, we should be grateful if you could carry out an eye/eyesight test and complete the duplicate copy of this letter enclosed informing us of whether [name] requires special corrective appliances for work with the display screen equipment, together with an indication of how frequent further tests should be undertaken.

We are grateful for your assistance and await hearing from you.

Yours sincerely

Personnel Manager

I [name] consent to the above information being supplied to my employer.

_____   _____
                                                                    [Date]

Are special corrective appliances required for display screen equipment work YES/NO

Interval of time suggested before repeat test _____ weeks/months/years

_____   _____
                                                                    [Date]

6 The Manual Handling Operations Regulations 1992
(The Manual Handling Regulations)

¶601 What is the purpose of the Manual Handling Regulations and why are they needed?

The HSE estimates that 34 per cent of all accidents at work result from manual handling activities at a current annual cost to UK industry of at least £90 million. A large number of those injuries are caused by people manually handling loads (not necessarily heavy ones) in the wrong manner. The main purpose of the Manual Handling Regulations, therefore, is to require employers to reduce the risk of injury to their employees who are involved in manual handling operations, by adopting better and safer practices. People are being urged to use what is known as an 'ergonomic' approach.

'Ergonomics' is the study of how efficiently a person carries out their duties. In this context, therefore, an ergonomic approach involves an employer studying the various factors relevant to manual handling and which can result in injury and, by improving the conditions within which the employee must work and/or by altering the work practices which are followed, reducing the risk of any injury.

The philosophy of the Manual Handling Regulations is very much that employers need to be proactive, not only in identifying the potential for injuries but also by implementing and policing measures designed to ensure that manual handling operations are carried out in such a way that the chances of injury to the employees are minimised.

¶602 Should I be concerned about the Manual Handling Regulations?

The Manual Handling Regulations have a far broader application than most people imagine. Not only are injuries of this sort experienced in all types of business, but it is also often forgotten that they result not only from the carrying or support of heavy loads but also from work requiring repeated or frequent manual handling of light loads, especially if the activity is linked with bad posture or difficult working conditions. Nor can you assume that manual handling injuries only occur with 'manual work'. There is, for example, a high incidence of injury in the banking, finance and retail industries.

You should therefore resist the temptation to think that the Manual Handling Regulations do not concern you because your business does not involve heavy lifting jobs.

It is easy to see that industries such as the construction, engineering and motor businesses will need to pay particular attention to the Manual Handling Regulations. So too will those industries where repetitive manual activities, for example on production lines, are involved or businesses which involve delivery work. Further, as the definition of 'load' includes humans and animals, then both the medical and veterinary professions will need to take notice too.

Example
Mark, Jim and Chris all work in a large warehouse. Mark helps to unload goods from a lorry by hauling on a rope which lifts goods from the lorry. Jim then steadies the load at the end of the rope and guides it clear of the lorry and positions it so that Mark is now free to lower the rope. Chris places boxes of goods on his shoulder and then climbs a ladder to store the boxes on a shelf.

Which of these men carry out manual handling operations? Answer – all three do. Even though the application of human effort may be indirect, or carried out in conjunction with mechanical assistance, Mark and Jim's work is 'manual handling' as defined by the regulations. So too is Chris's work even though the load is supported by a part of the body other than the hands.

The Manual Handling Regulations do not only affect employers but also impose duties on the self-employed making them responsible for their own safety during manual handling operations. They also require all employees to follow the systems of work provided by their employer to promote safety whilst handling loads.

¶603 What are the essential features of the Manual Handling Regulations upon which I should concentrate?

The Manual Handling Regulations are designed to supplement general duties imposed by the 1974 Act and the Framework Regulations. These two pieces of legislation taken together create general standards and obligations of health and safety, one of which is the duty imposed on employers to carry out a risk assessment covering all hazards to health and safety which employees are exposed to whilst at work. One of the risks or hazards which has to be assessed is that of injury arising from manual handling.

A risk assessment is therefore the key to compliance not only with the Framework Regulations but also the Manual Handling Regulations. Looking particularly at the Manual Handling Regulations, it is possible to set out a step by step process that should be followed (see points (1)–(5) below).

(1) Identify the potentially hazardous activities
The very first task is to identify by risk assessment exactly which manual handling

tasks being undertaken in the business actually involve a potential risk to health and safety.

The definition of 'manual handling' is deliberately broad so that it covers any situation involving the application of human effort for the purposes of carrying or supporting a load. This application of human effort may be direct or indirect, i.e. pulling a lever to make a machine lift a load is as much a manual handling operation as the lifting of the load itself. Manual handling also covers dropping or throwing loads.

The risk assessment also has to be 'suitable and sufficient', which is a fairly imprecise term. Simply put, it needs to be sufficiently thorough to identify hazards and risks associated with normal work activities but does not need to cover any possible eventuality.

Having identified which manual handling activities involve a risk of injury, the Manual Handling Regulations set out the next three steps which need to be taken.

(2) Avoid the need for employees to do manual handling work which may involve a risk of injury

The first option is that you should, so far as is reasonably practicable, simply discontinue the potentially hazardous manual handling activity. For example, at this stage you will be looking at solutions such as moving two processes or pieces of machinery closer together to remove the need to carry things between them, or the use of machinery or equipment to carry out the task instead.

Where you find yourself faced with a decision like this it is a good idea to approach your employers' association (if you have one) or even the HSE itself for their views. It is also a good idea to make and keep safe a written record of your thought process and decision. This will be valuable to you if you subsequently become involved in a dispute about whether your decision was the correct one.

Example

Brenda is employed as a tea lady in a large office. She is 50 years old. Every day she fills a tea urn in the office kitchen and then lifts the urn on to a four-wheel trolley which she pulls around the office, so that she can serve the tea to office staff at their desks.

A risk assessment reveals that the nature of the injuries that Brenda could suffer from lifting and pushing such an item are severe. A local doctor (who assisted with the assessment) has indicated that the likelihood of injury, especially at Brenda's age, is high.

Brenda's employer has decided that Brenda's kitchen will be used like a canteen in that staff will visit the kitchen whenever they want to buy a cup of tea or a snack. Hence the need for the tea urn to be moved has been avoided.

¶603

(3) Reassess those manual handling activities that cannot be avoided

Those potentially hazardous activities which have been identified during the risk assessment required by the Framework Regulations, but which cannot be removed altogether, have to be reassessed in much more detail.

In theory, this could be a substantial task as you would have to reassess nearly every manual handling activity which has been identified by the general risk assessment as possibly involving a risk of injury.

Having recognised this problem the HSE have, in their guidance notes, provided some useful and practical tips. Diagrams are used to show how, for example, a load should be handled and how the body should be positioned. By using this material it is easier for an employer to identify whether or not an individual activity exposes their employees to the risk of injury. This will help with the decision as to which manual handling operations can be ruled out as unlikely to pose a potential risk through injury and those which will (if they cannot be eradicated completely) require more detailed reassessment.

It is this reassessment, and the steps taken as a consequence of it in order to reduce the risks identified, which are the key areas to compliance with the Manual Handling Regulations. It is therefore worth examining the process of reassessment in more detail by considering the following questions.

(a) What factors should be considered in carrying out the reassessment?

The traditional approach of thinking only about the weight of the load is no longer acceptable. There are other relevant factors which need to be looked at and these are explained in the Manual Handling Regulations.

The task itself is the first factor. You should look to see exactly how the task *is* performed (rather than the way in which it *should* be performed) to see whether it involves actions, such as twisting, stretching or the use of excessive force, which increase the risk of injury. The Manual Handling Regulations themselves give useful guidance as to how a load should be handled in a perfect world.

Example

Billy works as a shelf packer in a large supermarket. Billy finds that the dog food shelves seem to clear quickly and always need to be fully stacked. Heavy sacks of dog mixer are placed on the top shelf which is approximately 6 feet high. To stock the lower shelves Billy keeps a fixed stooped posture for a prolonged period of time.

The supermarket manager has decided that it is not reasonably practicable to avoid the need for Billy to do this work, for example, by automating the process. Therefore, a more detailed reassessment has to be carried out. Risks of personal injury are identified by the fact that:

- Billy lifts relatively heavy loads from the floor to above shoulder height.

¶603

- Sustained stooping in order to stack the shelves is reducing Billy's muscular efficiency.

Examples of the remedial action which Billy's employer intends to implement following the reassessment include:

- Billy's work routine will be reorganised by rotating the jobs that he can do (such as clearing away boxes and sweeping, after short periods of shelf stacking) so that this will allow certain groups of muscles to rest whilst others are being used.
- The heavier items (such as mixer foods) will now be stacked on shelves that are at waist height and only small tins will be stacked on the top shelf.

The load itself is the second factor. You should try to ensure that the load is not made more difficult to handle than it needs to be because of its shape, bulk, the nature of its contents or its temperature.

Example

Andrew has just started work as a junior clerk in a bank. He is 16 years old. Each morning Andrew is told to carry two sacks containing small metal boxes filled with change. These are taken to the cashier's desk so that a float can be distributed amongst the six cashiers.

In carrying out a reassessment of Andrew's job, the bank has been made aware that, because these bags are so heavy, Andrew can bearly lift them off the floor. He takes both sacks together and walks stooping forwards. A risk of injury is therefore identified, especially in view of Andrew's young age.

One of the measures which the bank intends to take is that the float monies will now be divided into 12 separate bags each morning. Andrew will be told to carry one at a time even though this will extend the time needed to carry out the task. He is told that if he does not obey this instruction, this will be an act of misconduct and the bank's disciplinary procedure will be implemented. Andrew will also be given certain information and training regarding the small amount of manual handling which he undertakes.

The working environment is the third factor. Here you should think about the physical layout of the workplace. Is there anything in it which, for example, forces people to use bad posture or which gives them unstable footing, or do temperature, lighting and ventilation conditions affect their ability to handle loads in such a way that the risk of injury increases?

Example

Jack works on a construction site. He carries bricks on a hod up a temporary stairway and along a gangway. As it has been raining a great deal recently both the steps and the gangway are very slippery.

¶603

One of the measures which Jack's employer intends to take, following a reassessment having been carried out, is to construct a handrail along the stairs and gangways. Jack will also be provided with personal protective equipment, such as gloves, which will help him to grip onto surfaces.

The individual capability of the people carrying out the tasks is the fourth factor. Classic examples here will be whether the person is pregnant or has a particular health problem which might be aggravated by the manual handling of loads. However, it also covers the question of whether the person doing the job requires any special information or training in order to do the job more effectively and safely.

'Other' factors require you to look at, for example, whether any clothing or personal protective equipment (such as gloves) might hinder or impede an individual's ability to handle safely the load they are trying to move.

Different emphasis will have to be placed on these five factors according to the nature of your business. For instance, on a building site it may be difficult to change the *working environment* and therefore particular attention may need to be given to characteristics associated with *the load* or an *individual's capability*.

(b) Who should carry out the reassessment?
Because the assessor needs to have a good practical knowledge of the type of manual handling tasks carried out, the environment where work takes place, and of the types of loads handled, the ideal candidate will always be the employer or a member of the management team. However, the size of the business may make this impossible in which case the reassessment may have to be carried out by an outside third party. Depending upon the nature of the hazards in a particular business, it may be necessary to involve third parties such as ergonomic or medical experts in any case.

It is vital in any event that the employer involves employees in the process as their opinions and experience will be very valuable. They will often have suffered particular difficulties, injuries or strains which have gone unreported and will have a wealth of experience which can help identify potential risks.

The assessor also needs to know the likely costs incurred in implementing improvements so that an informed view can be taken as to whether the steps required to reduce hazards are 'reasonably practicable' (see ¶603(2) above).

(c) What record should be made of the reassessment?
Although the Manual Handling Regulations do not require you to keep a written record of reassessments which have been carried out in relation to manual handling, it is strongly recommended that you do so in any event as it will be a good source of evidence for the future.

The reassessment should be reviewed at suitable intervals and any changes (either to the reassessment or the remedial action being taken) should again be recorded in writing. For example, if you suspect that for some reason the reassessment is out of date, or if an injury of a type not previously identified is reported or if there is a significant change in the type of tasks being performed or loads being handled, then a review will be needed. In addition, it is a good idea for the reassessment to be reviewed at set time intervals in any event, unless it is perfectly clear that the risk of injury is minimal or unlikely to change.

(4) Take steps to reduce the risk of injury
Having completed your reassessment, the next step is to identify and implement the kind of preventative measures which will reduce or eradicate the risk or hazard. It is important to note once again the presence of the words 'reasonably practicable'.

Again, employees should be consulted as to the steps to be taken (and what, if any, equipment will be provided) to reduce risks, and the HSE's own guidance notes give practical help as to how certain risks can be reduced.

The reassessments discussed above are, in practice, directly linked to the identification of remedial action and it is almost certain that the steps which will need to be taken become clear actually while the reassessment is being carried out. To try and demonstrate this link you will find at the end of this chapter (see p. 51) a sample reassessment for an individual working in an office environment and whose duties include handling and moving office furniture, boxes of stationery supplies and large sacks of post (including parcels).

This sample reassessment form could also form the basis of a more detailed written record of the reassessment addressing points such as when and how the remedial action identified will be implemented and how this will be monitored.

Above all, any steps taken to reduce risks need to be regularly monitored to test their effectiveness. Measures which are not having the expected or desired result will almost certainly need to be changed.

(5) Provide information to those who may be affected
The Manual Handling Regulations also impose a duty on employers to provide employees involved in any manual handling which (as identified by the reassessment) involves a risk of injury with either a general indication or, where it is reasonably practicable to do so, precise information on:

- the weight of the load; and
- the heaviest side of any load whose centre of gravity is not positioned centrally.

Example
Paul is a school caretaker. He is often asked to lift and carry various pieces of school equipment such as computers, heavy science equipment, typewriters, etc.

Paul attends a meeting with the headmaster. He is given written information about the weight of the various pieces of equipment that he is normally asked to move.

¶603

He is told that he is to be given basic training so that he can:

- recognise loads which, because of their weight or shape might when handled, cause injury;
- estimate the weight of a load (for example in certain cases by rocking it from side to side before lifting); and
- learn good handling techniques and how to use handling aids such as trolleys, etc.

One class of children completed a project whereby each child had to identify a piece of equipment in the school whose centre of gravity was not positioned centrally (for example, a typewriter is heavier at the back than at the front). The children then produced sticky labels with 'heaviest side' written on them and placed them on the heaviest sides of all school equipment that Paul would normally be asked to lift or carry.

¶604 Complying with the Manual Handling Regulations – is it worth it?

Although some people may be horrified at the thought of adopting an ergonomic approach and reorganising the workplace or specific tasks so that the job fits the person rather than the other way round, it should be remembered that not only will this prevent suffering to your employees (and the associated costs of absenteeism and potential legal claims) but it will also result in an improvement in productivity and workplace efficiency.

The Manual Handling Operations Regulation 1992

ASSESSMENT

NAME: A N Other　　　　　　　　　　　　　　　　　JOB FUNCTION: General Office Operative

Questions to consider If the answer to a question is 'Yes' please tick against it and then consider the level of risk	Level of risk (Tick as appropriate)				Comments and possible remedial action (Make rough notes in this column in preparation for a more detailed report)	Costs (Tick as appropriate)		
	Yes	Low	Med	High		Low	Med	High
The tasks – do they involve:								
• holding loads away from trunk?	✓		✓		Heavy boxes stored on high shelves and behind other lighter items. Arrange for them to be moved to waist height shelves and in front of light items stored. Cost of extra storage space high			
• twisting?	✓		✓					
• stooping?	✓		✓					
• reaching upwards?	✓		✓					
• large vertical movement?	✓		✓					✓
• long carrying distances?	✗							
• strenuous pushing or pulling?	✗				*small microfiche printing machine. Drain chemical fluid before moving (NB hazardous substances legislation)			
• unpredictable movement of loads?	✓		✓					
• repetitive handling?	✗							✓
• insufficient rest of recovery?	✗							
• a workrate imposed by a process?	✗							
The loads – are they:								
• heavy?	✓			✓	Outside removal firm to be brought in to assist on office moves. High cost but risks even higher. Bulky storage boxes replaced by crates with hand grips. Plus porters and flat bed trolley to assist with post and parcels. Sharpish edge to printing machines. Provide protective gloves			✓
• bulky/unwieldly?	✓		✓					
• difficult to grasp?	✓		✓					
• unstable/unpredictable?*	✓		✓					
• intrinsically harmful (e.g. sharp/hot)	✓	✓						✓
								✓
The working environment – are there:								
• constraints on posture?	✗				General office staff complaining of dizziness due to high temperature. Fit extractor fan (approximately £400). High cost but even higher risk of injury			
• poor floors?	✗							
• variations in levels?	✗							
• hot/cold/humid conditions?	✓		✓					✓
• strong air movements?	✗							
• poor lighting conditions?								
Individual capacity – does the job:								
• require unusual capability?	✓		✓		Arrange for (1) special training course regarding manual handling (2) Ask HSE for information on how loads should be carried, to be provided to all general office operatives			✓
• hazard those with a health problem?	✗							
• hazard those who are pregnant?	✗							
• call for special training?	✓		✓					✓
Other factors:								
Is movement or posture hindered by clothing or personal protective equipment?	✗							

Signed....................................　　　　　　Review date: 1 March 1993
Assessment date : 1 January 1993

7 The Workplace (Health, Safety and Welfare) Regulations 1992
(The Workplace Regulations)

¶701 What is the purpose of the Workplace Regulations and why are they needed?

Before the Workplace Regulations were introduced an employer was under a general duty (created by the 1974 Act) to ensure, so far as reasonably practicable, the health, safety and welfare at work of all employees. The 1974 Act also obliged an employer to ensure, so far as is reasonably practicable, the maintenance of any place of work under their control in a condition that is safe and without risks to health and to provide and maintain safe means of access to and exit from it.

The Workplace Regulations complement these general objectives by providing greater detail as to how they can be met. Basically, the Workplace Regulations are intended to protect the health and safety of everyone in the workplace and to ensure that certain minimum welfare facilities are also provided.

The Workplace Regulations also amplify the 1974 Act by extending these duties to non-employee users of their premises such as visitors (including the general public) or contractors.

They are also designed to ensure that workplaces meet the health, safety and welfare needs of all members of the work-force, including persons with certain disabilities. The word 'suitable' is used throughout the Workplace Regulations and it is made clear that where this word is used about a particular act being done or a particular system being provided then it should be construed with reference to the particular person (including persons with disabilities) for whom the thing is being done or provided. Therefore, for example, when considering the obligation to provide 'suitable and sufficient lighting' regard should be given to anyone with impaired sight.

Compliance with the Workplace Regulations is phased as follows:

- Any workplace used for the first time after 31 December 1992 or any modifications, extensions or conversions to existing workplaces started after that date

should comply with the Workplace Regulations as at 1 January 1993 or, in the case of modifications/extensions/conversions, as soon as they are completed.
- All workplaces must, in any event, comply from 1 January 1996. Until then existing health and safety legislation will continue to apply.

Helpful definitions of 'conversion' and 'modification' are given in the HSC's ACOP which supplement the Workplace Regulations.

¶702 Should I be concerned about the Workplace Regulations?

The broad scope of the Workplace Regulations means that they are going to be of at least some relevance to all businesses.

Under the old law varying health and safety standards were applied to different types of business premises. The Workplace Regulations will replace that with a common standard of health, safety and welfare for every workplace. 'Workplace' is defined broadly to include private roads and paths on industrial estates as well as places within the premises (such as corridors) to which there is access while a person is at work. The only places excluded from the definition are:

- domestic premises;
- operational means of transport (e.g. boats, aircraft, trains and road vehicles whilst in use), as opposed to a non-operational means of transport such as a moored boat used as a restaurant;
- a workplace where only building operations or works of engineering construction are carried out; and
- a workplace where the only activities being undertaken are the exploration for, or extraction of, mineral resources.

There are different and less onerous duties concerning temporary work sites and the provision of certain minimum welfare benefits such as sanitary conveniences, washing facilities, drinking water, accommodation for clothing, changing facilities and rest facilities. These only have to be provided 'so far as is reasonably practicable'.

The Workplace Regulations create obligations for people falling into one of three categories as follows:

(1) every employer in respect of workplaces under their control;
(2) every person having, to any extent, control over a workplace in connection with their carrying on any kind of business; and
(3) every person deemed to be 'an occupier of a factory' within a specific definition.

Therefore, a tenant of a building must ensure that facilities required by the Workplace Regulations are provided in the areas they control while the landlord will be under a duty to ensure that the common areas under their control, such as stairwells or means of access, comply. The two will therefore have to co-operate to ensure that all requirements of the Workplace Regulations are met.

It will be unusual, but not unheard of, for an employer *not* to have control of the premises from which they operate their business. The best example would be a contractor whose employees are working on the business premises of a third party. Even though the Workplace Regulations will place no duties on that employer they will still be subject to the general duties imposed by the 1974 Act. The position of the employees is, however, protected as the third party on whose premises they are working will be under a duty to them by virtue of point (2) above.

> **Example**
> Tyrant Ltd is the landlord of an industrial estate which lets several units to business tenants. Tyrant, as landlord of the estate, is responsible for the upkeep of the estate roads. Tyrant therefore ensures that all estate roads are:
>
> - well-lit;
> - de-iced, gritted and cleared of snow in the winter;
> - repaired promptly when any defects likely to cause someone to trip or fall (such as large holes, bumps or uneven roads) occur. Until repaired the hole, bump, etc. must be surrounded by barriers; and
> - kept free from obstructions which may present a hazard (for example those near a corner or junction on estate roads). Until such time as the obstruction can be removed it must be surrounded by hazard cones.

¶703 What are the essential features of the Workplace Regulations upon which I should concentrate?

The Workplace Regulations list certain key requirements expressed in an essentially general way. These requirements are discussed in ¶704–¶724 below.

¶704 Maintenance (reg. 5)

Regulation 5 imposes an obligation to maintain in an efficient state, efficient working order, and good repair both the workplace and any pieces of equipment, devices and systems which, should they fail, would involve a failure to comply with other regulations. For example, this obligation covers an emergency lighting system because if it fails there would be a breach of reg. 8 which requires suitable and efficient emergency lighting to be provided.

This regulation also provides that 'where appropriate, the equipment ... shall be subject to a suitable system of maintenance'. This may mean that at certain intervals some pieces of equipment need to undergo safety testing. We would suggest that whilst carrying out the general risk assessment required by the Framework Regulations you identify and make a note of those pieces of equipment which are likely to require such a system being implemented.

¶705 Ventilation (reg. 6)

Regulation 6 requires that all enclosed workplaces must be ventilated by sufficient fresh or purified air. If provided by an air conditioning system, then the recirculated air must be filtered to ensure that any impurities are removed.

The regulation also requires the provision of a device to give warning of any breakdown in the ventilation system where that breakdown itself might have a health and safety implication as would be the case where there is a high concentration of noxious fumes in the workplace atmosphere which the ventilation system would normally clear.

¶706 Temperature (reg. 7)

Regulation 7 provides that a reasonable or comfortable temperature should be maintained in all workplaces inside a building. The ACOP advises different minimum temperatures depending upon the nature of the activity undertaken. In cases where it is not practicable to meet these minimum temperatures (for example in workplaces where food needs to be kept cold) then all reasonable steps should be taken to achieve a temperature as close as possible to those recommended. This regulation also prohibits the use of methods of heating/cooling which may generate offensive fumes, such as paraffin heaters.

More detailed guidance on temperature levels will be issued by the HSE at a later date in 1993.

There must also be enough thermometers provided to enable temperatures throughout the workplace to be monitored.

Example
Angela is a cook in a school kitchen. The kitchen tends to become very hot in the mornings when meals are being prepared. Angela has recently been experiencing symptoms associated with heat exhaustion and dehydration.

Angela's employer should:

- organise rest facilities and a rota of rest breaks for the kitchen staff in the mornings in an attempt to reduce the amount of time that staff are exposed to uncomfortable temperatures;
- investigate the cost of having insulated hot pipes running through the kitchen; and
- investigate the price of an improved ventilation system for the kitchen.

¶707 Lighting (reg. 8)

Regulation 8 provides that every workplace must be suitably and sufficiently lit to enable people to work, use facilities and move about safely and without experiencing eye strain. So far as is reasonably practicable lighting should be provided by natural light. The ACOP advises that windows and skylights should be regularly cleaned to allow in the maximum amount of daylight unless this would result in excessive heat or glare at a workstation.

Emergency lighting must also be provided wherever workers would be exposed to danger if the artificial lighting system failed. The ACOP advises that the emergency lighting system should be powered by a source independent from the normal lighting system.

¶708 Cleanliness and waste materials (reg. 9)

Regulation 9 imposes an obligation to keep workplaces and the furniture, furnishings and fittings in them clean. All surfaces of floors, walls and ceilings of workplaces inside buildings must also be *capable* of being sufficiently clean, which may involve sealing or coating. The ACOP points out that if it is likely that a floor is going to be contaminated by oil or other substances which are difficult to remove then any covering carpet should be avoided or removed.

¶709 Room dimensions and space (reg. 10)

Regulation 10 provides that every room where people work must have sufficient floor area, height and unoccupied space, and the ACOP gives suggested dimensions for the size of rooms and the height of ceilings.

¶710 Workstations and seating (reg. 11)

Regulation 11 provides that every workstation must be suitable both for the person using it and also for the work that is to be carried out there. The term 'suitable' will be judged by reference to any special needs of the individual worker including those with disabilities.

Particular reference is made to workstations outdoors. For them to be 'suitable' they must, so far as is reasonably practicable, provide protection from adverse weather. The layout of the workstation must enable the worker to leave it swiftly or to be assisted in case of an emergency and it should be arranged so that any person working at it is not likely to slip or fall.

Factors to be considered when judging suitability include the adequacy of freedom of movement and the ability to stand upright. This regulation also requires a suitable seat to be provided where the work carried out (or a substantial part of it) can or must be done while seated. A seat will not be considered suitable unless a footrest has been provided where necessary.

¶711 Traffic routes (reg. 12)

Regulation 12 requires that floors and the surfaces of 'traffic routes' must be suitable for the purposes for which they are used. The term 'traffic routes' is defined as a route for pedestrians and/or vehicles including stairs, doorways, ramps and ladders. To be 'suitable' they should have adequate strength and stability taking into account the persons/vehicles passing over or placed on them. Nor must they have any holes, slopes or uneven or slippery surfaces which might expose a person to a risk to their health and safety.

Floors must be adequately drained where necessary and, so far as is reasonably practicable, floors and traffic routes must be kept free from obstructions and any articles which might cause a person to slip, trip or fall.

Handrails and guards should be provided on all staircases except where the handrail would obstruct the staircase. The ACOP advises that a handrail should be provided on at least one side of every staircase and on both sides if there is a particular risk of falling, for example where staircases are liable to be subject to spillages.

Example
Two serious accidents have taken place in Jack's factory over the past month:

(1) a worker slipped close to a grinding machine, fell on to it and was seriously injured; and

(2) as a result of leakage from oil drums needed to be kept in the factory a worker slipped and broke his ankle.

Jack intends:

- to have the area surrounding the grinding machine coated with a slip resistant surface; and

- to have stop valves fitted to the filling points of the oil drums. Jack instructs the factory safety officer to inspect the area surrounding the oil drums once in the morning and once in the afternoon. If any leakage has occurred the safety office must arrange for the area to be fenced off and for the area to be covered with absorbent granules.

¶712 Falls or falling objects (reg. 13)

Regulation 13 requires that, so far as is reasonably practicable, measures must be taken to prevent people from:

- falling a distance likely to cause personal injury; or
- being struck by a falling object likely to cause personal injury,

and that any area where this is likely to happen must be clearly indicated.

The ACOP gives guidance on distances and other factors relevant to the likelihood of personal injury being caused by a fall. It also provides practical guidance in respect of the preventative measures that should be taken, such as fencing and covers.

This regulation also provides, that so far as is reasonably practicable, every tank, pit or structure should be securely covered or fenced where there is a risk of a person falling into a dangerous substance contained in it. A 'dangerous substance' is defined very widely. Further, every traffic route running over, across or in any covered tank/pit/structure containing a dangerous substance must be securely fenced.

¶713 Windows, transparent or translucent doors, gates and walls (reg. 14)

Regulation 14 requires that every window (or wall or partition which is transparent or translucent) and every transparent or translucent surface in a door or gate shall, where necessary, be of a safety material or be protected against breakage. The ACOP provides that this is necessary:

- where, in the case of doors and gates, the transparent or translucent surface is at shoulder level or below; and
- in the case of windows, walls and partitions where any part of the transparent or translucent surface is at waist level or below.

The ACOP also provides guidance as to 'safety materials'.

This regulation also provides that the windows or transparent or translucent surfaces should be made obvious. Marking may not be necessary if large handles or heavy tinting can make the surface apparent, but when it is needed then it should be conspicuous (for example coloured lines).

¶714 Windows, skylights and ventilators (reg. 15)

Regulation 15 provides that wherever a window, skylight or ventilator is capable of being opened then:

- it must not be designed in such a way that it is likely to be opened, closed or adjusted in a way that will expose the person doing the opening, etc. to a risk to their health and safety; and
- it should not be in a position when open which is likely to expose any person in a workplace to risks to their health and safety.

¶715 Ability to clean windows, etc. safely (reg. 16)

Regulation 16 requires that all windows and skylights must be designed or constructed so that they can be safely cleaned. In determining this question, account may be taken of any equipment used in conjunction with the window or skylight or devices fitted to the building (for example suspended cradles or travelling ladders).

¶716 Organisation, etc. of traffic routes (reg. 17)

Regulation 17 requires that workplaces should be organised so that pedestrians and vehicles can circulate safely. This regulation applies both to new and existing workplaces but in the case of those in existence before 1 January 1993 traffic routes need only comply 'so far as is reasonably practicable'.

Traffic routes must be suitable for the persons or vehicles using them especially in terms of position and dimensions. In order to be 'suitable':

- they should allow pedestrians/vehicles to use them without causing danger to others;
- there must be 'sufficient separation' between routes used by pedestrians (or doors or gates leading from those routes) and those used by vehicles; and
- when vehicles and pedestrians use the same route then there must be sufficient separation between them, i.e. it should be wide enough to allow vehicles to pass pedestrians safely.

All traffic routes must be suitably indicated where necessary for reasons of health and safety. For example, conspicuous signs must be erected showing maximum headroom for pedestrians or vehicles.

Example

An employer is concerned about the relatively large number of accidents that have been caused in his warehouse as a result of collisions between vehicles (such as fork-lift trucks).

The following measures are to be implemented:

- a one-way system for vehicles is to be introduced around the warehouse;
- signs indicating speed limits will be clearly displayed along vehicle traffic routes;
- speed humps (such that fork lift trucks can negotiate them safely) are to be fitted; and
- reversing alarm systems are to be fitted to all vehicles circulating around the warehouse.

¶717 Doors and gates (reg. 18)

Regulation 18 requires that doors and gates must be suitably constructed and must include any necessary safety devices. In particular, it requires that:

- sliding doors/gates have a device (such as a stop) which prevents them coming off their tracks;
- upward opening doors, etc. should have a device stopping them from falling back down;

- powered doors should have features (such as a sensitive edge) which prevent them from trapping anyone and should be able to be operated manually if the power fails; and

- doors, etc. which can be opened by being pushed from either side should provide a clear view of what is on the other side of the door. For example, a swing door should have a transparent panel in it unless it is low enough for you to see over.

¶718　Escalators and moving walkways (reg. 19)

Regulation 19 requires that escalators and moving walkways must function safely, be equipped with any necessary safety devices, and be fitted with one or more easily identifiable and readily accessible emergency stop controls.

¶719　Sanitary conveniences (reg. 20)

Regulation 20 requires that sanitary conveniences (i.e. toilets) must be provided at accessible places. The number of toilets to be provided in an existing workplace is specified in Part II of Schedule 1 of the regulations.

The toilets and the rooms they are in must be kept clean and in an orderly condition and must be adequately ventilated and lit. Separate rooms must be provided for men and women, although it will be acceptable for there to be a single convenience so long as this is a separate room which has a door which can be secured from the inside.

¶720　Washing facilities (reg. 21)

Regulation 21 requires that suitable and sufficient washing facilities must be provided at readily accessible places throughout the workplace. Showers may need to be provided if they are necessary for health reasons (for example there is a risk of workers' skin being contaminated) or because work being carried out is particularly dirty. Minimum numbers of washing facilities are set down by the ACOP.

To be 'suitable and sufficient' the washing facilities (e.g. wash-hand basins) must:

- whether or not they are provided elsewhere, be provided in any changing room and in the immediate facility of any sanitary convenience; and

- have soap (or other means of cleaning), towels (or other means of drying) and a supply of clean and, so far as is reasonably practicable, running hot and cold or warm water.

Both the washing facilities and the rooms they are in must be kept clean and in an orderly condition and should be sufficiently ventilated and lit. Separate facilities for washing should be provided for men and women except:

- if the facility (e.g. a shower) is in a room that is intended to be used by only one person at a time and has a door that can be secured from the inside; or

- if the washing facilities provided are needed only for washing hands, forearms and the face.

Example
Jane owns and runs a medium-sized travel agency where she employs 11 travel consultants/clerks, all of whom are women.

Above the travel shop are various rooms including storerooms, a kitchen and a cloakroom where all staff leave their coats and bags. Immediately behind the cloakroom is the washroom.

The washroom consists of two toilet cubicles, two wash-basins, a soap dispenser and two warm air hand-drying machines. The wash-basins provide hot and cold running water.

One of the water closets is adapted in terms of size, so as to be suitable for one member of staff who is disabled. This closet also has a handrail and is large enough to accommodate the manoeuvres of a wheelchair. The wash-basins are situated at a convenient height for this employee.

The washroom is ventilated by means of an extractor fan and is well lit. There is a large window which faces on to the street but this is glazed with frosted glass so that it is not possible to see in from the outside.

A cleaner is employed to clean the washroom every evening.

¶721 Drinking water (reg. 22)

Regulation 22 provides that there must be an adequate supply of wholesome drinking water in the workplace. The water should be in readily accessible places and, where necessary for reasons of health and safety (e.g. where there is a risk that people might drink water supplies which are not fit for drinking), should be conspicuously marked by an appropriate sign identifying it as drinking water.

¶722 Accommodation for clothing (reg. 23)

Regulation 23 provides that suitable and sufficient accommodation must be provided for clothing not worn during working hours and for any special clothing worn whilst at work which is not taken home (for example overalls).

¶723 Facilities for changing clothing (reg. 24)

Regulation 24 requires that suitable and sufficient facilities must be provided for people who need to change clothing where they have to wear special clothing for the purposes of their work and cannot, for reasons of health (for example, to avoid contamination), or propriety (if, for example, they remove more than their outer clothing), be expected to change in another room.

To be suitable there must be separate facilities for men and women where this is necessary to ensure privacy.

¶724 Facilities for rest and to eat meals (reg. 25)

Regulation 25 provides that suitable and sufficient rest facilities must be provided at readily accessible places. For example, persons who have to stand to carry out their work should be provided with seating which they can use during rest breaks.

Where meals are regularly eaten in the workplace, or where there is a risk that food eaten in the workplace will be likely to become contaminated, then suitable facilities should be provided for people to eat meals.

In addition there is an obligation to provide suitable rest facilities for pregnant women or nursing mothers.

Rest rooms and rest areas should be arranged to protect non-smokers from discomfort caused by tobacco smoke. This may be done either by prohibiting smoking in rest rooms/areas or by providing separate areas for smokers/non-smokers.

Example
David works in the childrens' ward of his local hospital as a nurse.

A rest room is provided near to the childrens' ward. This rest room has a table and a sufficient number of armchairs so that all members of staff, taking their lunch-break at the same time, can sit down.

An electric kettle is provided so that hot drinks can be made.

As the hospital canteen is some distance from the childrens' ward and, as it is always very busy at lunch-times, staff find they do not have enough time to make their way to the canteen, eat and return, all in their one hour lunch-break. A small electric cooker has been provided so that hot meals can be prepared by staff.

All hospital rest rooms are strictly no smoking zones.

On the wall is a notice setting out the cleaning rota which all members of staff must adhere to, in respect of the rest room.

¶725 Complying with the Workplace Regulations – is it worth it?

The consequences of non-compliance with the regulations are detailed at ¶104 above and will hopefully convince employers and others that it is worth complying with the regulations. There is however a more positive aspect in that the Workplace Regulations consolidate into one place various obligations and duties which have previously been contained in different pieces of legislation. This will certainly help employers to understand clearly the duties on them as regards health and safety standards of the workplace.

PART II
REGULATIONS

THE MANAGEMENT OF HEALTH AND SAFETY AT WORK REGULATIONS 1992

(SI 1992/2051)

Made on 26 August 1992 by The Secretary of State, in exercise of the powers conferred upon her by ss. 15(1), (2), (5) and (9), 47(2) and 52(2) and (3) of, and paras. 6(1), 7, 8(1), 14, 15(1) and 16 of Sch. 3 to, the Health and Safety at Work etc. Act 1974, and of all other powers enabling her in that behalf and for the purpose of giving effect without modifications to proposals submitted to her by the Health and Safety Commission under s. 11(2)(d) of the said Act after the carrying out by the said Commission of consultations in accordance with s. 50(3) of that Act. Operative from 1 January 1993.

ARRANGEMENT OF REGULATIONS

REGULATION
1. Citation, commencement and interpretation
2. Disapplication of these Regulations
3. Risk assessment
4. Health and safety arrangements
5. Health surveillance
6. Health and safety assistance
7. Procedures for serious and imminent danger and for danger areas
8. Information for employees
9. Co-operation and co-ordination
10. Persons working in host employers' or self-employed persons' undertakings
11. Capabilities and training
12. Employees' duties
13. Temporary workers
14. Exemption certificates
15. Exclusion of civil liability
16. Extension outside Great Britain
17. Modification of instrument
    The Schedule

CITATION, COMMENCEMENT AND INTERPRETATION

1(1) These Regulations may be cited as the Management of Health and Safety at Work Regulations 1992 and shall come into force on 1st January 1993.

1(2) In these Regulations –

"the assessment" means, in the case of an employer, the assessment made by him in accordance with regulation 3(1) and changed by him where necessary in accordance with regulation 3(3); and, in the case of a self-employed person, the assessment made by him in accordance with regulation 3(2) and changed by him where necessary in accordance with regulation 3(3);

"employment business" means a business (whether or not carried on with a view to profit and whether or not carried on in conjunction with any other business) which supplies persons (other than seafarers) who are employed in it to work for and under the control of other persons in any capacity;

"fixed-term contract of employment" means a contract of employment for a specific term which is fixed in advance or which can be ascertained in advance by reference to some relevant circumstance; and

"the preventive and protective measures" means the measures which have been identified by the employer or by the self-employed person in consequence of the assessment as the measures he needs to take to comply with the requirements and prohibitions imposed upon him by or under the relevant statutory provisions.

1(3) Any reference in these Regulations to –

(a) a numbered regulation is a reference to the regulation in these Regulations so numbered; or

(b) a numbered paragraph is a reference to the paragraph so numbered in the regulation in which the reference appears.

DISAPPLICATION OF THESE REGULATIONS

2 These Regulations shall not apply to or in relation to the master or crew of a sea-going ship or to the employer of such persons in respect of the normal ship-board activities of a ship's crew under the direction of the master.

RISK ASSESSMENT

3(1) Every employer shall make a suitable and sufficient assessment of –

(a) the risks to the health and safety of his employees to which they are exposed whilst they are at work; and

(b) the risks to the health and safety of persons not in his employment arising out of or in connection with the conduct by him of his undertaking,

for the purpose of identifying the measures he needs to take to comply with the requirements and prohibitions imposed upon him by or under the relevant statutory provisions.

3(2) Every self-employed person shall make a suitable and sufficient assessment of –

(a) the risks to his own health and safety to which he is exposed whilst he is at work; and

(b) the risks to the health and safety of persons not in his employment arising out of or in connection with the conduct by him of his undertaking,

for the purpose of identifying the measures he needs to take to comply with the requirements and prohibitions imposed upon him by or under the relevant statutory provisions.

3(3) Any assessment such as is referred to in paragraph (1) or (2) shall be reviewed by the employer or self-employed person who made it if –

(a) there is reason to suspect that it is no longer valid; or

(b) there has been a significant change in the matters to which it relates;

and where as a result of any such review changes to an assessment are required, the employer or self-employed person concerned shall make them.

3(4) Where the employer employs five or more employees, he shall record –

(a) the significant findings of the assessment; and

(b) any group of his employees identified by it as being especially at risk.

HEALTH AND SAFETY ARRANGEMENTS

4(1) Every employer shall make and give effect to such arrangements as are appropriate, having regard to the nature of his activities and the size of his undertaking, for the effective planning, organisation, control, monitoring and review of the preventive and protective measures.

4(2) Where the employer employs five or more employees, he shall record the arrangements referred to in paragraph (1).

HEALTH SURVEILLANCE

5 Every employer shall ensure that his employees are provided with such health surveillance as is appropriate having regard to the risks to their health and safety which are identified by the assessment.

HEALTH AND SAFETY ASSISTANCE

6(1) Every employer shall, subject to paragraphs (6) and (7), appoint one or more competent persons to assist him in undertaking the measures he needs to take to comply with the requirements and prohibitions imposed upon him by or under the relevant statutory provisions.

6(2) Where an employer appoints persons in accordance with paragraph (1), he shall make arrangements for ensuring adequate co-operation between them.

6(3) The employer shall ensure that the number of persons appointed under paragraph (1), the time available for them to fulfil their functions and the means at their disposal are adequate having regard to the size of his undertaking, the risks to which his employees are exposed and the distribution of those risks throughout the undertaking.

6(4) The employer shall ensure that –

(a) any person appointed by him in accordance with paragraph (1) who is not in his employment –

(i) is informed of the factors known by him to affect, or suspected by him of affecting, the health and safety of any other person who may be affected by the conduct of his undertaking, and

(ii) has access to the information referred to in regulation 8; and

(b) any person appointed by him in accordance with paragraph (1) is given such information about any person working in his undertaking who is –

(i) employed by him under a fixed-term contract of employment, or

(ii) employed in an employment business,

as is necessary to enable that person properly to carry out the function specified in that paragraph.

6(5) A person shall be regarded as competent for the purposes of paragraph (1) where he has sufficient training and experience or knowledge and other qualities to enable him properly to assist in undertaking the measures referred to in that paragraph.

6(6) Paragraph (1) shall not apply to a self-employed employer who is not in partnership with any other person where he has sufficient training and experience or knowledge and other qualities properly to undertake the measures referred to in that paragraph himself.

6(7) Paragraph (1) shall not apply to individuals who are employers and who are together carrying on business in partnership where at least one of the individuals concerned has sufficient training and experience or knowledge and other qualities –

(a) properly to undertake the measures he needs to take to comply with the requirements and prohibitions imposed upon him by or under the relevant statutory provisions; and

(b) properly to assist his fellow partners in undertaking the measures they need to take to comply with the requirements and prohibitions imposed upon them by or under the relevant statutory provisions.

PROCEDURES FOR SERIOUS AND IMMINENT DANGER AND FOR DANGER AREAS

7(1) Every employer shall –

(a) establish and where necessary give effect to appropriate procedures to be followed in the event of serious and imminent danger to persons at work in his undertaking;

(b) nominate a sufficient number of competent persons to implement those procedures insofar as they relate to the evacuation from premises of persons at work in his undertaking; and

(c) ensure that none of his employees has access to any area occupied by him to which it is necessary to restrict access on grounds of health and safety unless the employee concerned has received adequate health and safety instruction.

7(2) Without prejudice to the generality of paragraph (1)(a), the procedures referred to in that sub-paragraph shall –

(a) so far as is practicable, require any persons at work who are exposed to serious and imminent danger to be informed of the nature of the hazard and of the steps taken or to be taken to protect them from it;

SI 1992/2051, reg. 6(5)

(b) enable the persons concerned (if necessary by taking appropriate steps in the absence of guidance or instruction and in the light of their knowledge and the technical means at their disposal) to stop work and immediately proceed to a place of safety in the event of their being exposed to serious, imminent and unavoidable danger; and

(c) save in exceptional cases for reasons duly substantiated (which cases and reasons shall be specified in those procedures), require the persons concerned to be prevented from resuming work in any situation where there is still a serious and imminent danger.

7(3) A person shall be regarded as competent for the purposes of paragraph (1)(b) where he has sufficient training and experience or knowledge and other qualities to enable him properly to implement the evacuation procedures referred to in that sub-paragraph.

INFORMATION FOR EMPLOYEES

8 Every employer shall provide his employees with comprehensible and relevant information on –

(a) the risks to their health and safety identified by the assessment;

(b) the preventive and protective measures;

(c) the procedures referred to in regulation 7(1)(a);

(d) the identity of those persons nominated by him in accordance with regulation 7(1)(b); and

(e) the risks notified to him in accordance with regulation 9(1)(c).

CO-OPERATION AND CO-ORDINATION

9(1) Where two or more employers share a workplace (whether on a temporary or a permanent basis) each such employer shall –

(a) co-operate with the other employers concerned so far as is necessary to enable them to comply with the requirements and prohibitions imposed upon them by or under the relevant statutory provisions;

(b) (taking into account the nature of his activities) take all reasonable steps to co-ordinate the measures he takes to comply with the requirements and prohibitions imposed upon him by or under the relevant statutory provisions with the measures the other employers concerned are taking to comply with the requirements and prohibitions imposed upon them by or under the relevant statutory provisions; and

(c) take all reasonable steps to inform the other employers concerned of the risks to their employees' health and safety arising out of or in connection with the conduct by him of his undertaking.

9(2) Paragraph (1) shall apply to employers sharing a workplace with self-employed persons and to self-employed persons sharing a workplace with other self-employed persons as it applies to employers sharing a workplace with other employers; and the references in that paragraph to employers and the reference in the said paragraph to their employees shall be construed accordingly.

SI 1992/2051, reg. 9(2)

PERSONS WORKING IN HOST EMPLOYERS' OR SELF-EMPLOYED PERSONS' UNDERTAKINGS

10(1) Every employer and every self-employed person shall ensure that the employer of any employees from an outside undertaking who are working in his undertaking is provided with comprehensible information on –

(a) the risks to those employees' health and safety arising out of or in connection with the conduct by that first-mentioned employer or by that self-employed person of his undertaking; and

(b) the measures taken by that first-mentioned employer or by that self-employed person in compliance with the requirements and prohibitions imposed upon him by or under the relevant statutory provisions insofar as the said requirements and prohibitions relate to those employees.

10(2) Paragraph (1) shall apply to a self-employed person who is working in the undertaking of an employer or a self-employed person as it applies to employees from an outside undertaking who are working therein; and the reference in that paragraph to the employer of any employees from an outside undertaking who are working in the undertaking of an employer or a self-employed person and the references in the said paragraph to employees from an outside undertaking who are working in the undertaking of an employer or a self-employed person shall be construed accordingly.

10(3) Every employer shall ensure that any person working in his undertaking who is not his employee and every self-employed person (not being an employer) shall ensure that any person working in his undertaking is provided with appropriate instructions and comprehensible information regarding any risks to that person's health and safety which arise out of the conduct by that employer or self-employed person of his undertaking.

10(4) Every employer shall –

(a) ensure that the employer of any employees from an outside undertaking who are working in his undertaking is provided with sufficient information to enable that second-mentioned employer to identify any person nominated by that first-mentioned employer in accordance with regulation 7(1)(b) to implement evacuation procedures as far as those employees are concerned; and

(b) take all reasonable steps to ensure that any employees from an outside undertaking who are working in his undertaking receive sufficient information to enable them to identify any person nominated by him in accordance with regulation 7(1)(b) to implement evacuation procedures as far as they are concerned.

10(5) Paragraph (4) shall apply to a self-employed person who is working in an employer's undertaking as it applies to employees from an outside undertaking who are working therein; and the reference in that paragraph to the employer of any employees from an outside undertaking who are working in an employer's undertaking and the references in the said paragraph to employees from an outside undertaking who are working in an employer's undertaking shall be construed accordingly.

CAPABILITIES AND TRAINING

11(1) Every employer shall, in entrusting tasks to his employees, take into account their capabilities as regards health and safety.

SI 1992/2051, reg. 10(1)

11(2) Every employer shall ensure that his employees are provided with adequate health and safety training –
- (a) on their being recruited into the employer's undertaking; and
- (b) on their being exposed to new or increased risks because of –
  - (i) their being transferred or given a change of responsibilities within the employer's undertaking,
  - (ii) the introduction of new work equipment into or a change respecting work equipment already in use within the employer's undertaking,
  - (iii) the introduction of new technology into the employer's undertaking, or
  - (iv) the introduction of a new system of work into or a change respecting a system of work already in use within the employer's undertaking.

11(3) The training referred to in paragraph (2) shall –
- (a) be repeated periodically where appropriate;
- (b) be adapted to take account of any new or changed risks to the health and safety of the employees concerned; and
- (c) take place during working hours.

EMPLOYEES' DUTIES

12(1) Every employee shall use any machinery, equipment, dangerous substance, transport equipment, means of production or safety device provided to him by his employer in accordance both with any training in the use of the equipment concerned which has been received by him and the instructions respecting that use which have been provided to him by the said employer in compliance with the requirements and prohibitions imposed upon that employer by or under the relevant statutory provisions.

12(2) Every employee shall inform his employer or any other employee of that employer with specific responsibility for the health and safety of his fellow employees –
- (a) of any work situation which a person with the first-mentioned employee's training and instruction would reasonably consider represented a serious and immediate danger to health and safety; and
- (b) of any matter which a person with the first-mentioned employee's training and instruction would reasonably consider represented a shortcoming in the employer's protection arrangements for health and safety,

insofar as that situation or matter either affects the health and safety of that first-mentioned employee or arises out of or in connection with his own activities at work, and has not previously been reported to his employer or to any other employee of that employer in accordance with this paragraph.

TEMPORARY WORKERS

13(1) Every employer shall provide any person whom he has employed under a fixed-term contract of employment with comprehensible information on –
- (a) any special occupational qualifications or skills required to be held by that employee if he is to carry out his work safely; and

SI 1992/2051, reg. 13(1)

(b) any health surveillance required to be provided to that employee by or under any of the relevant statutory provisions,

and shall provide the said information before the employee concerned commences his duties.

13(2) Every employer and every self-employed person shall provide any person employed in an employment business who is to carry out work in his undertaking with comprehensible information on –

(a) any special occupational qualifications or skills required to be held by that employee if he is to carry out his work safely; and

(b) any health surveillance required to be provided to that employee by or under any of the relevant statutory provisions.

13(3) Every employer and every self-employed person shall ensure that every person carrying on an employment business whose employees are to carry out work in his undertaking is provided with comprehensible information on –

(a) any special occupational qualifications or skills required to be held by those employees if they are to carry out their work safely; and

(b) the specific features of the jobs to be filled by those employees (insofar as those features are likely to affect their health and safety);

and the person carrying on the employment business concerned shall ensure that the information so provided is given to the said employees.

EXEMPTION CERTIFICATES

14(1) The Secretary of State for Defence may, in the interests of national security, by a certificate in writing exempt –

(a) any of the home forces, any visiting force or any headquarters from those requirements of these Regulations which impose obligations on employers; or

(b) any member of the home forces, any member of a visiting force or any member of a headquarters from the requirements imposed by regulation 12;

and any exemption such as is specified in sub-paragraph (a) or (b) of this paragraph may be granted subject to conditions and to a limit of time and may be revoked by the said Secretary of State by a further certificate in writing at any time.

14(2) In this regulation –

(a) **"the home forces"** has the same meaning as in section 12(1) of the Visiting Forces Act 1952;

(b) **"headquarters"** has the same meaning as in article 3(2) of the Visiting Forces and International Headquarters (Application of Law) Order 1965;

(c) **"member of a headquarters"** has the same meaning as in paragraph 1(1) of the Schedule to the International Headquarters and Defence Organisations Act 1964; and

(d) **"visiting force"** has the same meaning as it does for the purposes of any provision of Part I of the Visiting Forces Act 1952.

EXCLUSION OF CIVIL LIABILITY

15 Breach of a duty imposed by these Regulations shall not confer a right of action in any civil proceedings.

EXTENSION OUTSIDE GREAT BRITAIN

16(1) These Regulations shall, subject to regulation 2, apply to and in relation to the premises and activities outside Great Britain to which sections 1 to 59 and 80 to 82 of the Health and Safety at Work etc. Act 1974 apply by virtue of the Health and Safety at Work etc. Act 1974 (Application Outside Great Britain) Order 1989 as they apply within Great Britain.

16(2) For the purposes of Part I of the 1974 Act, the meaning of **"at work"** shall be extended so that an employee or a self-employed person shall be treated as being at work throughout the time that he is present at the premises to and in relation to which these Regulations apply by virtue of paragraph (1); and, in that connection, these Regulations shall have effect subject to the extension effected by this paragraph.

MODIFICATION OF INSTRUMENT

17 The Safety Representatives and Safety Committees Regulations 1977 shall be modified to the extent specified in the Schedule to these Regulations.

THE SCHEDULE Regulation 17

The following regulation shall be inserted after regulation 4 of the Safety Representatives and Safety Committees Regulations 1977 –

"Employer's duty to consult and provide facilities and assistance

4A(1) Without prejudice to the generality of section 2(6) of the Health and Safety at Work etc. Act 1974, every employer shall consult safety representatives in good time with regard to –

(a) the introduction of any measure at the workplace which may substantially affect the health and safety of the employees the safety representatives concerned represent;

(b) his arrangements for appointing or, as the case may be, nominating persons in accordance with regulations 6(1) and 7(1)(b) of the Management of Health and Safety at Work Regulations 1992;

(c) any health and safety information he is required to provide to the employees the safety representatives concerned represent by or under the relevant statutory provisions;

(d) the planning and organisation of any health and safety training he is required to provide to the employees the safety representatives concerned represent by or under the relevant statutory provisions; and

(e) the health and safety consequences for the employees the safety representatives concerned represent of the introduction (including the planning thereof) of new technologies into the workplace.

4A(2) Without prejudice to regulations 5 and 6 of these Regulations, every employer shall provide such facilities and assistance as safety representatives may reasonably require for the purpose of carrying out their functions under section 2(4) of the 1974 Act and under these Regulations.".

EXPLANATORY NOTE

(This note is not part of the Regulations)

1 These Regulations (**"the Regulations"**) give effect as respects Great Britain (except to the extent specified below) to Council Directive 89/391/EEC on the introduction of measures to encourage improvements in the safety and health of workers at work (OJ No. L 183, 29.6.89, p. 1) [**"the Framework Directive"**] and to Council Directive 91/383/EEC supplementing the measures to encourage improvements in the safety and health at work of workers with a fixed-duration employment relationship or a temporary employment relationship (OJ No. L 206, 29.7.91, p. 19) [**"the Temporary Workers' Directive"**].

2 The Regulations do not apply in relation to sea transport (*regulation 2*).

3 Nor do the Regulations impose requirements with respect to the following matters:

  (a) accident reporting (*article 9(1)(c) and (d) and (2) of the Framework Directive*);

  (b) charging of workers in respect of health and safety measures (*article 6(5) of the Framework Directive*);

  (c) consultation and participation of workers and workers' representatives (*articles 10(3), 11(1), (3), (5) and (6) and 12(3) and (4) of the Framework Directive*);

  (d) employees' general safety obligations (*article 13(1) and (2)(e) and (f) of the Framework Directive*);

  (e) employers' general safety obligations (*articles 5 and 6(1) of the Framework Directive*);

  (f) employment protection rights (*articles 7(2), 8(4) and (5) and 11(4) of the Framework Directive*);

  (g) fire fighting (*articles 8(1) and (2) and 10(1) and (2) of the Framework Directive*);

  (h) first-aid (*articles 8(1) and (2) and 10(1) and (2) of the Framework Directive*);

  (i) risk groups (*article 15 of the Framework Directive*);

  (j) use of personal protective equipment (*article 13(2)(b) of the Framework Directive*); or

  (k) responsibility of host undertakings to temporary workers (*article 8 of the Temporary Workers' Directive*).

4 Regulation 3 requires employers and self-employed persons to make assessments of the health and safety risks to which their respective undertakings give rise, for the purpose of ascertaining what they have to do to comply with their obligations under health and safety legislation. Regulation 3 also makes provision for the review and recording of the results of risk assessments.

5 Regulation 4 requires employers to make, give effect to and in certain cases record appropriate health and safety arrangements.

6 Regulation 5 requires employers to ensure that their employees are provided with appropriate health surveillance.

7 Regulation 6 requires employers to appoint an adequate number of competent persons to assist them to comply with their obligations under health and safety legislation unless (in the case of a sole trader or a partnership) the employer concerned already has sufficient competence

to comply with the relevant obligations without assistance. Regulation 6, as well as defining **"competent person"** in this context, also requires employers –

- (a) to make arrangements for ensuring adequate co-operation between the competent persons they appoint; and
- (b) to provide the competent persons they appoint with –
    - (i) the facilities necessary to enable them to carry out their functions, and
    - (ii) specified health and safety information.

8 Regulation 7 requires employers –

- (a) to establish and give effect to procedures to be followed in the event of serious and imminent danger to persons working in their respective undertakings;
- (b) to nominate competent persons to implement those procedures insofar as they relate to the evacuation from premises of persons at work in their respective undertakings; and
- (c) restrict access to any danger areas occupied by them.

Regulation 7 also specifies in detail what the procedures referred to above must achieve and defines what is meant by **"competent person"** in this context.

9 Regulation 8 requires employers to provide their employees with specified health and safety information.

10 Regulation 9 requires every employer and self-employed person who shares a workplace with any other employer or self-employed person to –

- (a) co-operate with that other person so far as is necessary to enable him to comply with his statutory health and safety obligations;
- (b) co-ordinate the measures he takes in compliance with his statutory health and safety obligations with the measures being taken in that regard by that other person; and
- (c) take steps to provide that other person with specified health and safety information.

11 Regulation 10 requires employers and self-employed persons to ensure that –

- (a) the employers of any employees from outside undertakings who are working in their respective undertakings are provided with specified health and safety information;
- (b) self-employed persons who are working in their respective undertakings are provided with specified health and safety instructions and information; and
- (c) any employees from outside undertakings who are working in their respective undertakings are provided with specified health and safety instructions and information.

12 Regulation 11 requires employers –

- (a) to consider their employees' capabilities as regards health and safety when entrusting tasks to them; and
- (b) to ensure that in specified circumstances their employees are provided with adequate health and safety training.

Regulation 11 also specifies when the training referred to above is to be provided and the circumstances in which it is to be repeated or adapted.

SI 1992/2051, Note

13 Regulation 12 requires employees –

(a) to use machinery, equipment, dangerous substances, transport equipment, means of production and safety devices in accordance with any relevant training and instructions; and

(b) to inform their respective employers or any specified fellow employees of dangerous work situations and shortcomings in those employers' health and safety arrangements.

14 Regulation 13 –

(a) requires employers and self-employed persons to provide temporary workers in their respective undertakings with health and safety information before they commence their duties;

(b) requires employers and self-employed persons to provide any employment business whose employees are to carry out work in their respective undertakings with specified health and safety information about the work to be done by those employees; and

(c) requires any employment business provided with information by an employer or self-employed person in pursuance thereof to pass that information on to the employees to whom it relates.

15 Regulation 14 enables the Secretary of State for Defence to grant exemptions from the Regulations in the interests of national security.

16 Regulation 15 provides that breach of a duty imposed by the Regulations does not confer a right of action in civil proceedings.

17 Regulation 16 –

(a) extends the application of the Regulations to and in relation to certain premises and activities outside Great Britain; and

(b) extends the meaning of **"at work"** so that for the purposes of the Regulations an employee or a self-employed person is treated as being at work at all times when he is present at the premises to and in relation to which the Regulations apply by virtue of that regulation.

18 Regulation 17 and the Schedule modify the Safety Representatives and Safety Committees Regulations 1977 (S.I. 1977/500) by inserting a new regulation therein, regulation 4A.

SI 1992/2051, Note

THE PERSONAL PROTECTIVE EQUIPMENT AT WORK REGULATIONS 1992

(SI 1992/2966)

Made on 25 November 1992 by The Secretary of State, in exercise of the powers conferred upon her by ss. 15(1), (2), (3)(a) and (b), (5)(b) and (9) of, and paras. 11 and 14 of Sch. 3 to the Health and Safety at Work etc. Act 1974, and of all other powers enabling her in that behalf and for the purpose of giving effect without modifications to proposals submitted to her by the Health and Safety Commission under s. 11(2)(d) of the said Act after the carrying out by the said Commission of consultations in accordance with s. 50(3) of that Act. Operative from 1 January 1993.

ARRANGEMENT OF REGULATIONS

REGULATION
1. Citation and commencement
2. Interpretation
3. Disapplication of these Regulations
4. Provision of personal protective equipment
5. Compatibility of personal protective equipment
6. Assessment of personal protective equipment
7. Maintenance and replacement of personal protective equipment
8. Accommodation for personal protective equipment
9. Information, instruction and training
10. Use of personal protective equipment
11. Reporting loss or defect
12. Exemption certificates
13. Extension outside Great Britain
14. Modifications, repeal and revocations

SCHEDULE
1. Relevant Community directive
2. Modifications
    - Part I   The Factories Act 1961
    - Part II   The Coal and Other Mines (Fire and Rescue) Order 1956
    - Part III   The Shipbuilding and Ship-Repairing Regulations 1960
    - Part IV   The Coal Mines (Respirable Dust) Regulations 1975

Part V   The Control of Lead at Work Regulations 1980
Part VI   The Ionising Radiations Regulations 1985
Part VII   The Control of Asbestos at Work Regulations 1987
Part VIII   The Control of Substances Hazardous to Health Regulations 1988
Part IX   The Noise at Work Regulations 1989
Part X   The Construction (Head Protection) Regulations 1989
3. Revocations

CITATION AND COMMENCEMENT

1 These Regulations may be cited as the Personal Protective Equipment at Work Regulations 1992 and shall come into force on 1st January 1993.

INTERPRETATION

2(1) In these Regulations, unless the context otherwise requires, **"personal protective equipment"** means all equipment (including clothing affording protection against the weather) which is intended to be worn or held by a person at work and which protects him against one or more risks to his health or safety, and any addition or accessory designed to meet that objective.

2(2) Any reference in these Regulations to –

(a) a numbered regulation or Schedule is a reference to the regulation or Schedule in these Regulations so numbered; and

(b) a numbered paragraph is a reference to the paragraph so numbered in the regulation in which the reference appears.

DISAPPLICATION OF THESE REGULATIONS

3(1) These Regulations shall not apply to or in relation to the master or crew of a sea-going ship or to the employer of such persons in respect of the normal ship-board activities of a ship's crew under the direction of the master.

3(2) Regulations 4 to 12 shall not apply in respect of personal protective equipment which is –

(a) ordinary working clothes and uniforms which do not specifically protect the health and safety of the wearer;

(b) an offensive weapon within the meaning of section 1(4) of the Prevention of Crime Act 1953 used as self-defence or as deterrent equipment;

(c) portable devices for detecting and signalling risks and nuisances;

(d) personal protective equipment used for protection while travelling on a road within the meaning (in England and Wales) of section 192(1) of the Road Traffic Act 1988, and (in Scotland) of section 151 of the Roads (Scotland) Act 1984;

(e) equipment used during the playing of competitive sports.

3(3) Regulations 4 and 6 to 12 shall not apply where any of the following Regulations apply and in respect of any risk to a person's health or safety for which any of them require the provision or use of personal protective equipment, namely –

(a) the Control of Lead at Work Regulations 1980;

(b) the Ionising Radiations Regulations 1985;
(c) the Control of Asbestos at Work Regulations 1987;
(d) the Control of Substances Hazardous to Health Regulations 1988;
(e) the Noise at Work Regulations 1989;
(f) the Construction (Head Protection) Regulations 1989.

PROVISION OF PERSONAL PROTECTIVE EQUIPMENT

4(1) Every employer shall ensure that suitable personal protective equipment is provided to his employees who may be exposed to a risk to their health or safety while at work except where and to the extent that such risk has been adequately controlled by other means which are equally or more effective.

4(2) Every self-employed person shall ensure that he is provided with suitable personal protective equipment where he may be exposed to a risk to his health or safety while at work except where and to the extent that such risk has been adequately controlled by other means which are equally or more effective.

4(3) Without prejudice to the generality of paragraphs (1) and (2), personal protective equipment shall not be suitable unless –

(a) it is appropriate for the risk or risks involved and the conditions at the place where exposure to the risk may occur;

(b) it takes account of ergonomic requirements and the state of health of the person or persons who may wear it;

(c) it is capable of fitting the wearer correctly, if necessary, after adjustments within the range for which it is designed;

(d) so far as is practicable, it is effective to prevent or adequately control the risk or risks involved without increasing overall risk;

(e) it complies with any enactment (whether in an Act or instrument) which implements in Great Britain any provision on design or manufacture with respect to health or safety in any relevant Community directive listed in Schedule 1 which is applicable to that item of personal protective equipment.

COMPATIBILITY OF PERSONAL PROTECTIVE EQUIPMENT

5(1) Every employer shall ensure that where the presence of more than one risk to health or safety makes it necessary for his employee to wear or use simultaneously more than one item of personal protective equipment, such equipment is compatible and continues to be effective against the risk or risks in question.

5(2) Every self-employed person shall ensure that where the presence of more than one risk to health or safety makes it necessary for him to wear or use simultaneously more than one item of personal protective equipment, such equipment is compatible and continues to be effective against the risk or risks in question.

ASSESSMENT OF PERSONAL PROTECTIVE EQUIPMENT

6(1) Before choosing any personal protective equipment which by virtue of regulation 4 he is required to ensure is provided, an employer or self-employed person shall ensure that an assessment is made to determine whether the personal protective equipment he intends will be provided is suitable.

6(2) The assessment required by paragraph (1) shall include –

(a) an assessment of any risk or risks to health or safety which have not been avoided by other means;

(b) the definition of the characteristics which personal protective equipment must have in order to be effective against the risks referred to in sub-paragraph (a) of this paragraph, taking into account any risks which the equipment itself may create;

(c) comparison of the characteristics of the personal protective equipment available with the characteristics referred to in sub-paragraph (b) of this paragraph.

6(3) Every employer or self-employed person who is required by paragraph (1) to ensure that any assessment is made shall ensure that any such assessment is reviewed if –

(a) there is reason to suspect that it is no longer valid; or

(b) there has been a significant change in the matters to which it relates,

and where as a result of any such review changes in the assessment are required, the relevant employer or self-employed person shall ensure that they are made.

MAINTENANCE AND REPLACEMENT OF PERSONAL PROTECTIVE EQUIPMENT

7(1) Every employer shall ensure that any personal protective equipment provided to his employees is maintained (including replaced or cleaned as appropriate) in an efficient state, in efficient working order and in good repair.

7(2) Every self-employed person shall ensure that any personal protective equipment provided to him is maintained (including replaced or cleaned as appropriate) in an efficient state, in efficient working order and in good repair.

ACCOMMODATION FOR PERSONAL PROTECTIVE EQUIPMENT

8 Where an employer or self-employed person is required, by virtue of regulation 4, to ensure personal protective equipment is provided, he shall also ensure that appropriate accommodation is provided for that personal protective equipment when it is not being used.

INFORMATION, INSTRUCTION AND TRAINING

9(1) Where an employer is required to ensure that personal protective equipment is provided to an employee, the employer shall also ensure that the employee is provided with such information, instruction and training as is adequate and appropriate to enable the employee to know –

(a) the risk or risks which the personal protective equipment will avoid or limit;

(b) the purpose for which and the manner in which personal protective equipment is to be used; and

SI 1992/2966, reg. 6(1)

(c) any action to be taken by the employee to ensure that the personal protective equipment remains in an efficient state, in efficient working order and in good repair as required by regulation 7(1).

9(2) Without prejudice to the generality of paragraph (1), the information and instruction provided by virtue of that paragraph shall not be adequate and appropriate unless it is comprehensible to the persons to whom it is provided.

USE OF PERSONAL PROTECTIVE EQUIPMENT

10(1) Every employer shall take all reasonable steps to ensure that any personal protective equipment provided to his employees by virtue of regulation 4(1) is properly used.

10(2) Every employee shall use any personal protective equipment provided to him by virtue of these Regulations in accordance both with any training in the use of the personal protective equipment concerned which has been received by him and the instructions respecting that use which have been provided to him by virtue of regulation 9.

10(3) Every self-employed person shall make full and proper use of any personal protective equipment provided to him by virtue of regulation 4(2).

10(4) Every employee and self-employed person who has been provided with personal protective equipment by virtue of regulation 4 shall take all reasonable steps to ensure that it is returned to the accommodation provided for it after use.

REPORTING LOSS OR DEFECT

11 Every employee who has been provided with personal protective equipment by virtue of regulation 4(1) shall forthwith report to his employer any loss of or obvious defect in that personal protective equipment.

EXEMPTION CERTIFICATES

12(1) The Secretary of State for Defence may, in the interests of national security, by a certificate in writing exempt –

(a) any of the home forces, any visiting force or any headquarters from those requirements of these Regulations which impose obligations on employers; or

(b) any member of the home forces, any member of a visiting force or any member of a headquarters from the requirements imposed by regulation 10 or 11;

and any exemption such as is specified in sub-paragraph (a) or (b) of this paragraph may be granted subject to conditions and to a limit of time and may be revoked by the said Secretary of State by a further certificate in writing at any time.

12(2) In this regulation –

(a) **"the home forces"** has the same meaning as in section 12(1) of the Visiting Forces Act 1952;

(b) **"headquarters"** has the same meaning as in article 3(2) of the Visiting Forces and International Headquarters (Application of Law) Order 1965;

(c) **"member of a headquarters"** has the same meaning as in paragraph 1(1) of the Schedule to the International Headquarters and Defence Organisations Act 1964; and

(d) **"visiting force"** has the same meaning as it does for the purposes of any provision of Part I of the Visiting Forces Act 1952.

EXTENSION OUTSIDE GREAT BRITAIN

13 These Regulations shall apply to and in relation to the premises and activities outside Great Britain to which sections 1 to 59 and 80 to 82 of the Health and Safety at Work etc. Act 1974 apply by virtue of the Health and Safety at Work etc. Act 1974 (Application Outside Great Britain) Order 1989 as they apply within Great Britain.

MODIFICATIONS, REPEAL AND REVOCATIONS

14(1) The Act and Regulations specified in Schedule 2 shall be modified to the extent specified in the corresponding Part of that Schedule.

14(2) Section 65 of the Factories Act 1961 is repealed.

14(3) The instruments specified in column 1 of Schedule 3 are revoked to the extent specified in column 3 of that Schedule.

Schedule 1 – Relevant Community Directive

Regulation 4(3)(e)

Council Directive of 21 December 1989 on the approximation of the laws of the Member States relating to personal protective equipment (89/686/EEC).

Schedule 2 – Modifications

Regulation 14(1)

Part I – The Factories Act 1961

1 In section 30(6), for "breathing apparatus of a type approved by the chief inspector", substitute "suitable breathing apparatus".

Part II – The Coal and Other Mines (Fire and Rescue) Order 1956

2 In Schedule 1, in regulation 23(a), for "breathing apparatus of a type approved by the Minister", substitute "suitable breathing apparatus".

3 In Schedule 1, in regulation 23(b), for "smoke helmets or other apparatus serving the same purpose, being helmets or apparatus of a type approved by the Minister,", substitute "suitable smoke helmets or other suitable apparatus serving the same purpose".

4 In Schedule 1, in regulation 24(a), for "smoke helmet or other apparatus serving the same purpose, being a helmet or other apparatus of a type approved by the Minister,", substitute "suitable smoke helmet or other suitable apparatus serving the same purpose".

Part III – The Shipbuilding and Ship-Repairing Regulations 1960

5   In each of regulations 50, 51(1) and 60(1), for "breathing apparatus of a type approved for the purpose of this Regulation", substitute "suitable breathing apparatus".

Part IV – The Coal Mines (Respirable Dust) Regulations 1975

6   In regulation 10(a), for "dust respirators of a type approved by the Executive for the purpose of this Regulation", substitute "suitable dust respirators".

Part V – The Control of Lead at Work Regulations 1980

7   In regulation 7 –
   (a) after "respiratory protective equipment", insert "which complies with regulation 8A or, where the requirements of that regulation do not apply, which is"; and
   (b) after "as will", insert ", in either case,".

8   In regulation 8, for "adequate protective clothing", substitute "protective clothing which complies with regulation 8A or, where no requirement is imposed by virtue of that regulation, is adequate".

9   After regulation 8, insert the following new regulations –

"Compliance with relevant Community directives

8A   Any respiratory protective equipment or protective clothing shall comply with any enactment (whether in an Act or instrument) which implements any provision on design or manufacture with respect to health or safety in any relevant Community directive listed in Schedule 1 to the Personal Protective Equipment at Work Regulations 1992 which is applicable to that item of respiratory protective equipment or protective clothing.

Assessment of respiratory protective equipment or protective clothing

8B(1)   Before choosing respiratory protective equipment or protective clothing, an employer shall make an assessment to determine whether it will satisfy regulation 7 or 8, as appropriate.

8B(2)   The assessment required by paragraph (1) shall involve –
   (a) definition of the characteristics necessary to comply with regulation 7 or, as the case may be, 8, and
   (b) comparison of the characteristics of respiratory protective equipment or protective clothing available with the characteristics referred to in sub-paragraph (a) of this paragraph.

8B(3)   The assessment required by paragraph (1) shall be revised if –
   (a) there is reason to suspect that it is no longer valid; or
   (b) there has been a significant change in the work to which it relates,

and, where, as a result of the review, changes in the assessment are required, the employer shall make them.".

10   In regulation 9, for sub-paragraph (b), substitute the following sub-paragraph –
   "(b) where he is required under regulations 7 or 8 to provide respiratory protective

equipment or protective clothing, adequate changing facilities and adequate facilities for the storage of –
  (i) the respiratory protective equipment or protective clothing, and
  (ii) personal clothing not worn during working hours.".

11 At the end of regulation 13, add the following new paragraph –

"(3) Every employee shall take all reasonable steps to ensure that any respiratory protective equipment provided to him pursuant to regulation 7 and protective clothing provided to him pursuant to regulation 8 is returned to the accommodation provided for it after use."

12 In regulation 18(2), omit the full stop and add "and that any provision imposed by the European Communities in respect of the encouragement of improvements in the safety and health of workers at work will be satisfied.".

Part VI – The Ionising Radiations Regulations 1985

13 In regulation 23(1), after "that respiratory protective equipment", insert "complies with paragraph (1A) or, where no requirement is imposed by that paragraph,".

14 After regulation 23(1), insert the following paragraphs –

"(1A) For the purposes of paragraph (1), personal protective equipment complies with this paragraph if it complies with any enactment (whether in an Act or instrument) which implements in Great Britain any provision on design or manufacture with respect to health or safety in any relevant Community directive listed in Schedule 1 to the Personal Protective Equipment at Work Regulations 1992 which is applicable to that item of personal protective equipment.

(1B) Before choosing personal protective equipment, an employer shall make an assessment to determine whether it will satisfy regulation 6(3).

(1C) The assessment required by paragraph (1B) shall involve –
  (a) definition of the characteristics necessary to comply with regulation 6(3), and
  (b) comparison of the characteristics of available personal protective equipment with the characteristics referred to in sub-paragraph (a) of this paragraph.

(1D) The assessment required by paragraph (1B) shall be reviewed if –
  (a) there is reason to suspect that it is no longer valid; or
  (b) there has been a significant change in the work to which it relates,

and where, as a result of the review, changes in the assessment are required, the employer shall make them.".

15 Add at the end of regulation 23 the following additional paragraphs –

"(2A) Every employer shall ensure that appropriate accommodation is provided for personal protective equipment when it is not being worn.

(2B) Every employee shall take all reasonable steps to ensure that personal protective equipment provided to him is returned to the accommodation provided for it after use.".

Part VII – The Control of Asbestos at Work Regulations 1987

16 In regulation 8(3), after "shall" the first time that word appears, insert "comply with paragraph (3A) or, where no requirement is imposed by that paragraph, shall".

SI 1992/2966, Sch. 2, para. 11

17 Insert the following new paragraph after regulation 8(3) –

"(3A) Any respiratory protective equipment provided in pursuance of paragraph (2) or protective clothing provided in pursuance of regulation 11(1) shall comply with this paragraph if it complies with any enactment (whether in an Act or instrument) which implements in Great Britain any provision on design or manufacture with respect to health or safety in any relevant Community directive listed in Schedule 1 to the Personal Protective Equipment at Work Regulations 1992 which is applicable to that item of respiratory protective equipment or protective clothing.".

18 In regulation 20(2), omit the fullstop and add "and that any provision imposed by the European Communities in respect of the encouragement of improvements in the safety and health of workers at work will be satisfied.".

Part VIII – The Control of Substances Hazardous to Health Regulations 1988

19 In regulation 7, after paragraph (3), insert the following new paragraph –

"(3A) Any personal protective equipment provided by an employer in pursuance of this regulation shall comply with any enactment (whether in an Act or instrument) which implements in Great Britain any provision on design or manufacture with respect to health or safety in any relevant Community directive listed in Schedule 1 to the Personal Protective Equipment at Work Regulations 1992 which is applicable to that item of personal protective equipment.".

20 In regulation 7, in paragraph (6)(b), insert at the beginning "complies with paragraph (3A) or, where no requirement is imposed by virtue of that paragraph,".

21 In regulation 8(2), after "these regulations", insert "and shall take all reasonable steps to ensure it is returned after use to any accommodation provided for it".

Part IX – The Noise at Work Regulations 1989

22 Add the following new paragraph at the end of regulation 8 –

"(3) Any personal ear protectors provided by virtue of this regulation shall comply with any enactment (whether in an Act or instrument) which implements in Great Britain any provision on design or manufacture with respect to health or safety in any relevant Community directive listed in Schedule 1 to the Personal Protective Equipment at Work Regulations 1992 which is applicable to those ear protectors.".

Part X – The Construction (Head Protection) Regulations 1989

23 Add the following paragraphs at the end of regulation 3 –

"(3) Any head protection provided by virtue of this regulation shall comply with any enactment (whether in an Act or instrument) which implements any provision on design or manufacture with respect to health or safety in any relevant Community directive listed in Schedule 1 to the Personal Protective Equipment at Work Regulations 1992 which is applicable to that head protection.

(4) Before choosing head protection, an employer or self-employed person shall make an assessment to determine whether it is suitable.

(5) The assessment required by paragraph (4) of this regulation shall involve –

   (a) the definition of the characteristics which head protection must have in order to be suitable;

   (b) comparison of the characteristics of the protection available with the characteristics referred to in sub-paragraph (a) of this paragraph.

(6) The assessment required by paragraph (4) shall be reviewed if –

   (a) there is reason to suspect that it is no longer valid; or

   (b) there has been a significant change in the work to which it relates,

and where as a result of the review changes in the assessment are required, the relevant employer or self-employed person shall make them.

(7) Every employer and every self-employed person shall ensure that appropriate accommodation is available for head protection provided by virtue of these Regulations when it is not being used.".

24 For regulation 6(4), substitute the following paragraph –

"(4) Every employee or self-employed person who is required to wear suitable head protection by or under these Regulations shall –

   (a) make full and proper use of it; and

   (b) take all reasonable steps to return it to the accommodation provided for it after use.".

25 In regulation 9(2), omit the full stop and add "and that any provision imposed by the European Communities in respect of the encouragement of improvements in the safety and health of workers at work will be satisfied.".

Schedule 3 – Revocations

Regulation 14(3)

(1) Title	(2) Reference	(3) Extent of Revocation
Regulations dated 26th February 1906 in respect of the processes of spinning and weaving of flax and tow and the processes incidental thereto (the Flax and Tow-Spinning and Weaving Regulations 1906).	S.R. & O. 1906/177, amended by S.I. 1988/1657.	In regulation 9, the words "unless waterproof skirts, and bibs of suitable material, are provided by the occupier and worn by the workers". Regulation 13.
Order dated 5th October 1917 (the Tin or Terne Plates Manufacture Welfare Order 1917).	S.R. & O. 1917/1035.	Paragraph 1.

SI 1992/2966, Sch. 2, para. 24

(1) Title	(2) Reference	(3) Extent of Revocation
Order dated 15th August 1919 (the Fruit Preserving Welfare Order 1919).	S.R. & O. 1919/1136, amended by S.I. 1988/1657.	Paragraph 1.
Order dated 23rd April 1920 (the Laundries Welfare Order 1920).	S.R. & O. 1920/654.	Paragraph 1.
Order dated 28th July 1920 (the Gut-Scrapping, Tripe Dressing, etc. Welfare Order 1920).	S.R. & O. 1920/1437.	Paragraph 1.
Order dated 3rd March 1921 (the Glass Bevelling Welfare Order 1921).	S.R. & O. 1921/288.	Paragraph 1.
The Aerated Water Regulations 1921.	S.R. & O. 1921/1932; amended by S.I. 1981/686.	The whole Regulations.
The Sacks (Cleaning and Repairing) Welfare Order 1927.	S.R. & O. 1927/860.	Paragraph 1.
The Oil Cake Welfare Order 1929.	S.R. & O. 1929/534.	Paragraph 1.
The Cement Works Welfare Order 1930.	S.R. & O. 1930/94.	Paragraph 1.
The Tanning Welfare Order 1930.	S.R. & O. 1930/312.	Paragraph 1 and the Schedule.
The Magnesium (Grinding of Castings and Other Articles) Special Regulations 1946.	S.R. & O. 1946/2107.	Regulation 12.
The Clay Works (Welfare) Special Regulations 1948.	S.I. 1948/1547.	Regulation 5.
The Iron and Steel Foundries Regulations 1953.	S.I. 1953/1464; amended by S.I. 1974/1681 and S.I. 1981/1332.	Regulation 8.

SI 1992/2966, Sch. 3

(1) Title	(2) Reference	(3) Extent of Revocation
The Shipbuilding and Ship-Repairing Regulations 1960.	S.I. 1960/1932; amended by S.I. 1974/1681.	Regulations 73 and 74.
The Non-Ferrous Metals (Melting and Founding) Regulations 1962.	S.I. 1962/1667; amended by S.I. 1974/1681.	Regulation 13.
The Abstract of Special Regulations (Aerated Water) Order 1963.	S.I. 1963/2058.	The whole Order.
The Construction (Health and Welfare) Regulations 1966.	S.I. 1966/95; to which there are amendments not relevant to these regulations.	Regulation 15.
The Foundries (Protective Footwear and Gaiters) Regulations 1971.	S.I. 1971/476.	The whole Regulations.
The Protection of Eyes Regulations 1974.	S.I. 1974/1681; amended by S.I. 1975/303.	The whole Regulations.
The Aerated Water Regulations (Metrication) Regulations 1981.	S.I. 1981/686.	The whole Regulations.

EXPLANATORY NOTE

(This note is not part of the Regulations)

1   These Regulations impose health and safety requirements with respect to the provision for, and use by, persons at work of personal protective equipment. Personal protective equipment is defined in regulation 2(1) and certain types of such equipment are excluded from the application of regulations 4 to 12 by regulation 3(2).

2   The Regulations do not apply in relation to sea transport (*regulation 3(1)*). With that exception, the Regulations, together with the existing Regulations listed in regulation 3(3) (which are modified by Parts V to X of Schedule 2), give effect as respects Great Britain to Council Directive 89/656/EEC (OJ No. L 393, 30.12.89, p. 18) on the minimum health and safety requirements for the use by workers of personal protective equipment at the workplace.

The Personal Protective Equipment at Work Regulations 1992

3 Regulations 4 and 6 to 12 do not apply in respect of risks to health and safety for which personal protective equipment is required by specified existing Regulations (*regulation 3(3)*).

4 The Regulations require employers to ensure suitable personal protective equipment is provided for their employees and also require self-employed persons to ensure suitable personal protective equipment is provided for themselves. The circumstances in which personal protective equipment must be provided and minimum conditions of what is "suitable" are specified (*regulation 4*).

5 The Regulations also impose requirements with respect to –

(a) compatibility of items of personal protective equipment where it is necessary to wear or use more than one item simultaneously (*regulation 5*);

(b) the making, review and changing of assessments in relation to the choice of personal protective equipment (*regulation 6*);

(c) the maintenance (including replacement and cleaning as appropriate) of personal protective equipment (*regulation 7*);

(d) the provision of accommodation for personal protective equipment (*regulation 8*);

(e) the provision of information, instruction and training (*regulation 9*); and

(f) ensuring personal protective equipment is used (*regulation 10(1)*).

6 Requirements are imposed on employees and self-employed persons in respect of the use of personal protective equipment and in respect of returning it to accommodation provided for it (*regulation 10(2) to (4)*). Employees are also required to report to their employer the loss of or any obvious defect in personal protective equipment (*regulation 11*).

7 The Secretary of State for Defence may grant exemptions from the Regulations in the interests of national security (*regulation 12*).

8 The Regulations extend to and in relation to certain premises and activities outside Great Britain (*regulation 13*).

9 Certain existing provisions relating to personal protective equipment are modified (*Schedule 2*). Provisions replaced by these Regulations are repealed or revoked (*regulation 14(2) and Schedule 3*).

SI 1992/2966, Note

THE PROVISION AND USE OF WORK EQUIPMENT REGULATIONS 1992

(SI 1992/2932)

Made on 17 November 1992 by The Secretary of State, in the exercise of the powers conferred on her by ss. 15(1), (2), (3)(a), (5)(b) and (9), and 82(3)(a) of, and paras. 1(1), (2) and (3), 13(1) and 14 of Sch. 3 to, the Health and Safety at Work etc. Act 1974 ("the 1974 Act") and of all other powers enabling her in that behalf and for the purpose of giving effect without modifications to proposals submitted to her by the Health and Safety Commission under s. 11(2)(d) of the 1974 Act, after the carrying out by the said Commission of consultations in accordance with s. 50(3) of that Act. Operative from 1 January 1993 (the whole regulations except regs. 11 to 24 and 27 and Sch. 2 to the extent specified in reg. 1(3)) and 1 January 1997 (regs. 11 to 24 and 27 and Sch. 2 to the extent specified in reg. 1(3)).

ARRANGEMENT OF REGULATIONS

REGULATION
1. Citation and commencement
2. Interpretation
3. Disapplication of these Regulations
4. Application of requirements under these Regulations
5. Suitability of work equipment
6. Maintenance
7. Specific risks
8. Information and instructions
9. Training
10. Conformity with Community requirements
11. Dangerous parts of machinery
12. Protection against specified hazards
13. High or very low temperature
14. Controls for starting or making a significant change in operating conditions
15. Stop controls
16. Emergency stop controls
17. Controls
18. Control systems
19. Isolation from sources of energy
20. Stability
21. Lighting

22. Maintenance operations
23. Markings
24. Warnings
25. Exemption certificates
26. Extension outside Great Britain
27. Repeals, saving and revocations

SCHEDULE
 1. Relevant Community directives
 2. Repeals and revocations

CITATION AND COMMENCEMENT

1(1) These Regulations may be cited as the Provision and Use of Work Equipment Regulations 1992.

1(2) Subject to paragraph (3), these Regulations shall come into force on 1st January 1993.

1(3) Regulations 11 to 24 and 27 and Schedule 2 in so far as they apply to work equipment first provided for use in the premises or undertaking before 1st January 1993 shall come into force on 1st January 1997.

INTERPRETATION

2(1) In these Regulations, unless the context otherwise requires –

"**use**" in relation to work equipment means any activity involving work equipment and includes starting, stopping, programming, setting, transporting, repairing, modifying, maintaining, servicing and cleaning, and related expressions shall be construed accordingly;

"**work equipment**" means any machinery, appliance, apparatus or tool and any assembly of components which, in order to achieve a common end, are arranged and controlled so that they function as a whole.

2(2) Any reference in these Regulations to –

(a) a numbered regulation or Schedule is a reference to the regulation or Schedule in these Regulations so numbered; and

(b) a numbered paragraph is a reference to the paragraph so numbered in the regulation in which the reference appears.

DISAPPLICATION OF THESE REGULATIONS

3 These Regulations shall not apply to or in relation to the master or crew of a sea-going ship or to the employer of such persons, in respect of the normal ship-board activities of a ship's crew under the direction of the master.

APPLICATION OF REQUIREMENTS UNDER THESE REGULATIONS

4(1) The requirements imposed by these Regulations on an employer shall apply in respect of work equipment provided for use or used by any of his employees who is at work or who is on an offshore installation within the meaning assigned to that term by section 1(4) of the Offshore Safety Act 1992.

4(2) The requirements imposed by these Regulations on an employer shall also apply –
- (a) to a self-employed person, in respect of work equipment he uses at work;
- (b) to any person who has control, to any extent, of non-domestic premises made available to persons as a place of work, in respect of work equipment used in such premises by such persons and to the extent of his control; and
- (c) to any person to whom the provisions of the Factories Act 1961 apply by virtue of section 175(5) of that Act as if he were the occupier of a factory, in respect of work equipment used in the premises deemed to be a factory by that section.

4(3) Any reference in paragraph (2)(b) to a person having control of any premises or matter is a reference to the person having control of the premises or matter in connection with the carrying on by him of a trade, business or other undertaking (whether for profit or not).

SUITABILITY OF WORK EQUIPMENT

5(1) Every employer shall ensure that work equipment is so constructed or adapted as to be suitable for the purpose for which it is used or provided.

5(2) In selecting work equipment, every employer shall have regard to the working conditions and to the risks to the health and safety of persons which exist in the premises or undertaking in which that work equipment is to be used and any additional risk posed by the use of that work equipment.

5(3) Every employer shall ensure that work equipment is used only for operations for which, and under conditions for which, it is suitable.

5(4) In this regulation **"suitable"** means suitable in any respect which it is reasonably foreseeable will affect the health or safety of any person.

MAINTENANCE

6(1) Every employer shall ensure that work equipment is maintained in an efficient state, in efficient working order and in good repair.

6(2) Every employer shall ensure that where any machinery has a maintenance log, the log is kept up to date.

SPECIFIC RISKS

7(1) Where the use of work equipment is likely to involve a specific risk to health or safety, every employer shall ensure that –
- (a) the use of that work equipment is restricted to those persons given the task of using it; and
- (b) repairs, modifications, maintenance or servicing of that work equipment is restricted to those persons who have been specifically designated to perform operations of that description (whether or not also authorised to perform other operations).

7(2) The employer shall ensure that the persons designated for the purposes of subparagraph (b) of paragraph (1) have received adequate training related to any operations in respect of which they have been so designated.

SI 1992/2932, reg. 4(2)

INFORMATION AND INSTRUCTIONS

8(1) Every employer shall ensure that all persons who use work equipment have available to them adequate health and safety information and, where appropriate, written instructions pertaining to the use of the work equipment.

8(2) Every employer shall ensure that any of his employees who supervises or manages the use of work equipment has available to him adequate health and safety information and, where appropriate, written instructions pertaining to the use of the work equipment.

8(3) Without prejudice to the generality of paragraphs (1) or (2), the information and instructions required by either of those paragraphs shall include information and, where appropriate, written instructions on –

(a) the conditions in which and the methods by which the work equipment may be used;

(b) foreseeable abnormal situations and the action to be taken if such a situation were to occur; and

(c) any conclusions to be drawn from experience in using the work equipment.

8(4) Information and instructions required by this regulation shall be readily comprehensible to those concerned.

TRAINING

9(1) Every employer shall ensure that all persons who use work equipment have received adequate training for purposes of health and safety, including training in the methods which may be adopted when using the work equipment, any risks which such use may entail and precautions to be taken.

9(2) Every employer shall ensure that any of his employees who supervises or manages the use of work equipment has received adequate training for purposes of health and safety, including training in the methods which may be adopted when using the work equipment, any risks which such use may entail and precautions to be taken.

CONFORMITY WITH COMMUNITY REQUIREMENTS

10(1) Every employer shall ensure that any item of work equipment provided for use in the premises or undertaking of the employer complies with any enactment (whether in an Act or instrument) which implements in Great Britain any of the relevant Community directives listed in Schedule 1 which is applicable to that item of work equipment.

10(2) Where it is shown that an item of work equipment complies with an enactment (whether in an Act or instrument) to which it is subject by virtue of paragraph (1), the requirements of regulations 11 to 24 shall apply in respect of that item of work equipment only to the extent that the relevant Community directive implemented by that enactment is not applicable to that item of work equipment.

10(3) This regulation applies to items of work equipment provided for use in the premises or undertaking of the employer for the first time after 31st December 1992.

SI 1992/2932, reg. 10(3)

DANGEROUS PARTS OF MACHINERY

11(1) Every employer shall ensure that measures are taken in accordance with paragraph (2) which are effective –

(a) to prevent access to any dangerous part of machinery or to any rotating stock-bar; or

(b) to stop the movement of any dangerous part of machinery or rotating stock-bar before any part of a person enters a danger zone.

11(2) The measures required by paragraph (1) shall consist of –

(a) the provision of fixed guards enclosing every dangerous part or rotating stock-bar where and to the extent that it is practicable to do so, but where or to the extent that it is not, then

(b) the provision of other guards or protection devices where and to the extent that it is practicable to do so, but where or to the extent that it is not, then

(c) the provision of jigs, holders, push-sticks or similar protection appliances used in conjunction with the machinery where and to the extent that it is practicable to do so, but where or to the extent that it is not, then

(d) the provision of information, instruction, training and supervision.

11(3) All guards and protection devices provided under sub-paragraphs (a) or (b) of paragraph (2) shall –

(a) be suitable for the purpose for which they are provided;

(b) be of good construction, sound material and adequate strength;

(c) be maintained in an efficient state, in efficient working order and in good repair;

(d) not give rise to any increased risk to health or safety;

(e) not be easily bypassed or disabled;

(f) be situated at sufficient distance from the danger zone;

(g) not unduly restrict the view of the operating cycle of the machinery, where such a view is necessary;

(h) be so constructed or adapted that they allow operations necessary to fit or replace parts and for maintenance work, restricting access so that it is allowed only to the area where the work is to be carried out and, if possible, without having to dismantle the guard or protection device.

11(4) All protection appliances provided under sub-paragraph (c) of paragraph (2) shall comply with sub-paragraphs (a) to (d) and (g) of paragraph (3).

11(5) In this regulation –

"danger zone" means any zone in or around machinery in which a person is exposed to a risk to health or safety from contact with a dangerous part of machinery or a rotating stock-bar;

"stock-bar" means any part of a stock-bar which projects beyond the head-stock of a lathe.

PROTECTION AGAINST SPECIFIED HAZARDS

12(1) Every employer shall take measures to ensure that the exposure of a person using work

SI 1992/2932, reg. 11(1)

equipment to any risk to his health or safety from any hazard specified in paragraph (3) is either prevented, or, where that is not reasonably practicable, adequately controlled.

12(2) The measures required by paragraph (1) shall –

    (a) be measures other than the provision of personal protective equipment or of information, instruction, training and supervision, so far as is reasonably practicable; and

    (b) include, where appropriate, measures to minimise the effects of the hazard as well as to reduce the likelihood of the hazard occurring.

12(3) The hazards referred to in paragraph (1) are –

    (a) any article or substance falling or being ejected from work equipment;

    (b) rupture or disintegration of parts of work equipment;

    (c) work equipment catching fire or overheating;

    (d) the unintended or premature discharge of any article or of any gas, dust, liquid, vapour or other substance which, in each case, is produced, used or stored in the work equipment;

    (e) the unintended or premature explosion of the work equipment or any article or substance produced, used or stored in it.

12(4) For the purposes of this regulation **"adequate"** means adequate having regard only to the nature of the hazard and the nature and degree of exposure to the risk, and **"adequately"** shall be construed accordingly.

12(5) This regulation shall not apply where any of the following Regulations apply in respect of any risk to a person's health or safety for which such Regulations require measures to be taken to prevent or control such risk, namely –

    (a) the Control of Lead at Work Regulations 1980;

    (b) the Ionising Radiations Regulations 1985;

    (c) the Control of Asbestos at Work Regulations 1987;

    (d) the Control of Substances Hazardous to Health Regulations 1988;

    (e) the Noise at Work Regulations 1989;

    (f) the Construction (Head Protection) Regulations 1989.

HIGH OR VERY LOW TEMPERATURE

13 Every employer shall ensure that work equipment, parts of work equipment and any article or substance produced, used or stored in work equipment which, in each case, is at a high or very low temperature shall have protection where appropriate so as to prevent injury to any person by burn, scald or sear.

CONTROLS FOR STARTING OR MAKING A SIGNIFICANT CHANGE IN OPERATING CONDITIONS

14(1) Every employer shall ensure that, where appropriate, work equipment is provided with one or more controls for the purposes of –

    (a) starting the work equipment (including re-starting after a stoppage for any reason); or

SI 1992/2932, reg. 14(1)

(b) controlling any change in the speed, pressure or other operating conditions of the work equipment where such conditions after the change result in risk to health and safety which is greater than or of a different nature from such risks before the change.

14(2) Subject to paragraph (3), every employer shall ensure that where a control is required by paragraph (1), it shall not be possible to perform any operation mentioned in sub-paragraph (a) or (b) of that paragraph except by a deliberate action on such control.

14(3) Paragraph (1) shall not apply to re-starting or changing operating conditions as a result of the normal operating cycle of an automatic device.

STOP CONTROLS

15(1) Every employer shall ensure that, where appropriate, work equipment is provided with one or more readily accessible controls the operation of which will bring the work equipment to a safe condition in a safe manner.

15(2) Any control required by paragraph (1) shall bring the work equipment to a complete stop where necessary for reasons of health and safety.

15(3) Any control required by paragraph (1) shall, if necessary for reasons of health and safety, switch off all sources of energy after stopping the functioning of the work equipment.

15(4) Any control required by paragraph (1) shall operate in priority to any control which starts or changes the operating conditions of the work equipment.

EMERGENCY STOP CONTROLS

16(1) Every employer shall ensure that, where appropriate, work equipment is provided with one or more readily accessible emergency stop controls unless it is not necessary by reason of the nature of the hazards and the time taken for the work equipment to come to a complete stop as a result of the action of any control provided by virtue of regulation 15(1).

16(2) Any control required by paragraph (1) shall operate in priority to any control required by regulation 15(1).

CONTROLS

17(1) Every employer shall ensure that all controls for work equipment shall be clearly visible and identifiable, including by appropriate marking where necessary.

17(2) Except where necessary, the employer shall ensure that no control for work equipment is in a position where any person operating the control is exposed to a risk to his health or safety.

17(3) Every employer shall ensure where appropriate –

(a) that, so far as is reasonably practicable, the operator of any control is able to ensure from the position of that control that no person is in a place where he would be exposed to any risk to his health or safety as a result of the operation of that control, but where or to the extent that it is not reasonably practicable;

(b) that, so far as is reasonably practicable, systems of work are effective to ensure that, when work equipment is about to start, no person is in a place where he would be exposed to a risk to his health or safety as a result of the work equipment starting, but where neither of these is reasonably practicable;

SI 1992/2932, reg. 14(2)

(c) that an audible, visible or other suitable warning is given by virtue of regulation 24 whenever work equipment is about to start.

17(4) Every employer shall take appropriate measures to ensure that any person who is in a place where he would be exposed to a risk to his health or safety as a result of the starting or stopping of work equipment has sufficient time and suitable means to avoid that risk.

CONTROL SYSTEMS

18(1) Every employer shall ensure, so far as is reasonably practicable, that all control systems of work equipment are safe.

18(2) Without prejudice to the generality of paragraph (1), a control system shall not be safe unless –

(a) its operation does not create any increased risk to health or safety;

(b) it ensures, so far as is reasonably practicable, that any fault in or damage to any part of the control system or the loss of supply of any source of energy used by the work equipment cannot result in additional or increased risk to health or safety;

(c) it does not impede the operation of any control required by regulation 15 or 16.

ISOLATION FROM SOURCES OF ENERGY

19(1) Every employer shall ensure that where appropriate work equipment is provided with suitable means to isolate it from all its sources of energy.

19(2) Without prejudice to the generality of paragraph (1), the means mentioned in that paragraph shall not be suitable unless they are clearly identifiable and readily accessible.

19(3) Every employer shall take appropriate measures to ensure that re-connection of any energy source to work equipment does not expose any person using the work equipment to any risk to his health or safety.

STABILITY

20 Every employer shall ensure that work equipment or any part of work equipment is stabilised by clamping or otherwise where necessary for purposes of health or safety.

LIGHTING

21 Every employer shall ensure that suitable and sufficient lighting, which takes account of the operations to be carried out, is provided at any place where a person uses work equipment.

MAINTENANCE OPERATIONS

22 Every employer shall take appropriate measures to ensure that work equipment is so constructed or adapted that, so far as is reasonably practicable, maintenance operations which involve a risk to health or safety can be carried out while the work equipment is shut down or, in other cases –

(a) maintenance operations can be carried out without exposing the person carrying them out to a risk to his health or safety; or

(b) appropriate measures can be taken for the protection of any person carrying out maintenance operations which involve a risk to his health or safety.

MARKINGS

23 Every employer shall ensure that work equipment is marked in a clearly visible manner with any marking appropriate for reasons of health and safety.

WARNINGS

24(1) Every employer shall ensure that work equipment incorporates any warnings or warning devices which are appropriate for reasons of health and safety.

24(2) Without prejudice to the generality of paragraph (1), warnings given by warning devices on work equipment shall not be appropriate unless they are unambiguous, easily perceived and easily understood.

EXEMPTION CERTIFICATES

25(1) The Secretary of State for Defence may, in the interests of national security, by a certificate in writing exempt any of the home forces, any visiting force or any headquarters from any of the requirements of these Regulations and any such exemption may be granted subject to conditions and to a limit of time and may be revoked by the said Secretary of State by a further certificate in writing at any time.

25(2) In this regulation –

(a) **"the home forces"** has the same meaning as in section 12(1) of the Visiting Forces Act 1952;

(b) **"headquarters"** has the same meaning as in article 3(2) of the Visiting Forces and International Headquarters (Application of Law) Order 1965;

(c) **"visiting force"** has the same meaning as it does for the purposes of any provision of Part I of the Visiting Forces Act 1952.

EXTENSION OUTSIDE GREAT BRITAIN

26 These Regulations shall, subject to regulation 3, apply to and in relation to the premises and activities outside Great Britain to which sections 1 to 59 and 80 to 82 of the 1974 Act apply by virtue of the Health and Safety at Work etc. Act 1974 (Application outside Great Britain) Order 1989 as they apply within Great Britain.

REPEALS, SAVING AND REVOCATIONS

27(1) Subject to paragraph (2), the enactments mentioned in Part I of Schedule 2 are repealed to the extent specified in column 3 of that Part.

27(2) Nothing in this regulation shall affect the operation of any provision of the Offices, Shops and Railway Premises Act 1963 as that provision has effect by virtue of section 90(4) of that Act.

27(3) The instruments mentioned in Part II of Schedule 2 are revoked to the extent specified in column 3 of that Part.

Schedule 1 – Relevant Community Directives

Regulation 10

1 Council Directive 73/23/EEC on the harmonization of the laws of Member States relating to electrical equipment designed for use within certain voltage limits (OJ No. L77, 26.3.1973, p.29).

2 Council Directive 79/113/EEC on the approximation of the laws of the Member States relating to the determination of the noise emission of construction plant and equipment (OJ No. L33, 8.2.1979, p.15).

3 Council Directive 81/1051/EEC amending Directive 79/113/EEC on the approximation of the laws of the Member States relating to the determination of the noise emission of construction plant and equipment (OJ No. L376, 30.12.1981, p.49).

4 Council Directive 84/532/EEC on the approximation of the laws of the Member States relating to common provisions for construction plant and equipment (OJ No. L300, 19.11.1984, p.111).

5 Council Directive 84/533/EEC on the approximation of the laws of the Member States relating to the permissible sound power level of compressors (OJ No. L300, 19.11.1984, p.123).

6 Council Directive 84/534/EEC on the approximation of the laws of the Member States relating to the permissible sound power level of tower cranes (OJ No. L300, 19.11.1984, p.130).

7 Council Directive 84/535/EEC on the approximation of the laws of the Member States relating to the permissible sound power level of welding generators (OJ No. L300, 19.11.1984, p.142).

8 Council Directive 84/536/EEC on the approximation of the laws of the Member States relating to the permissible sound power level of power generators (OJ No. L300, 19.11.1984, p.149).

9 Council Directive 84/537/EEC on the approximation of the laws of the Member States relating to the permissible sound power level of powered hand-held concrete-breakers and picks (OJ No. L300, 19.11.1984, p.156).

10 Council Directive 84/538/EEC on the approximation of the laws of the Member States relating to the permissible sound power level of lawn mowers (OJ No. L300, 19.11.1984, p.171).

11 Commission Directive 85/405/EEC adapting to technical progress Council Directive 79/113/EEC on the approximation of the laws of the Member States relating to the determination of the noise emission of construction plant and equipment (OJ No. L233, 30.8.1985, p.9).

12 Commission Directive 85/406/EEC adapting to technical progress Council Directive 84/533/EEC on the approximation of the laws of the Member States relating to the permissible sound power level of compressors (OJ No. L233, 30.8.1985, p.11).

13 Commission Directive 85/407/EEC adapting to technical progress Council Directive 84/535/EEC on the approximation of the laws of the Member States relating to the permissible sound power level of welding generators (OJ No. L233, 30.8.1985, p.16).

SI 1992/2932, Sch. 1, para. 13

14 Commission Directive 85/408/EEC adapting to technical progress Council Directive 84/536/EEC on the approximation of the laws of the Member States relating to the permissible sound power level of power generators (OJ No. L233, 30.8.1985, p.18).

15 Commission Directive 85/409/EEC adapting to technical progress Council Directive 84/537/EEC on the approximation of the laws of the Member States relating to the permissible sound power level of powered hand-held concrete-breakers and picks (OJ No. L233, 30.8.1985, p.20).

16 Commission Directive 87/252/EEC adapting to technical progress Council Directive 84/538/EEC on the approximation of the laws of the Member States relating to the permissible sound power level of lawn mowers (OJ No. L117, 5.5.1987, p.22 with corrigenda at OJ No. L158, 18.6.1987, p.31).

17 Council Directive 87/405/EEC amending Council Directive 84/534/EEC on the approximation of the laws of the Member States relating to the permissible sound power level of tower cranes (OJ No. L220, 8.8.1987, p.60).

18 Council Directive 88/180/EEC amending Council Directive 84/538/EEC on the approximation of the laws of the Member States relating to the permissible sound power level of lawn-mowers (OJ No. L81, 26.3.1988, p.69).

19 Council Directive 88/181/EEC amending Council Directive 84/538/EEC on the approximation of the laws of the Member States relating to the permissible sound power level of lawn-mowers (OJ No. L81, 26.3.1988, p.71).

20 Council Directive 84/539/EEC on the approximation of the laws of the Member States relating to electro-medical equipment used in human or veterinary medicine (OJ No. L300, 19.11.1984, p.179).

21 Council Directive 86/295/EEC on the approximation of the laws of the Member States relating to roll-over protective structures (ROPS) for certain construction plant (OJ No. L186, 8.7.1986, p.1).

22 Council Directive 86/296/EEC on the approximation of the laws of the Member States relating to falling-object protective structures (FOPS) for certain construction plant (OJ No. L186, 8.7.1986, p.10).

23 Council Directive 86/662/EEC on the limitation of noise emitted by hydraulic excavators, rope-operated excavators, dozers, loaders and excavator-loaders (OJ No. L384, 31.12.1986, p.1).

24 Council Directive 86/663/EEC on the approximation of the laws of the Member States relating to self-propelled industrial trucks (OJ No. L384, 31.12.1986, p.12).

25 Council Directive 87/404/EEC on the harmonization of the laws of the Member States relating to simple pressure vessels (OJ No. L220, 8.8.1987, p.48).

26 Council Directive 89/106/EEC on the approximation of laws, regulations and administrative provisions of the Member States relating to construction products (OJ No. L40, dated 11.2.1989 p.12).

27 Commission Directive 89/240/EEC adapting to technical progress Council Directive 86/663/EEC on the approximation of the laws of the Member States relating to self-propelled industrial trucks (OJ No. L100, 12.4.1989, p.1).

SI 1992/2932, Sch. 1, para. 14

28 Council Directive 89/336/EEC on the approximation of the laws of the Member States relating to electromagnetic compatibility (OJ No. L139, 23.5.1989, p.19).

29 Council Directive 89/392/EEC on the approximation of the laws of the Member States relating to machinery (OJ No. L183, 29.6.1989, p.9).

30 Commission Directive 89/514/EEC adapting to technical progress Council Directive 86/662/EEC on the limitation of noise emitted by hydraulic excavators, rope-operated excavators, dozers, loaders and excavator-loaders (OJ No. L253, 30.8.1989, p.35).

31 Council Directive 89/686/EEC on the approximation of the laws of the Member States relating to personal protective equipment (OJ No. L399, 30.12.1989, p.18).

32 Council Directive 90/385/EEC on the approximation of the laws of the Member States relating to active implantable medical devices (OJ No. L189, 20.7.1990, p.17).

33 Council Directive 90/396/EEC on the approximation of the laws of the Member States relating to appliances burning gaseous fuels (OJ No. L196, 26.7.1990, p.15).

34 Council Directive 91/368/EEC amending Directive 89/392/EEC on the approximation of the laws of the Member States relating to machinery (OJ No. L198, 22.7.1991, p.16).

35 Council Directive 92/31/EEC amending Directive 89/336/EEC on the approximation of the laws of the Member States relating to electromagnetic compatibility (OJ No. L126, 12.5.92, p.11).

Schedule 2

Regulation 27

Part I – Repeals

(1) *Chapter*	(2) *Short title*	(3) *Extent of repeal*
1954 c.70.	The Mines and Quarries Act 1954.	Sections 81(1) and 82.
1961 c.34.	The Factories Act 1961.	Sections 12 to 16, 17 and 19.
1963 c.41.	The Offices, Shops and Railway Premises Act 1963.	Section 17.

Part II – Revocations

(1) *Title*	(2) *Reference*	(3) *Extent of revocation*
Regulations dated 17th October 1905 (The Spinning by Self-Acting Mules Regulations 1905).	S.R. & O. 1905/1103, amended by the Employment Act 1989 (c.38), section 29(5), Schedule 8.	The whole Regulations.

(1) Chapter	(2) Short title	(3) Extent of repeal
The Aerated Water Regulations 1921.	S.R. & O. 1921/1932, amended by S.I. 1981/686.	Regulations 1, 2 and 8.
The Horizontal Milling Machines Regulations 1928.	S.R. & O. 1928/548, amended by S.R. & O. 1934/207.	The exemptions and regulations 2 to 7.
The Operations at Unfenced Machinery Regulations 1938.	S.R. & O. 1938/641, amended by S.R. & O. 1946/156 and S.I. 1976/955.	The whole Regulations.
The Jute (Safety, Health and Welfare) Regulations 1948.	S.I. 1948/1696, to which there are amendments not relevant to these Regulations.	Regulations 15, 27 and 28 and the First Schedule.
The Iron and Steel Foundries Regulations 1953.	S.I. 1953/1464, amended by S.I. 1974/1681 and S.I. 1981/1332.	Regulation 5.
The Agriculture (Power Take-Off) Regulations 1957.	S.I. 1957/1386, amended by S.I. 1976/1247, S.I. 1981/1414 and S.I. 1991/1913.	The whole Regulations.
The Agriculture (Circular Saws) Regulations 1959.	S.I. 1959/427, amended by S.I. 1981/1414.	(i) In regulation 1, in sub-paragraph (b), from the beginning to "and" where it first occurs; and sub-paragraph (c); (ii) regulations 3 and 4; (iii) in regulation 5(1), the words from "unless" to "or"; and (iv) Schedule 1.
The Agriculture (Stationary Machinery) Regulations 1959.	S.I. 1959/1216, amended by S.I. 1976/1247 and S.I. 1981/1414.	The whole Regulations.
The Agriculture (Threshers and Balers) Regulations 1960.	S.I. 1960/1199, amended by S.I. 1976/1247 and S.I. 1981/1414.	In the Schedule, paragraphs 2, 3, 6, 7, 8, 9, 10, 11, 12, 16 and 17.
The Shipbuilding and Ship-Repairing Regulations 1960.	S.I. 1960/1932, to which there are amendments not relevant to these Regulations.	Regulation 67.
The Construction (General Provisions) Regulations 1961.	S.I. 1961/1580, to which there are amendments not relevant to these Regulations.	Regulations 42, 43 and 57.

SI 1992/2932, Sch. 2

(1) Chapter	(2) Short title	(3) Extent of repeal
The Agriculture (Field Machinery) Regulations 1962.	S.I. 1962/1472, amended by S.I. 1976/1247 and S.I. 1981/1414.	In the Schedule, paragraphs 2 to 6 and 15 to 19.
The Abrasive Wheels Regulations 1970.	S.I. 1970/535.	In regulation 3, paragraphs (2), (3) and (4); and regulations 4, 6 to 8, 10 to 16, 18 and 19.
The Woodworking Machines Regulations 1974.	S.I. 1974/903, amended by S.I. 1978/1126.	In regulation 1, paragraphs (2) and (3); in regulation 2, the definitions of "cutters", "machine table", "narrow band sawing machine", "sawmill" and "squared stock"; in , regulation 3 paragraph (2); regulations 5 to 9, 14 to 19, 21 to 38, and 40 to 43.
The Offshore Installations (Operational Safety, Health and Welfare) Regulations 1976.	S.I. 1976/1019, which has effect as an existing statutory provision under the 1974 Act by virtue of section 1(1) of the Offshore Safety Act 1992 (c.15).	Regulations 10 and 12.
The Agriculture (Power Take-off) (Amendment) Regulations 1991.	S.I. 1991/1913.	The whole Regulations.

EXPLANATORY NOTE

(This note is not part of the Regulations)

1 These Regulations impose health and safety requirements with respect to the provision and use of work equipment, which is defined in regulation 2. Existing provisions which are replaced by these Regulations are repealed or revoked (*Schedule 2*).

2 The Regulations give effect as respects Great Britain to Council Directive 89/655/EEC (OJ No. L393, 30.12.89, p.13) on the minimum safety and health requirements for the use of work equipment by workers at work ("the Directive") with the exception of the following matters –

- (a) the Regulations do not extend to sea transport (*regulation 3*);
- (b) a general requirement to ensure that work equipment may be used without impairment to safety or health (*Article 3.1 of the Directive*);
- (c) a general requirement to minimise risks where they cannot be eliminated (*Article 3.2 of the Directive*);
- (d) a requirement for containment or extraction devices in certain cases (*point 2.5, second indent of the Annex to the Directive*);

(e) a requirement for safe means of access to and safe places of work (*point 2.16 of the Annex to the Directive*);

(f) protection from electrical risks (*point 2.19 of the Annex to the Directive*).

3 The Regulations impose requirements upon employers in respect of work equipment provided for or used by their employees at work. The requirements are also applied to self-employed persons and persons in control of specified premises in the circumstances set out in regulation 4.

4 The Regulations make provision with respect to –

(a) the suitability of work equipment (*regulation 5*);

(b) the maintenance of work equipment and keeping up to date of any maintenance log (*regulation 6*);

(c) steps to be taken where the use of work equipment is likely to involve a specific risk to health or safety (*regulation 7*);

(d) information, instruction and training for persons who use work equipment and certain other employees (*regulations 8 and 9*);

(e) conformity with European Community requirements (*regulation 10 and Schedule 1*);

(f) the protection of persons from dangerous parts of machinery and rotating stock-bars (*regulation 11*);

(g) the prevention or control of exposure of any person to any risk caused by certain specified hazards (*regulation 12*);

(h) protection from high or very low temperature (*regulation 13*);

(i) controls (including emergency and other stop controls) and control systems (*regulations 14 to 18*);

(j) the isolation of work equipment from sources of energy (*regulation 19*);

(k) the stability of work equipment (*regulation 20*);

(l) lighting at any place where work equipment is used (*regulation 21*);

(m) taking measures to ensure that work equipment is so constructed or adapted that maintenance operations can be carried out in specified ways (*regulation 22*);

(n) appropriate markings, warnings, or warning devices (*regulations 23 and 24*).

5 The Secretary of State for Defence may grant exemptions from the Regulations in the interests of national security (*regulation 25*).

6 The Regulations extend to and in relation to certain premises and activities outside Great Britain (*regulation 26*).

SI 1992/2932, Note

THE HEALTH AND SAFETY (DISPLAY SCREEN EQUIPMENT) REGULATIONS 1992

(SI 1992/2792)

Made on 5 November 1992 by The Secretary of State, in exercise of the powers conferred on her by ss. 15(1), (2), (5)(b) and (9) and 82(3)(a) of, and paras. 1(1)(a) and (c) and (2), 7, 8(1), 9 and 14 of Sch. 3 to, the Health and Safety at Work etc. Act 1974 and of all other powers enabling her in that behalf and for the purpose of giving effect without modifications to proposals submitted to her by the Health and Safety Commission under s. 11(2)(d) of the said Act after the carrying out by the said Commission of consultations in accordance with s. 50(3) of that Act. Operative from 1 January 1993.

CITATION, COMMENCEMENT, INTERPRETATION AND APPLICATION

1(1) These Regulations may be cited as the Health and Safety (Display Screen Equipment) Regulations 1992 and shall come into force on 1st January 1993.

1(2) In these Regulations –

(a) **"display screen equipment"** means any alphanumeric or graphic display screen, regardless of the display process involved;

(b) **"operator"** means a self-employed person who habitually uses display screen equipment as a significant part of his normal work;

(c) **"use"** means use for or in connection with work;

(d) **"user"** means an employee who habitually uses display screen equipment as a significant part of his normal work; and

(e) **"workstation"** means an assembly comprising –

  (i) display screen equipment (whether provided with software determining the interface between the equipment and its operator or user, a keyboard or any other input device),

  (ii) any optional accessories to the display screen equipment,

  (iii) any disk drive, telephone, modem, printer, document holder, work chair, work desk, work surface or other item peripheral to the display screen equipment, and

  (iv) the immediate work environment around the display screen equipment.

1(3) Any reference in these Regulations to –
  (a) a numbered regulation is a reference to the regulation in these Regulations so numbered; or
  (b) a numbered paragraph is a reference to the paragraph so numbered in the regulation in which the reference appears.

1(4) Nothing in these Regulations shall apply to or in relation to –
  (a) drivers' cabs or control cabs for vehicles or machinery;
  (b) display screen equipment on board a means of transport;
  (c) display screen equipment mainly intended for public operation;
  (d) portable systems not in prolonged use;
  (e) calculators, cash registers or any equipment having a small data or measurement display required for direct use of the equipment; or
  (f) window typewriters.

ANALYSIS OF WORKSTATIONS

2(1) Every employer shall perform a suitable and sufficient analysis of those workstations which –
  (a) (regardless of who has provided them) are used for the purposes of his undertaking by users; or
  (b) have been provided by him and are used for the purposes of his undertaking by operators.

for the purpose of assessing the health and safety risks to which those persons are exposed in consequence of that use.

2(2) Any assessment made by an employer in pursuance of paragraph (1) shall be reviewed by him if –
  (a) there is reason to suspect that it is no longer valid; or
  (b) there has been a significant change in the matters to which it relates;

and where as a result of any such review changes to an assessment are required, the employer concerned shall make them.

2(3) The employer shall reduce the risks identified in consequence of an assessment to the lowest extent reasonably practicable.

2(4) The reference in paragraph (3) to **"an assessment"** is a reference to an assessment made by the employer concerned in pursuance of paragraph (1) and changed by him where necessary in pursuance of paragraph (2).

REQUIREMENTS FOR WORKSTATIONS

3(1) Every employer shall ensure that any workstation first put into service on or after 1st January 1993 which –
  (a) (regardless of who has provided it) may be used for the purposes of his undertaking by users; or

The Health and Safety (Display Screen Equipment) Regulations 1992

(b) has been provided by him and may be used for the purposes of his undertaking by operators,

meets the requirements laid down in the Schedule to these Regulations to the extent specified in paragraph 1 thereof.

3(2) Every employer shall ensure that any workstation first put into service on or before 31st December 1992 which –

(a) (regardless of who provided it) may be used for the purposes of his undertaking by users; or

(b) was provided by him and may be used for the purposes of his undertaking by operators,

meets the requirements laid down in the Schedule to these Regulations to the extent specified in paragraph 1 thereof not later than 31st December 1996.

DAILY WORK ROUTINE OF USERS

4 Every employer shall so plan the activities of users at work in his undertaking that their daily work on display screen equipment is periodically interrupted by such breaks or changes of activity as reduce their workload at that equipment.

EYES AND EYESIGHT

5(1) Where a person –

(a) is already a user on the date of coming into force of these Regulations; or

(b) is an employee who does not habitually use display screen equipment as a significant part of his normal work but is to become a user in the undertaking in which he is already employed,

his employer shall ensure that he is provided at his request with an appropriate eye and eyesight test, any such test to be carried out by a competent person.

5(2) Any eye and eyesight test provided in accordance with paragraph (1) shall –

(a) in any case to which sub-paragraph (a) of that paragraph applies, be carried out as soon as practicable after being requested by the user concerned; and

(b) in any case to which sub-paragraph (b) of that paragraph applies, be carried out before the employee concerned becomes a user.

5(3) At regular intervals after an employee has been provided with an eye and eyesight test in accordance with paragraphs (1) and (2), his employer shall, subject to paragraph (6), ensure that he is provided with a further eye and eyesight test of an appropriate nature, any such test to be carried out by a competent person.

5(4) Where a user experiences visual difficulties which may reasonably be considered to be caused by work on display screen equipment, his employer shall ensure that he is provided at his request with an appropriate eye and eyesight test, any such test to be carried out by a competent person as soon as practicable after being requested as aforesaid.

5(5) Every employer shall ensure that each user employed by him is provided with special corrective appliances appropriate for the work being done by the user concerned where –

(a) normal corrective appliances cannot be used; and

(b) the result of any eye and eyesight test which the user has been given in accordance with this regulation shows such provision to be necessary.

5(6) Nothing in paragraph (3) shall require an employer to provide any employee with an eye and eyesight test against that employee's will.

PROVISION OF TRAINING

6(1) Where a person –

(a) is already a user on the date of coming into force of these Regulations; or

(b) is an employee who does not habitually use display screen equipment as a significant part of his normal work but is to become a user in the undertaking in which he is already employed,

his employer shall ensure that he is provided with adequate health and safety training in the use of any workstation upon which he may be required to work.

6(2) Every employer shall ensure that each user at work in his undertaking is provided with adequate health and safety training whenever the organisation of any workstation in that undertaking upon which he may be required to work is substantially modified.

PROVISION OF INFORMATION

7(1) Every employer shall ensure that operators and users at work in his undertaking are provided with adequate information about –

(a) all aspects of health and safety relating to their workstations; and

(b) such measures taken by him in compliance with his duties under regulations 2 and 3 as relate to them and their work.

7(2) Every employer shall ensure that users at work in his undertaking are provided with adequate information about such measures taken by him in compliance with his duties under regulations 4 and 6(2) as relate to them and their work.

7(3) Every employer shall ensure that users employed by him are provided with adequate information about such measures taken by him in compliance with his duties under regulations 5 and 6(1) as relate to them and their work.

EXEMPTION CERTIFICATES

8(1) The Secretary of State for Defence may, in the interests of national security, exempt any of the home forces, any visiting force or any headquarters from any of the requirements imposed by these Regulations.

8(2) Any exemption such as is specified in paragraph (1) may be granted subject to conditions and to a limit of time and may be revoked by the Secretary of State for Defence by a further certificate in writing at any time.

8(3) In this regulation –

(a) **"the home forces"** has the same meaning as in section 12(1) of the Visiting Forces Act 1952;

(b) **"headquarters"** has the same meaning as in article 3(2) of the Visiting Forces and International Headquarters (Application of Law) Order 1965; and

(c) **"visiting force"** has the same meaning as it does for the purposes of any provision of Part I of the Visiting Forces Act 1952.

EXTENSION OUTSIDE GREAT BRITAIN

9 These Regulations shall, subject to regulation 1(4), apply to and in relation to the premises and activities outside Great Britain to which sections 1 to 59 and 80 to 82 of the Health and Safety at Work etc. Act 1974 apply by virtue of the Health and Safety at Work etc. Act 1974 (Application Outside Great Britain) Order 1989 as they apply within Great Britain.

THE SCHEDULE

(which sets out the minimum requirements for workstations which are contained in the annex to Council Directive 90/270/EEC on the minimum safety and health requirements for work with display screen equipment)

Regulation 3

1 Extent to which employers must ensure that workstations meet the requirements laid down in this schedules

An employer shall ensure that a workstation meets the requirements laid down in this Schedule to the extent that –

(a) those requirements relate to a component which is present in the workstation concerned;

(b) those requirements have effect with a view to securing the health, safety and welfare of persons at work; and

(c) the inherent characteristics of a given task make compliance with those requirements appropriate as respects the workstation concerned.

2 Equipment

(a) *General comment*
The use as such of the equipment must not be a source of risk for operators or users.

(b) *Display screen*
The characters on the screen shall be well-defined and clearly formed, of adequate size and with adequate spacing between the characters and lines.

The image on the screen should be stable, with no flickering or other forms of instability.

The brightness and the contrast between the characters and the background shall be easily adjustable by the operator or user, and also be easily adjustable to ambient conditions.

The screen must swivel and tilt easily and freely to suit the needs of the operator or user.

It shall be possible to use a separate base for the screen or an adjustable table.

SI 1992/2792, Schedule

The screen shall be free of reflective glare and reflections liable to cause discomfort to the operator or user.

(c) *Keyboard*

The keyboard shall be tiltable and separate from the screen so as to allow the operator or user to find a comfortable working position avoiding fatigue in the arms or hands.

The space in front of the keyboard shall be sufficient to provide support for the hands and arms of the operator or user.

The keyboard shall have a matt surface to avoid reflective glare.

The arrangement of the keyboard and the characteristics of the keys shall be such as to facilitate the use of the keyboard.

The symbols on the keys shall be adequately contrasted and legible from the design working position.

(d) *Work desk or work surface*

The work desk or work surface shall have a sufficiently large, low-reflectance surface and allow a flexible arrangement of the screen, keyboard, documents and related equipment.

The document holder shall be stable and adjustable and shall be positioned so as to minimise the need for uncomfortable head and eye movements.

There shall be adequate space for operators or users to find a comfortable position.

(e) *Work chair*

The work chair shall be stable and allow the operator or user easy freedom of movement and a comfortable position.

The seat shall be adjustable in height.

The seat back shall be adjustable in both height and tilt.

A footrest shall be made available to any operator or user who wishes one.

3 Environment

(a) *Space requirements*

The workstation shall be dimensioned and designed so as to provide sufficient space for the operator or user to change position and vary movements.

(b) *Lighting*

Any room lighting or task lighting provided shall ensure satisfactory lighting conditions and an appropriate contrast between the screen and the background environment, taking into account the type of work and the vision requirements of the operator or user.

Possible disturbing glare and reflections on the screen or other equipment shall be prevented by co-ordinating workplace and workstation layout with the positioning and technical characteristics of the artificial light sources.

(c) *Reflections and glare*

Workstations shall be so designed that sources of light, such as windows and other openings, transparent or translucid walls, and brightly coloured fixtures or walls cause no direct glare and no distracting reflections on the screen.

Windows shall be fitted with a suitable system of adjustable covering to attenuate the daylight that falls on the workstation.

SI 1992/2792, Schedule

The Health and Safety (Display Screen Equipment) Regulations 1992   111

(d) *Noise*

Noise emitted by equipment belonging to any workstation shall be taken into account when a workstation is being equipped, with a view in particular to ensuring that attention is not distracted and speech is not disturbed.

(e) *Heat*

Equipment belonging to any workstation shall not produce excess heat which could cause discomfort to operators or users.

(f) *Radiation*

All radiation with the exception of the visible part of the electromagnetic spectrum shall be reduced to negligible levels from the point of view of the protection of operators' or users' health and safety.

(g) *Humidity*

An adequate level of humidity shall be established and maintained.

4 Interface between computer and operator/user

In designing, selecting, commissioning and modifying software, and in designing tasks using display screen equipment, the employer shall take into account the following principles:

(a) software must be suitable for the task;

(b) software must be easy to use and, where appropriate, adaptable to the level of knowledge or experience of the operator or user; no quantitative or qualitative checking facility may be used without the knowledge of the operators or users;

(c) systems must provide feedback to operators or users on the performance of those systems;

(d) systems must display information in a format and at a pace which are adapted to operators or users;

(e) the principles of software ergonomics must be applied, in particular to human data processing.

EXPLANATORY NOTE

(This note is not part of the Regulations)

1 Subject to the exception specified in paragraph 2 below, these Regulations give effect as respects Great Britain to the substantive provisions of Council Directive 90/270/EEC on the minimum safety and health requirements for work with display screen equipment (OJ No. L156, 21.6.90, p.14).

2 These Regulations do not purport to give effect to paragraphs 2 and 4 of article 9 of the Directive specified in paragraph 1 above.

3 Regulation 2 requires each employer –

(a) to make a suitable and sufficient analysis of those workstations which –

(i) (regardless of who has provided them) are used for the purposes of his undertaking by users, or

(ii) have been provided by him and are used for the purposes of his undertaking by operators;

SI 1992/2792, Note

(b) to assess the health and safety risks to which those operators or users are exposed in consequence of that use;

(c) to reduce those risks to the lowest extent reasonably practicable; and

(d) in the circumstances specified in paragraph (2) of that regulation, to review (and where necessary change) any assessment such as is referred to in sub-paragraph (b) above.

4 Regulation 1(2) defines not only the words **"operator"**, **"user"** and **"workstation"**, but also the phrase **"display screen equipment"**.

5 Regulation 3 requires each employer to ensure that any workstation which –

(a) (regardless of who has provided it) may be used for the purposes of his undertaking by users; or

(b) has been provided by him and may be used for the purposes of his undertaking by operators,

meets the requirements laid down in the Schedule to these Regulations. In the case of workstations first put into service on or before 31st December 1992, the employer has until 31st December 1996 to ensure compliance with the above-mentioned requirements.

6 Regulation 4 requires each employer to plan the activities of users at work in his undertaking in such a way that their daily work on display screen equipment is periodically interrupted by such breaks or changes of activity as reduce their workload at that equipment.

7 Regulation 5 requires each employer to ensure that users employed by him are provided –

(a) with initial eye and eyesight tests on request;

(b) at regular intervals thereafter and with the consent of the users concerned, with subsequent eye and eyesight tests;

(c) with additional eye and eyesight tests on request, where the users concerned are experiencing visual difficulties which might reasonably be considered to be caused by work on display screen equipment; and

(d) with appropriate special corrective appliances, where normal corrective appliances cannot be used and any eye and eyesight tests carried out on the users concerned in accordance with regulation 5 show such provision to be necessary.

8 Regulation 6 requires each employer to ensure that –

(a) users employed by him are provided with adequate health and safety training in the use of their workstations; and

(b) users at work in his undertaking are provided with adequate health and safety training whenever their workstations are substantially modified.

9 Regulation 7 requires each employer to ensure that operators and users at work in his undertaking are provided with adequate health and safety information, both about their workstations and about such measures taken by him to comply with regulations 2 to 6 of these Regulations as relate to them and their work.

10 Regulation 8 enables the Secretary of State for Defence to grant certificates of exemption from these Regulations in the interests of national security.

11 Regulation 9 extends the application of these Regulations to and in relation to certain premises and activities outside Great Britain.

SI 1992/2792, Note

THE MANUAL HANDLING OPERATIONS REGULATIONS 1992

(SI 1992/2793)

Made on 5 November 1992 by The Secretary of State, in exercise of the powers conferred on her by ss. 15(1), (2), (3)(a), (5)(a) and (9) and 80(1), (2)(a) and (4) of, and paras. 1(1)(a) and (c) and 8 of Sch. 3 to, the Health and Safety at Work etc. Act 1974 ("the 1974 Act") and of all other powers enabling her in that behalf and –

(a) *for the purpose of giving effect without modifications to proposals submitted to her by the Health and Safety Commission under s. 11(2)(d) of the 1974 Act after the carrying out by the said Commission of consultations in accordance with s. 50(3) of that Act; and*

(b) *it appearing to her that the repeal of s. 18(1)(f) of the Children and Young Persons Act 1933 and s. 28(1)(f) of the Children and Young Persons (Scotland) Act 1937 except insofar as those provisions apply to such employment as is permitted under s. 1(2) of the Employment of Women, Young Persons, and Children Act 1920 is expedient in consequence of the Regulations referred to below after the carrying out by her of consultations in accordance with s. 80(4) of the 1974 Act.*

Operative from 1 January 1993.

CITATION AND COMMENCEMENT

1 These Regulations may be cited as the Manual Handling Operations Regulations 1992 and shall come into force on 1st January 1993.

INTERPRETATION

2(1) In these Regulations, unless the context otherwise requires –

"injury" does not include injury caused by any toxic or corrosive substance which –

(a) has leaked or spilled from a load;

(b) is present on the surface of a load but has not leaked or spilled from it; or

(c) is a constituent part of a load;

and **"injured"** shall be construed accordingly;

"load" includes any person and any animal;

"manual handling operations" means any transporting or supporting of a load (including the lifting, putting down, pushing, pulling, carrying or moving thereof) by hand or by bodily force.

2(2) Any duty imposed by these Regulations on an employer in respect of his employees shall also be imposed on a self-employed person in respect of himself.

DISAPPLICATION OF REGULATIONS

3 These Regulations shall not apply to or in relation to the master or crew of a sea-going ship or to the employer of such persons in respect of the normal ship-board activities of a ship's crew under the direction of the master.

DUTIES OF EMPLOYERS

4(1) Each employer shall –
- (a) so far as is reasonably practicable, avoid the need for his employees to undertake any manual handling operations at work which involve a risk of their being injured; or
- (b) where it is not reasonably practicable to avoid the need for his employees to undertake any manual handling operations at work which involve a risk of their being injured –
  - (i) make a suitable and sufficient assessment of all such manual handling operations to be undertaken by them, having regard to the factors which are specified in column 1 of Schedule 1 to these Regulations and considering the questions which are specified in the corresponding entry in column 2 of that Schedule,
  - (ii) take appropriate steps to reduce the risk of injury to those employees arising out of their undertaking any such manual handling operations to the lowest level reasonably practicable, and
  - (iii) take appropriate steps to provide any of those employees who are undertaking any such manual handling operations with general indications and, where it is reasonably practicable to do so, precise information on –
    - (aa) the weight of each load, and
    - (bb) the heaviest side of any load whose centre of gravity is not positioned centrally.

4(2) Any assessment such as is referred to in paragraph (1)(b)(i) of this regulation shall be reviewed by the employer who made it if –
- (a) there is reason to suspect that it is no longer valid; or
- (b) there has been a significant change in the manual handling operations to which it relates;

and where as a result of any such review changes to an assessment are required, the relevant employer shall make them.

DUTY OF EMPLOYEES

5 Each employee while at work shall make full and proper use of any system of work provided for his use by his employer in compliance with regulation 4(1)(b)(ii) of these Regulations.

EXEMPTION CERTIFICATES

6(1) The Secretary of State for Defence may, in the interests of national security, by a certificate in writing exempt –

SI 1992/2793, reg. 2(2)

(a) any of the home forces, any visiting force or any headquarters from any requirement imposed by regulation 4 of these Regulations; or

(b) any member of the home forces, any member of a visiting force or any member of a headquarters from the requirement imposed by regulation 5 of these Regulations;

and any exemption such as is specified in sub-paragraph (a) or (b) of this paragraph may be granted subject to conditions and to a limit of time and may be revoked by the said Secretary of State by a further certificate in writing at any time.

6(2) In this regulation –
(a) **"the home forces"** has the same meaning as in section 12(1) of the Visiting Forces Act 1952;
(b) **"headquarters"** has the same meaning as in article 3(2) of the Visiting Forces and International Headquarters (Application of Law) Order 1965;
(c) **"member of a headquarters"** has the same meaning as in paragraph 1(1) of the Schedule to the International Headquarters and Defence Organisations Act 1964; and
(d) **"visiting force"** has the same meaning as it does for the purposes of any provision of Part I of the Visiting Forces Act 1952.

EXTENSION OUTSIDE GREAT BRITAIN

7 These Regulations shall, subject to regulation 3 hereof, apply to and in relation to the premises and activities outside Great Britain to which sections 1 to 59 and 80 to 82 of the Health and Safety at Work etc. Act 1974 apply by virtue of the Health and Safety at Work etc. Act 1974 (Application Outside Great Britain) Order 1989 as they apply within Great Britain.

REPEALS AND REVOCATIONS

8(1) The enactments mentioned in column 1 of Part I of Schedule 2 to these Regulations are repealed to the extent specified in the corresponding entry in column 3 of that part.

8(2) The Regulations mentioned in column 1 of Part II of Schedule 2 to these Regulations are revoked to the extent specified in the corresponding entry in column 3 of that part.

Schedule 1 – Factors to Which The Employer Must Have Regard and Questions He Must Consider When Making an Assessment of Manual Handling Operations

Regulation 4(1)(b)(i)

Column 1 *Factors*	Column 2 *Questions*

1. The tasks	**Do they involve:**
	—holding or manipulating loads at distance from trunk?
	—unsatisfactory bodily movement or posture, especially:
	  —twisting the trunk?
	  —stooping?

Column 1 *Factors*	Column 2 *Questions*
	—reaching upwards? —excessive movement of loads, especially: 　　—excessive lifting or lowering distances? 　　—excessive carrying distances? —excessive pushing or pulling of loads? —risk of sudden movement of loads? —frequent or prolonged physical effort? —insufficient rest or recovery periods? —a rate of work imposed by a process?
2. The loads	**Are they:** —heavy? —bulky or unwieldy? —difficult to grasp? —unstable, or with contents likely to shift? —sharp, hot or otherwise potentially damaging?
3. The working environment	**Are there:** —space constraints preventing good posture? —uneven, slippery or unstable floors? —variations in level of floors or work surfaces? —extremes of temperature or humidity? —conditions causing ventilation problems or gusts of wind? —poor lighting conditions?
4. Individual capability	**Does the job:** —require unusual strength, height, etc? —create a hazard to those who might reasonably be considered to be pregnant or to have a health problem? —require special information or training for its safe performance?
5. Other factors	**Is movement or posture hindered by personal protective equipment or by clothing?**

SI 1992/2793, Sch. 1

Schedule 2 – Repeals and Revocations

Regulation 8

Part I – Repeals

Column 1 *Short title of enactment*	Column 2 *Reference*	Column 3 *Extent of repeal*
The Children and Young Persons Act 1933.	1933 c.12.	Section 18(1)(f) except insofar as that paragraph applies to such employment as is permitted under section 1(2) of the Employment of Women, Young Persons, and Children Act 1920 (1920 c.65).
The Children and Young Persons (Scotland) Act 1937.	1937 c.37.	Section 28(1)(f) except insofar as that paragraph applies to such employment as is permitted under section 1(2) of the Employment of Women, Young Persons, and Children Act 1920.
The Mines and Quarries Act 1954.	1954 c.70.	Section 93; in section 115 the word "ninety-three".
The Agriculture (Safety, Health and Welfare Provisions) Act 1956.	1956 c.49.	Section 2.
The Factories Act 1961.	1961 c.34.	Section 72.
The Offices, Shops and Railway Premises Act 1963.	1963 c.41.	Section 23 except insofar as the prohibition contained in that section applies to any person specified in section 90(4) of the same Act. In section 83(1) the number "23".

Part II – Revocations

Column 1 *Title of instrument*	Column 2 *Reference*	Column 3 *Extent of revocation*
The Agriculture (Lifting of Heavy Weights) Regulations 1959.	S.I. 1959/2120.	The whole Regulations.
The Construction (General Provisions) Regulations 1961.	S.I. 1961/1580.	In regulation 3(1)(a) the phrase "and 55"; regulation 55.

SI 1992/2793, Sch. 2

EXPLANATORY NOTE

(This note is not part of the Regulations)

1 Subject to the exceptions specified in paragraph 2 below, these Regulations give effect as respects Great Britain to the substantive provisions of Council Directive 90/269/EEC on the minimum health and safety requirements for the manual handling of loads where there is a risk particularly of back injury to workers (OJ No. L156, 21.6.90, p.9).

2 These Regulations do not extend to sea transport (*regulation 3*); nor do they give effect to the first indent of article 6.1 of the Directive referred to in paragraph 1 above.

3 Regulation 4 requires each employer –

    (a) so far as it is reasonably practicable to do so, to avoid the need for his employees to undertake manual handling operations at work which involve a risk of their being injured; or

    (b) where it is not reasonably practicable to avoid the need for his employees to undertake any manual handling operations at work which involve a risk of their being injured –

        (i) to assess all such manual handling operations to be undertaken by them having regard to Schedule 1 to these Regulations,

        (ii) to reduce the risk of injury to those employees arising out of their undertaking any such manual handling operations to the lowest level reasonably practicable, and

        (iii) to provide any of those employees who are undertaking any such manual handling operations with certain information about the loads to be carried by them; and

    (c) in the circumstances specified in paragraph (2) of that regulation, to review (and where necessary change) any assessment such as is referred to in sub-paragraph (b)(i) above.

4 Regulation 2(1) defines, among other expressions, what is meant by **"injury"**, **"injured"** and **"manual handling operations"** and regulation 2(2) provides that where these Regulations impose duties on employers in respect of their employees those duties are also imposed on self-employed persons in respect of themselves.

5 Regulation 5 requires each employee while at work to make full and proper use of systems of work provided for his use by his employer in compliance with that employer's duty under regulation 4(1)(b)(ii) of these Regulations.

6 Regulation 6 enables the Secretary of State for Defence to grant certificates of exemption from these Regulations in the interests of national security.

7 Regulation 7 extends the application of these Regulations to and in relation to certain premises and activities outside Great Britain.

8 Regulation 8 (together with Schedule 2) repeals a number of enactments and revokes a number of instruments.

THE WORKPLACE (HEALTH, SAFETY AND WELFARE) REGULATIONS 1992

(SI 1992/3004)

Made on 1 December 1992 by The Secretary of State, in exercise of the powers conferred on her by ss. 15(1), (2), (3)(a) and (5)(b), and 82(3)(a) of, and paras. 1(2), 9 and 10 of Sch. 3 to, the Health and Safety at Work etc. Act 1974 ("the 1974 Act") and of all other powers enabling her in that behalf and for the purpose of giving effect without modifications to proposals submitted to her by the Health and Safety Commission under s. 11(2)(d) of the 1974 Act after the carrying out by the said Commission of consultations in accordance with s. 50(3) of that Act. Operative from 1 January 1993 (the whole regulations except regs. 5 to 27 and the Schedules, to the extent specified in reg. 1(3)) and 1 January 1996 (regs. 5 to 27 and the Schedules, to the extent specified in reg. 1(3)).

ARRANGEMENT OF REGULATIONS

REGULATION
1. Citation and commencement
2. Interpretation
3. Application of these Regulations
4. Requirements under these Regulations
5. Maintenance of workplace, and of equipment, devices and systems
6. Ventilation
7. Temperature in indoor workplaces
8. Lighting
9. Cleanliness and waste materials
10. Room dimensions and space
11. Workstations and seating
12. Condition of floors and traffic routes
13. Falls or falling objects
14. Windows, and transparent or translucent doors, gates and walls
15. Windows, skylights and ventilators
16. Ability to clean windows etc. safely
17. Organisation etc. of traffic routes
18. Doors and gates
19. Escalators and moving walkways
20. Sanitary conveniences
21. Washing facilities

SI 1992/3004

22. Drinking water
23. Accommodation for clothing
24. Facilities for changing clothing
25. Facilities for rest and to eat meals
26. Exemption certificates
27. Repeals, saving and revocations

SCHEDULE
1. Provisions applicable to factories which are not new workplaces, extensions or conversions
2. Repeals and revocations

CITATION AND COMMENCEMENT

1(1) These Regulations may be cited as the Workplace (Health, Safety and Welfare) Regulations 1992.

1(2) Subject to paragraph (3), these Regulations shall come into force on 1st January 1993.

1(3) Regulations 5 to 27 and the Schedules shall come into force on 1st January 1996 with respect to any workplace or part of a workplace which is not –

  (a) a new workplace; or

  (b) a modification, an extension or a conversion.

INTERPRETATION

2(1) In these Regulations, unless the context otherwise requires –

"new workplace" means a workplace used for the first time as a workplace after 31st December 1992;

"public road" means (in England and Wales) a highway maintainable at public expense within the meaning of section 329 of the Highways Act 1980 and (in Scotland) a public road within the meaning assigned to that term by section 151 of the Roads (Scotland) Act 1984;

"traffic route" means a route for pedestrian traffic, vehicles or both and includes any stairs, staircase, fixed ladder, doorway, gateway, loading bay or ramp;

"workplace" means, subject to paragraph (2), any premises or part of premises which are not domestic premises and are made available to any person as a place of work, and includes –

  (a) any place within the premises to which such person has access while at work; and

  (b) any room, lobby, corridor, staircase, road or other place used as a means of access to or egress from that place of work or where facilities are provided for use in connection with the place of work other than a public road;

but shall not include a modification; an extension or a conversion of any of the above until such modification, extension or conversion is completed.

2(2) Any reference in these Regulations, except in paragraph (1), to a modification, an extension or a conversion is a reference, as the case may be, to a modification, an extension or a conversion of a workplace started after 31st December 1992.

2(3) Any requirement that anything done or provided in pursuance of these Regulations shall

SI 1992/3004, reg. 1(1)

be suitable shall be construed to include a requirement that it is suitable for any person in respect of whom such thing is so done or provided.

2(4) Any reference in these Regulations to –
- (a) a numbered regulation or Schedule is a reference to the regulation in or Schedule to these Regulations so numbered; and
- (b) a numbered paragraph is a reference to the paragraph so numbered in the regulation in which the reference appears.

APPLICATION OF THESE REGULATIONS

3(1) These Regulations apply to every workplace but shall not apply to –
- (a) a workplace which is or is in or on a ship within the meaning assigned to that word by regulation 2(1) of the Docks Regulations 1988;
- (b) a workplace where the only activities being undertaken are building operations or works of engineering construction within, in either case, section 176 of the Factories Act 1961 and activities for the purpose of or in connection with the first-mentioned activities;
- (c) a workplace where the only activities being undertaken are the exploration for or extraction of mineral resources; or
- (d) a workplace which is situated in the immediate vicinity of another workplace or intended workplace where exploration for or extraction of mineral resources is being or will be undertaken, and where the only activities being undertaken are activities preparatory to, for the purposes of, or in connection with such exploration for or extraction of mineral resources at that other workplace.

3(2) In their application to temporary work sites, any requirement to ensure a workplace complies with any of regulations 20 to 25 shall have effect as a requirement to so ensure so far as is reasonably practicable.

3(3) As respects any workplace which is or is in or on an aircraft, locomotive or rolling stock, trailer or semi-trailer used as a means of transport or a vehicle for which a licence is in force under the Vehicles (Excise) Act 1971 or a vehicle exempted from duty under that Act –
- (a) regulations 5 to 12 and 14 to 25 shall not apply to any such workplace; and
- (b) regulation 13 shall apply to any such workplace only when the aircraft, locomotive or rolling stock, trailer or semi-trailer or vehicle is stationary inside a workplace and, in the case of a vehicle for which a licence is in force under the Vehicles (Excise) Act 1971, is not on a public road.

3(4) As respects any workplace which is in fields, woods or other land forming part of an agricultural or forestry undertaking but which is not inside a building and is situated away from the undertaking's main buildings –
- (a) regulations 5 to 19 and 23 to 25 shall not apply to any such workplace; and
- (b) any requirement to ensure that any such workplace complies with any of regulations 20 to 22 shall have effect as a requirement to so ensure so far as is reasonably practicable.

SI 1992/3004, reg. 3(4)

REQUIREMENTS UNDER THESE REGULATIONS

4(1) Every employer shall ensure that every workplace, modification, extension or conversion which is under his control and where any of his employees works complies with any requirement of these Regulations which –

(a) applies to that workplace or, as the case may be, to the workplace which contains that modification, extension or conversion; and

(b) is in force in respect of the workplace, modification, extension or conversion.

4(2) Subject to paragraph (4), every person who has, to any extent, control of a workplace, modification, extension or conversion shall ensure that such workplace, modification, extension or conversion complies with any requirement of these Regulations which –

(a) applies to that workplace or, as the case may be, to the workplace which contains that modification, extension or conversion;

(b) is in force in respect of the workplace, modification, extension, or conversion; and

(c) relates to matters within that person's control.

4(3) Any reference in this regulation to a person having control of any workplace, modification, extension or conversion is a reference to a person having control of the workplace, modification, extension or conversion in connection with the carrying on by him of a trade, business or other undertaking (whether for profit or not).

4(4) Paragraph (2) shall not impose any requirement upon a self-employed person in respect of his own work or the work of any partner of his in the undertaking.

4(5) Every person who is deemed to be the occupier of a factory by virtue of section 175(5) of the Factories Act 1961 shall ensure that the premises which are so deemed to be a factory comply with these Regulations.

MAINTENANCE OF WORKPLACE, AND OF EQUIPMENT, DEVICES AND SYSTEMS

5(1) The workplace and the equipment, devices and systems to which this regulation applies shall be maintained (including cleaned as appropriate) in an efficient state, in efficient working order and in good repair.

5(2) Where appropriate, the equipment, devices and systems to which this regulation applies shall be subject to a suitable system of maintenance.

5(3) The equipment, devices and systems to which this regulation applies are –

(a) equipment and devices a fault in which is liable to result in a failure to comply with any of these Regulations; and

(b) mechanical ventilation systems provided pursuant to regulation 6 (whether or not they include equipment or devices within sub-paragraph (a) of this paragraph).

VENTILATION

6(1) Effective and suitable provision shall be made to ensure that every enclosed workplace is ventilated by a sufficient quantity of fresh or purified air.

SI 1992/3004, reg. 4(1)

6(2) Any plant used for the purpose of complying with paragraph (1) shall include an effective device to give visible or audible warning of any failure of the plant where necessary for reasons of health or safety.

6(3) This regulation shall not apply to any enclosed workplace or part of a workplace which is subject to the provisions of –

    (a)   section 30 of the Factories Act 1961;

    (b)   regulations 49 to 52 of the Shipbuilding and Ship-Repairing Regulations 1960;

    (c)   regulation 21 of the Construction (General Provisions) Regulations 1961;

    (d)   regulation 18 of the Docks Regulations 1988.

TEMPERATURE IN INDOOR WORKPLACES

7(1) During working hours, the temperature in all workplaces inside buildings shall be reasonable.

7(2) A method of heating or cooling shall not be used which results in the escape into a workplace of fumes, gas or vapour of such character and to such extent that they are likely to be injurious or offensive to any person.

7(3) A sufficient number of thermometers shall be provided to enable persons at work to determine the temperature in any workplace inside a building.

LIGHTING

8(1) Every workplace shall have suitable and sufficient lighting.

8(2) The lighting mentioned in paragraph (1) shall, so far as is reasonably practicable, be by natural light.

8(3) Without prejudice to the generality of paragraph (1), suitable and sufficient emergency lighting shall be provided in any room in circumstances in which persons at work are specially exposed to danger in the event of failure of artificial lighting.

CLEANLINESS AND WASTE MATERIALS

9(1) Every workplace and the furniture, furnishings and fittings therein shall be kept sufficiently clean.

9(2) The surfaces of the floors, walls and ceilings of all workplaces inside buildings shall be capable of being kept sufficiently clean.

9(3) So far as is reasonably practicable, waste materials shall not be allowed to accumulate in a workplace except in suitable receptacles.

ROOM DIMENSIONS AND SPACE

10(1) Every room where persons work shall have sufficient floor area, height and unoccupied space for purposes of health, safety and welfare.

10(2) It shall be sufficient compliance with this regulation in a workplace which is not a new workplace, a modification, an extension and which, immediately before this regulation came into force in respect of it, was subject to the provisions of the Factories Act 1961, if the workplace does not contravene the provisions of Part I of Schedule 1.

WORKSTATIONS AND SEATING

11(1) Every workstation shall be so arranged that it is suitable both for any person at work in the workplace who is likely to work at that workstation and for any work of the undertaking which is likely to be done there.

11(2) Without prejudice to the generality of paragraph (1), every workstation outdoors shall be so arranged that –

(a) so far as is reasonably practicable, it provides protection from adverse weather;

(b) it enables any person at the workstation to leave it swiftly or, as appropriate, to be assisted in the event of an emergency; and

(c) it ensures that any person at the workstation is not likely to slip or fall.

11(3) A suitable seat shall be provided for each person at work in the workplace whose work includes operations of a kind that the work (or a substantial part of it) can or must be done sitting.

11(4) A seat shall not be suitable for the purpose of paragraph (3) unless –

(a) it is suitable for the person for whom it is provided as well as for the operations to be performed; and

(b) a suitable footrest is also provided where necessary.

CONDITION OF FLOORS AND TRAFFIC ROUTES

12(1) Every floor in a workplace and the surface of every traffic route in a workplace shall be of a construction such that the floor or surface of the traffic route is suitable for the purpose for which it is used.

12(2) Without prejudice to the generality of paragraph (1), the requirements in that paragraph shall include requirements that –

(a) the floor, or surface of the traffic route, shall have no hole or slope, or be uneven or slippery so as, in each case, to expose any person to a risk to his health or safety; and

(b) every such floor shall have effective means of drainage where necessary.

12(3) So far as is reasonably practicable, every floor in a workplace and the surface of every traffic route in a workplace shall be kept free from obstructions and from any article or substance which may cause a person to slip, trip or fall.

12(4) In considering whether for the purposes of paragraph (2)(a) a hole or slope exposes any person to a risk to his health or safety –

(a) no account shall be taken of a hole where adequate measures have been taken to prevent a person falling; and

(b) account shall be taken of any handrail provided in connection with any slope.

12(5) Suitable and sufficient handrails and, if appropriate, guards shall be provided on all traffic routes which are staircases except in circumstances in which a handrail can not be provided without obstructing the traffic route.

FALLS OR FALLING OBJECTS

13(1) So far as is reasonably practicable, suitable and effective measures shall be taken to prevent any event specified in paragraph (3).

SI 1992/3004, reg. 11(1)

13(2) So far as is reasonably practicable, the measures required by paragraph (1) shall be measures other than the provision of personal protective equipment, information, instruction, training or supervision.

13(3) The events specified in this paragraph are –
   (a) any person falling a distance likely to cause personal injury;
   (b) any person being struck by a falling object likely to cause personal injury.

13(4) Any area where there is a risk to health or safety from any event mentioned in paragraph (3) shall be clearly indicated where appropriate.

13(5) So far as is practicable, every tank, pit or structure where there is a risk of a person in the workplace falling into a dangerous substance in the tank, pit or structure, shall be securely covered or fenced.

13(6) Every traffic route over, across or in an uncovered tank, pit or structure such as is mentioned in paragraph (5) shall be securely fenced.

13(7) In this regulation, **"dangerous substance"** means –
   (a) any substance likely to scald or burn;
   (b) any poisonous substance;
   (c) any corrosive substance;
   (d) any fume, gas or vapour likely to overcome a person; or
   (e) any granular or free-flowing solid substance, or any viscous substance which, in any case, is of a nature of quantity which is likely to cause danger to any person.

WINDOWS, AND TRANSPARENT OR TRANSLUCENT DOORS, GATES AND WALLS

14(1) Every window or other transparent or translucent surface in a wall or partition and every transparent or translucent surface in a door or gate shall, where necessary for reasons of health or safety –
   (a) be of safety material or be protected against breakage of the transparent or translucent material; and
   (b) be appropriately marked or incorporate features so as, in either case, to make it apparent.

WINDOWS, SKYLIGHTS AND VENTILATORS

15(1) No window, skylight or ventilator which is capable of being opened shall be likely to be opened, closed or adjusted in a manner which exposes any person performing such operation to a risk to his health or safety.

15(2) No window, skylight or ventilator shall be in a position when open which is likely to expose any person in the workplace to a risk to his health or safety.

ABILITY TO CLEAN WINDOWS ETC. SAFELY

16(1) All windows and skylights in a workplace shall be of a design or be so constructed that they may be cleaned safely.

SI 1992/3004, reg. 16(1)

16(2) In considering whether a window or skylight is of a design or so constructed as to comply with paragraph (1), account may be taken of equipment used in conjunction with the window or skylight or of devices fitted to the building.

ORGANISATION ETC. OF TRAFFIC ROUTES

17(1) Every workplace shall be organised in such a way that pedestrians and vehicles can circulate in a safe manner.

17(2) Traffic routes in a workplace shall be suitable for the persons or vehicles using them, sufficient in number, in suitable positions and of sufficient size.

17(3) Without prejudice to the generality of paragraph (2), traffic routes shall not satisfy the requirements of that paragraph unless suitable measures are taken to ensure that –

- (a) pedestrians or, as the case may be, vehicles may use a traffic route without causing danger to the health or safety of persons at work near it;
- (b) there is sufficient separation of any traffic route for vehicles from doors or gates or from traffic routes for pedestrians which lead onto it; and
- (c) where vehicles and pedestrians use the same traffic route, there is sufficient separation between them.

17(4) All traffic routes shall be suitably indicated where necessary for reasons of health or safety.

17(5) Paragraph (2) shall apply so far as is reasonably practicable, to a workplace which is not a new workplace, a modification, an extension or a conversion.

DOORS AND GATES

18(1) Doors and gates shall be suitably constructed (including being fitted with any necessary safety devices).

18(2) Without prejudice to the generality of paragraph (1), doors and gates shall not comply with that paragraph unless –

- (a) any sliding door or gate has a device to prevent it coming off its track during use;
- (b) any upward opening door or gate has a device to prevent it falling back;
- (c) any powered door or gate has suitable and effective features to prevent it causing injury by trapping any person;
- (d) where necessary for reasons of health or safety, any powered door or gate can be operated manually unless it opens automatically if the power fails; and
- (e) any door or gate which is capable of opening by being pushed from either side is of such a construction as to provide, when closed, a clear view of the space close to both sides.

ESCALATORS AND MOVING WALKWAYS

19 Escalators and moving walkways shall –
- (a) function safely;
- (b) be equipped with any necessary safety devices;

SI 1992/3004, reg. 16(2)

(c) be fitted with one or more emergency stop controls which are easily identifiable and readily accessible.

SANITARY CONVENIENCES

20(1) Suitable and sufficient sanitary conveniences shall be provided at readily accessible places.

20(2) Without prejudice to the generality of paragraph (1), sanitary conveniences shall not be suitable unless –

(a) the rooms containing them are adequately ventilated and lit;

(b) they and the rooms containing them are kept in a clean and orderly condition; and

(c) separate rooms containing conveniences are provided for men and women except where and so far as each convenience is in a separate room the door of which is capable of being secured from inside.

20(3) It shall be sufficient compliance with the requirement in paragraph (1) to provide sufficient sanitary conveniences in a workplace which is not a new workplace, a modification, an extension or a conversion and which, immediately before this regulation came into force in respect of it, was subject to the provisions of the Factories Act 1961, if sanitary conveniences are provided in accordance with the provisions of Part II of Schedule 1.

WASHING FACILITIES

21(1) Suitable and sufficient washing facilities, including showers if required by the nature of the work or for health reasons, shall be provided at readily accessible places.

21(2) Without prejudice to the generality of paragraph (1), washing facilities shall not be suitable unless –

(a) they are provided in the immediate vicinity of every sanitary convenience, whether or not provided elsewhere as well;

(b) they are provided in the vicinity of any changing rooms required by these Regulations, whether or not provided elsewhere as well;

(c) they include a supply of clean hot and cold, or warm, water (which shall be running water so far as is practicable);

(d) they include soap or other suitable means of cleaning;

(e) they include towels or other suitable means of drying;

(f) the rooms containing them are sufficiently ventilated and lit;

(g) they and the rooms containing them are kept in a clean and orderly condition; and

(h) separate facilities are provided for men and women, except where and so far as they are provided in a room the door of which is capable of being secured from inside and the facilities in each such room are intended to be used by only one person at a time.

21(3) Paragraph (2)(h) shall not apply to facilities which are provided for washing hands, forearms and face only.

SI 1992/3004, reg. 21(3)

DRINKING WATER

22(1) An adequate supply of wholesome drinking water shall be provided for all persons at work in the workplace.

22(2) Every supply of drinking water required by paragraph (1) shall –

    (a) be readily accessible at suitable places; and

    (b) be conspicuously marked by an appropriate sign where necessary for reasons of health or safety.

23(3) Where a supply of drinking water is required by paragraph (1), there shall also be provided a sufficient number of suitable cups or other drinking vessels unless the supply of drinking water is in a jet from which persons can drink easily.

ACCOMMODATION FOR CLOTHING

23(1) Suitable and sufficient accommodation shall be provided –

    (a) for the clothing of any person at work which is not worn during working hours; and

    (b) for special clothing which is worn by any person at work but which is not taken home.

23(2) Without prejudice to the generality of paragraph (1), the accommodation mentioned in that paragraph shall not be suitable unless –

    (a) where facilities to change clothing are required by regulation 24, it provides suitable security for the clothing mentioned in paragraph (1)(a);

    (b) where necessary to avoid risks to health or damage to the clothing, it includes separate accommodation for clothing worn at work and for other clothing;

    (c) so far as is reasonably practicable, it allows or includes facilities for drying clothing; and

    (d) it is in a suitable location.

FACILITIES FOR CHANGING CLOTHING

24(1) Suitable and sufficient facilities shall be provided for any person at work in the workplace to change clothing in all cases where –

    (a) the person has to wear special clothing for the purpose of work; and

    (b) the person can not, for reasons of health or propriety, be expected to change in another room.

24(2) Without prejudice to the generality of paragraph (1), the facilities mentioned in that paragraph shall not be suitable unless they include separate facilities for, or separate use of facilities by, men and women where necessary for reasons of propriety.

FACILITIES FOR REST AND TO EAT MEALS

25(1) Suitable and sufficient rest facilities shall be provided at readily accessible places.

25(2) Rest facilities provided by virtue of paragraph (1) shall –

    (a) where necessary for reasons of health or safety include, in the case of a new workplace, an extension or a conversion, rest facilities provided in one or more rest rooms, or, in other cases, in rest rooms or rest areas;

SI 1992/3004, reg. 22(1)

(b) include suitable facilities to eat meals where food eaten in the workplace would otherwise be likely to become contaminated.

25(3) Rest rooms and rest areas shall include suitable arrangements to protect non-smokers from discomfort caused by tobacco smoke.

25(4) Suitable facilities shall be provided for any person at work who is a pregnant woman or nursing mother to rest.

25(5) Suitable and sufficient facilities shall be provided for persons at work to eat meals where meals are regularly eaten in the workplace.

EXEMPTION CERTIFICATES

26(1) The Secretary of State for Defence may, in the interests of national security, by a certificate in writing exempt any of the home forces, any visiting force or any headquarters from the requirements of these Regulations and any exemption may be granted subject to conditions and to a limit of time and may be revoked by the said Secretary of State by a further certificate in writing at any time.

26(2) In this regulation –

(a) **"the home forces"** has the same meaning as in section 12(1) of the Visiting Forces Act 1952;

(b) **"headquarters"** has the same meaning as in article 3(2) of the Visiting Forces and International Headquarters (Application of Law) Order 1965;

(c) **"visiting force"** has the same meaning as it does for the purposes of any provision of Part I of the Visiting Forces Act 1952.

REPEALS, SAVING AND REVOCATIONS

27(1) The enactments mentioned in column 2 of Part I of Schedule 2 are repealed to the extent specified in column 3 of that Part.

27(2) Nothing in this regulation shall affect the operation of any provision of the Offices, Shops and Railway Premises Act 1963 as that provision has effect by virtue of section 90(4) of that Act.

27(3) The instruments mentioned in column 1 of Part II of Schedule 2 are revoked to the extent specified in column 3 of that Part.

Schedule 1 – Provisions Applicable to Factories Which Are Not New Workplaces, Modifications, Extensions or Conversions

Regulations 10 and 20

Part I – Space

1 No room in the workplace shall be so overcrowded as to cause risk to the health or safety of persons at work in it.

SI 1992/3004, Sch. 1, para. 1

2 Without prejudice to the generality of paragraph 1, the number of persons employed at a time in any workroom shall not be such that the amount of cubic space allowed for each is less than 11 cubic metres.

3 In calculating for the purposes of this Part of this Schedule the amount of cubic space in any room no space more than 4.2 metres from the floor shall be taken into account and, where a room contains a gallery, the gallery shall be treated for the purposes of this Schedule as if it were partitioned off from the remainder of the room and formed a separate room.

Part II – Number of Sanitary Conveniences

4 In workplaces where females work, there shall be at least one suitable water closet for use by females only for every 25 females.

5 In workplaces where males work, there shall be at least one suitable water closet for use by males only for every 25 males.

6 In calculating the number of males or females who work in any workplace for the purposes of this Part of this Schedule, any number not itself divisible by 25 without fraction or remainder shall be treated as the next number higher than it which is so divisible.

Schedule 2 – Repeals and Revocations

Regulation 27

Part I – Repeals

1 Chapter	2 Short title	3 Extent of repeal
1961 c.34	The Factories Act 1961	Sections 1 to 7, 18, 28, 29, 57 to 60 and 69
1963 c.41	The Offices, Shops and Railway Premises Act 1963	Sections 4 to 16
1956 c.49	The Agriculture (Safety, Health and Welfare Provisions) Act 1956	Sections 3 and 5 and, in section 25, sub-sections (3) and (6)

Part II – Revocations

(1) Title	(2) Reference	(3) Extent of revocation
The Flax and Tow Spinning and Weaving Regulations 1906	S.R. & O. 1906/177, amended by S.I. 1988/1657	Regulation 3, 8, 10, 11 and 14
The Hemp Spinning and Weaving Regulations 1907	S.R. & O. 1907/660, amended by S.I. 1988/1657	Regulations 3 to 5 and 8

SI 1992/3004, Sch. 1, para. 2

The Workplace (Health, Safety and Welfare) Regulations 1992

(1) Title	(2) Reference	(3) Extent of revocation
Order dated 5 October 1917 (the Tin or Terne Plates Manufacture Welfare Order 1917)	S.R. & O. 1917/1035	The whole Order
Order dated 15 May 1918 (the Glass Bottle, etc. Manufacture Welfare Order 1918)	S.R. & O. 1918/558	The whole Order
Order dated 15 August 1919 (the Fruit Preserving Welfare Order 1919)	S.R. & O. 1919/1136, amended by S.I. 1988/1657	The whole Order
Order dated 23 April 1920 (the Laundries Welfare Order 1920)	S.R. & O. 1920/654	The whole Order
Order dated 28 July 1920 (the Gut Scraping, Tripe Dressing, etc Welfare Order 1920)	S.R. & O. 1920/1437	The whole Order
Order dated 9 September 1920 (the Herring Curing (Norfolk and Suffolk) Welfare Order 1920)	S.R. & O. 1920/1662	The whole Order
Order dated 3 March 1921 (the Glass Bevelling Welfare Order 1921)	S.R. & O. 1921/288	The whole Order
The Herring Curing (Scotland) Welfare Order 1926	S.R. & O. 1926/535 (S.24)	The whole Order
The Herring Curing Welfare Order 1927	S.R. & O. 1927/813, amended by S.I. 1960/1690 and 917	The whole Order
The Sacks (Cleaning and Repairing) Welfare Order 1927	S.R. & O. 1927/860	The whole Order
The Horizontal Milling Machines Regulations 1928	S.R. & O. 1928/548	The whole Regulations
The Cotton Cloth Factories Regulations 1929	S.I. 1929/300	Regulations 5 to 10, 11 and 12
The Oil Cake Welfare Order 1929	S.R. & O. 1929/534	Articles 3 to 6
The Cement Works Welfare Order 1930	S.R. & O. 1930/94	The whole Order
The Tanning Welfare Order 1930	S.R. & O. 1930/312	The whole Order
The Kiers Regulations 1938	S.R. & O. 1938/106 amended by S.I. 1981/1152	Regulations 12 to 15

SI 1992/3004, Sch. 2

(1) Title	(2) Reference	(3) Extent of revocation
The Sanitary Accommodation Regulations 1938	S.R. & O. 1938/611, amended by S.I. 1974/426	The whole Regulations
The Clay Works (Welfare) Special Regulations 1948	S.I. 1948/1547	Regulations 3, 4, 6, 8 and 9
The Jute (Safety, Health and Welfare) Regulations 1948	S.I. 1948/1696, amended by S.I. 1988/1657	Regulations 11, 13, 14 to 16 and 19 to 26
The Pottery (Health and Welfare) Special Regulations 1950	S.I. 1950/65, amended by S.I. 1963/879, 1973/36, 1980/1248, 1982/877, 1988/1657, 1989/2311 and 1990/305	Regulation 15
The Iron and Steel Foundries Regulations 1953	S.I. 1953/1464, amended by S.I. 1974/1681 and 1981/1332	The whole Regulations
The Washing Facilities (Running Water) Exemption Regulations 1960	S.I. 1960/1029	The whole Regulations
The Washing Facilities (Miscellaneous Industries) Regulations 1960	S.I. 1960/1214	The whole Regulations
The Factories (Cleanliness of Walls and Ceilings) Order 1960	S.I. 1960/1794, amended by S.I. 1974/427	The whole Order
The Non-ferrous Metals (Melting and Founding) Regulations 1962	S.I. 1962/1667, amended by S.I. 1974/1681, 1981/1332 and 1988/165	Regulations 5, 6 to 10, 14 to 17 and 20
The Offices, Shops and Railway Premises Act 1963 (Exemption No. 1) Order 1964	S.I. 1964/964	The whole Order
The Washing Facilities Regulations 1964	S.I. 1964/965	The whole Regulations
The Sanitary Conveniences Regulations 1964	S.I. 1964/966, amended by S.I. 1982/827	The whole Regulations
The Offices, Shops and Railway Premises Act 1963 (Exemption No. 7) Order 1968	S.I. 1968/1947, amended by S.I. 1982/827	The whole Order
The Abrasive Wheels Regulations 1970	S.I. 1970/535	Regulation 17
The Sanitary Accommodation (Amendment) Regulations 1974	S.I. 1974/426	The whole Regulations

SI 1992/3004, Sch. 2

The Workplace (Health, Safety and Welfare) Regulations 1992

(1) Title	(2) Reference	(3) Extent of revocation
The Factories (Cleanliness of Walls and Ceilings) (Amendment) Regulations 1974	S.I. 1974/427	The whole Regulations
The Woodworking Machines Regulations 1974	S.I. 1974/903, amended by S.I. 1978/1126	Regulations 10 to 12
The Offices, Shops and Railway Premises Act 1963 etc. (Metrication) Regulations 1982	S.I. 1982/827	The whole Regulations

EXPLANATORY NOTE

(This note is not part of the Regulations)

1 These Regulations impose requirements with respect to the health, safety and welfare of persons in a **"workplace"**, defined in regulation 2(1).

2 Except to the extent specified below, the Regulations give effect as respects Great Britain to Council Directive 89/654/EEC (OJ L. 393, 30.12.89, p.1) concerning the minimum safety and health requirements for the workplace (**"the Directive"**).

3 The Regulations do not apply to a workplace which is or is in or on a ship (*regulation 3(1)(a)*). Nor do they impose requirements with respect to –

   (a)   stability and solidity (*Annex I, point 2; and Annex II, point 2 of the Directive*);

   (b)   electrical installations (*Annex I, point 3; and Annex II, point 3 of the Directive*);

   (c)   emergency routes and exits (*Annex I, point 4; and Annex II, point 4 of the Directive*);

   (d)   fire detection and fire fighting (*Annex I, point 5; and Annex II, point 5 of the Directive*);

   (e)   thermal insulation (*Annex I, point 9.1, second paragraph, of the Directive*); and

   (f)   first aid rooms or equipment (*Annex I, point 19; and Annex II, point 14 of the Directive*).

4 The Regulations are disapplied in relation to construction sites and sites where mineral exploration or extraction is undertaken. The application of specified regulations is modified in their application to temporary work sites, specified means of transport and specified parts of agricultural undertakings (*regulation 3*).

5 Requirements are imposed upon employers, persons who have, to any extent, control of a workplace, and persons who are deemed to be the occupiers of factories for the purposes of section 175(5) of the Factories Act 1961 (c. 54) (*regulation 4*).

6 The Regulations impose requirements with respect to –

   (a)   maintenance (*regulation 5*);

   (b)   ventilation of enclosed workplaces (*regulation 6*);

(c) temperature indoors and the provision of thermometers (*regulation 7*);

(d) lighting (including emergency lighting) (*regulation 8*);

(e) cleanliness of the workplace, furniture, furnishings and fittings; the ability to clean the surface of floors, walls and ceilings; and the accumulation of waste materials (*regulation 9*);

(f) room dimensions and unoccupied space (*regulation 10 and Schedule 1, Part I*);

(g) the suitability of workstations (including workstations outdoors) and the provision of suitable seats (*regulation 11*);

(h) the condition of floors (*regulation 12*);

(i) the condition and arrangement of routes for pedestrians or vehicles (*regulations 12 and 17*);

(j) protection from falling objects and from persons falling from a height or falling into a dangerous substance (*regulation 13*);

(k) the material or protection of windows and other transparent or translucent walls, doors or gates and to them being apparent (*regulation 14*);

(l) the way in which windows, skylights or ventilators are opened and the position they are left in when open (*regulation 15*);

(m) the ability to clean windows and skylights (*regulation 16*);

(n) the construction of doors and gates (including the fitting of necessary safety devices) (*regulation 18*);

(o) escalators and moving walkways (*regulation 19*);

(p) the provision of suitable sanitary conveniences (*regulation 20 and Schedule 1, Part II*);

(q) the provision of suitable washing facilities (*regulation 21*);

(r) the provision of a supply of drinking water and of cups or other drinking vessels (*regulation 22*);

(s) the provision of suitable accommodation for clothing and of facilities for changing clothing (*regulations 23 and 24*); and

(t) the provision of suitable facilities for rest and to eat meals (*regulation 25*).

7 The Secretary of State for Defence may grant exemption from the requirements of the Regulations in the interests of national security (*regulation 26*).

8 Provisions replaced by the Regulations are repealed or revoked. There is a saving for provisions of the Offices, Shops and Railway Premises Act 1963 (c. 41) in specified circumstances (*regulation 27 and Schedule 2*).

PART III
EC DIRECTIVES

COUNCIL DIRECTIVE 89/391

On the introduction of measures to encourage improvements in the safety and health of workers at work

(12 June 1989, OJ 1989 L183/1)

The Council of the European Communities,

Having regard to the Treaty establishing the European Economic Community, and in particular Article 118a thereof,

Having regard to the proposal from the Commission, drawn up after consultation with the Advisory Committee on Safety, Hygiene and Health Protection at Work,

In cooperation with the European Parliament,

Having regard to the opinion of the Economic and Social Committee,

[1] Whereas Article 118a of the Treaty provides that the Council shall adopt, by means of directives, minimum requirements for encouraging improvements, especially in the working environment, to guarantee a better level of protection of the safety and health of workers;

[2] Whereas this directive does not justify any reduction in levels of protection already achieved in individual member states, the member state being committed, under the Treaty, to encouraging improvements in conditions in this area and to harmonising conditions while maintaining the improvements made;

[3] Whereas it is known that workers can be exposed to the effects of dangerous environmental factors at the work place during the course of their working life;

[4] Whereas, pursuant to Article 118a of the Treaty, such directives must avoid imposing administrative, financial and legal constraints which would hold back the creation and development of small and medium-sized undertakings;

[5] Whereas the communication from the Commission on its programme concerning safety, hygiene and health at work provides for the adoption of directives designed to guarantee the safety and health of workers;

[6] Whereas the Council, in its resolution of 21 December 1987 on safety, hygiene and health at work, took note of the Commission's intention to submit to the Council in the near future a directive on the organisation of the safety and health of workers at the work place;

[7] Whereas in February 1988 the European Parliament adopted four resolutions following the debate on the internal market and worker protection; whereas these resolutions specifically invited the Commission to draw up a framework directive to serve as a basis for more specific directives covering all the risks connected with safety and health at the work place;

[8] Whereas member states have a responsibility to encourage improvements in the safety and health of workers on their territory; whereas taking measures to protect the health and safety of workers at work also helps, in certain cases, to preserve the health and possibly the safety of persons residing with them;

[9] Whereas member states' legislative systems covering safety and health at the work place differ widely and need to be improved; whereas national provisions on the subject, which often include technical specifications and/or self-regulatory standards, may result in different levels of safety and health protection and allow competition at the expense of safety and health;

[10] Whereas the incidence of accidents at work and occupational diseases is still too high; whereas preventive measures must be introduced or improved without delay in order to safeguard the safety and health of workers and ensure a higher degree of protection;

[11] Whereas, in order to ensure an improved degree of protection, workers and/or their representatives must be informed of the risks to their safety and health and of the measures required to reduce or eliminate these risks; whereas they must also be in a position to contribute, by means of balanced participation in accordance with national laws and/or practices, to seeing that the necessary protective measures are taken;

[12] Whereas information, dialogue and balanced participation on safety and health at work must be developed between employers and workers and/or their representatives by means of appropriate procedures and instruments, in accordance with national laws and/or practices;

[13] Whereas the improvement of workers' safety, hygiene and health at work is an objective which should not be subordinated to purely economic considerations;

[14] Whereas employers shall be obliged to keep themselves informed of the latest advances in technology and scientific findings concerning work-place design, account being taken of the inherent dangers in their undertaking, and to inform accordingly the workers' representatives exercising participation rights under this directive, so as to be able to guarantee a better level of protection of workers' health and safety;

[15] Whereas the provisions of this directive apply, without prejudice to more stringent present or future Community provisions, to all risks, and in particular to those arising from the use at work of chemical, physical and biological agents covered by Directive 80/1107/EEC, as last amended by Directive 88/642/EEC;

[16] Whereas, pursuant to Decision 74/325/EEC, the Advisory Committee on Safety, Hygiene and Health Protection at Work is consulted by the Commission on the drafting of proposals in this field;

[17] Whereas a Committee composed of members nominated by the member states needs to be set up to assist the Commission in making the technical adaptations to the individual directives provided for in this directive.

has adopted this directive:

SECTION I – GENERAL PROVISIONS

ART. 1 Object

1(1) The object of this directive is to introduce measures to encourage improvements in the safety and health of workers at work.

1(2) To that end it contains general principles concerning the prevention of occupational risks, the protection of safety and health, the elimination of risk and accident factors, the informing, consultation, balanced participation in accordance with national laws and/or practices and training of workers and their representatives, as well as general guidelines for the implementation of the said principles.

1(3) This directive shall be without prejudice to existing or future national and Community provisions which are more favourable to protection of the safety and health of workers at work.

ART. 2 Scope

2(1) This directive shall apply to all sectors of activity, both public and private (industrial, agricultural, commercial, administrative, service, educational, cultural, leisure, etc.).

2(2) This directive shall not be applicable where characteristics peculiar to certain specific public service activities, such as the armed forces or the police, or to certain specific activities in the civil protection services inevitably conflict with it.

In that event, the safety and health of workers must be ensured as far as possible in the light of the objectives of this directive.

ART. 3 Definitions

3 For the purposes of this directive, the following terms shall have the following meanings:

(a) **worker:** any person employed by an employer, including trainees and apprentices but excluding domestic servants;

(b) **employer:** any natural or legal person who has an employment relationship with the worker and has responsibility for the undertaking and/or establishment;

(c) **workers' representative with specific responsibility for the safety and health of workers:** any person elected, chosen or designated in accordance with national laws and/or practices to represent workers where problems arise relating to the safety and health protection of workers at work;

(d) **prevention:** all the steps or measures taken or planned at all stages of work in the undertaking to prevent or reduce occupational risks.

ART. 4 [Legal provisions]

4(1) Member states shall take the necessary steps to ensure that employers, workers and workers' representatives are subject to the legal provisions necessary for the implementation of this directive.

4(2) In particular, member states shall ensure adequate controls and supervision.

SECTION II – EMPLOYERS' OBLIGATIONS

ART. 5 General provision

5(1) The employer shall have a duty to ensure the safety and health of workers in every aspect related to the work.

5(2) Where, pursuant to Article 7(3), an employer enlists competent external services or persons, this shall not discharge him from his responsibilities in this area.

5(3) The workers' obligations in the field of safety and health at work shall not affect the principle of the responsibility of the employer.

5(4) This directive shall not restrict the option of member states to provide for the exclusion or the limitation of employers' responsibility where occurrences are due to unusual and unforeseeable circumstances, beyond the employers' control, or to exceptional events, the consequences of which could not have been avoided despite the exercise of all due care.

Member states need not exercise the option referred to in the first subparagraph.

ART. 6 General obligations on employers

6(1) Within the context of his responsibilities, the employer shall take the measures necessary for the safety and health protection of workers, including prevention of occupational risks and provision of information and training, as well as provision of the necessary organisation and means.

The employer shall be alert to the need to adjust these measures to take account of changing circumstances and aim to improve existing situations.

6(2) The employer shall implement the measures referred to in the first subparagraph of paragraph 1 on the basis of the following general principles of prevention:

(a) avoiding risks;

(b) evaluating the risks which cannot be avoided;

(c) combating the risks at source;

(d) adapting the work to the individual, especially as regards the design of work places, the choice of work equipment and the choice of working and production methods, with a view, in particular, to alleviating monotonous work and work at a predetermined work-rate and to reducing their effect on health.

(e) adapting to technical progress;

(f) replacing the dangerous by the non-dangerous or the less dangerous;

(g) developing a coherent overall prevention policy which covers technology, organisation of work, working conditions, social relationships and the influence of factors related to the working environment;

(h) giving collective protective measures priority over individual protective measures;

(i) giving appropriate instructions to the workers.

6(3) Without prejudice to the other provisions of this directive, the employer shall, taking into account the nature of the activities of the enterprise and/or establishment:

(a) evaluate the risks to the safety and health of workers, *inter alia* in the choice of work equipment, the chemical substances or preparations used, and the fitting-out of work places.

Dir. 89/391, Art. 5(1)

Subsequent to this evaluation and as necessary, the preventive measures and the working and production methods implemented by the employer must:
- assure an improvement in the level of protection afforded to workers with regard to safety and health;
- be integrated into all the activities of the undertaking and/or establishment and at all hierarchical levels;

(b) where he entrusts tasks to a worker, take into consideration the worker's capabilities as regards health and safety;

(c) ensure that the planning and introduction of new technologies are the subject of consultation with the workers and/or their representatives, as regards the consequences of the choice of equipment, the working conditions and the working environment for the safety and health of workers;

(d) take appropriate steps to ensure that only workers who have received adequate instructions may have access to areas where there is serious and specific danger.

6(4) Without prejudice to the other provisions of this directive, where several undertakings share a work place, the employers shall cooperate in implementing the safety, health and occupational hygiene provisions and, taking into account the nature of the activities, shall coordinate their actions in matters of the protection and prevention of occupational risks, and shall inform one another and their respective workers and/or workers' representatives of these risks.

6(5) Measures related to safety, hygiene and health at work may in no circumstances involve the workers in financial cost.

ART. 7 Protective and preventive services

7(1) Without prejudice to the obligations referred to in Articles 5 and 6, the employer shall designate one or more workers to carry out activities related to the protection and prevention of occupational risks for the undertaking and/or establishment.

7(2) Designated workers may not be placed at any disadvantage because of their activities related to the protection and prevention of occupational risks.

Designated workers shall be allowed adequate time to enable them to fulfil their obligations arising from this directive.

7(3) If such protective and preventive measures cannot be organised for lack of competent personnel in the undertaking and/or establishment, the employer shall enlist competent external services or persons.

7(4) Where the employer enlists such services or persons, he shall inform them of the factors known to affect, or suspected of affecting, the safety and health of the workers and they must have access to the information referred to in Article 10(2).

7(5) In all cases:
- the workers designated must have the necessary capabilities and the necessary means,
- the external services or persons consulted must have the necessary aptitudes and the necessary personal and professional means, and
- the workers designated and the external services or persons consulted must be sufficient in number

to deal with the organisation of protective and preventive measures, taking into account the size of the undertaking and/or establishment and/or the hazards to which the workers are exposed and their distribution throughout the entire undertaking and/or establishment.

7(6) The protection from, and prevention of, the health and safety risks which form the subject of this Article shall be the responsibility of one or more workers, of one service or of separate services whether from inside or outside the undertaking and/or establishment.

The worker(s) and/or agency(ies) must work together whenever necessary.

7(7) Member states may define, in the light of the nature of the activities and size of the undertakings, the categories of undertakings in which the employer, provided he is competent, may himself take responsibility for the measures referred to in paragraph 1.

7(8) Member states shall define the necessary capabilities and aptitudes referred to in paragraph 5.

They may determine the sufficient number referred to in paragraph 5.

ART. 8 First aid, fire-fighting and evacuation of workers, serious and imminent danger

8(1) The employer shall:
- take the necessary measures for first aid, fire-fighting and evacuation of workers, adapted to the nature of the activities and the size of the undertaking and/or establishment and taking into account other persons present,
- arrange any necessary contacts with external services, particularly as regards first aid, emergency medical care, rescue work and fire-fighting.

8(2) Pursuant to paragraph 1, the employer shall, *inter alia*, for first aid, fire-fighting and the evacuation of workers, designate the workers required to implement such measures.

The number of such workers, their training and the equipment available to them shall be adequate, taking account of the size and/or specific hazards of the undertaking and/or establishment.

8(3) The employer shall:
(a) as soon as possible, inform all workers who are, or may be, exposed to serious and imminent danger of the risk involved and of the steps taken or to be taken as regards protection;
(b) take action and give instructions to enable workers in the event of serious, imminent and unavoidable danger to stop work and/or immediately to leave the work place and proceed to a place of safety;
(c) save in exceptional cases for reasons duly substantiated, refrain from asking workers to resume work in a working situation where there is still a serious and imminent danger.

8(4) Workers who, in the event of serious, imminent and unavoidable danger, leave their workstation and/or a dangerous area may not be placed at any disadvantage because of their action and must be protected against any harmful and unjustified consequences, in accordance with national laws and/or practices.

8(5) The employer shall ensure that all workers are able, in the event of serious and imminent danger to their own safety and/or that of other persons, and where the immediate superior

Dir. 89/391, Art. 7(6)

responsible cannot be contacted, to take the appropriate steps in the light of their knowledge and the technical means at their disposal, to avoid the consequences of such danger.

Their actions shall not place them at any disadvantage, unless they acted carelessly or there was negligence on their part.

ART. 9   Various obligations on employers

9(1) The employer shall:
- (a) be in possession of an assessment of the risks to safety and health at work, including those facing groups of workers exposed to particular risks;
- (b) decide on the protective measures to be taken and, if necessary, the protective equipment to be used;
- (c) keep a list of occupational accidents resulting in a worker being unfit for work for more than three working days;
- (d) draw up, for the responsible authorities and in accordance with national laws and/or practices, reports on occupational accidents suffered by his workers.

9(2) Member states shall define, in the light of the nature of the activities and size of the undertakings, the obligations to be met by the different categories of undertakings in respect of the drawing-up of the documents provided for in paragraph 1(a) and (b) and when preparing the documents provided for in paragraph 1(c) and (d).

ART. 10   Worker information

10(1) The employer shall take appropriate measures so that workers and/or their representatives in the undertaking and/or establishment receive, in accordance with national laws and/or practices which may take account, *inter alia*, of the size of the undertaking and/or establishment, all the necessary information concerning:
- (a) the safety and health risks and protective and preventive measures and activities in respect of both the undertaking and/or establishment in general and each type of workstation and/or job;
- (b) the measures taken pursuant to Article 8(2).

10(2) The employer shall take appropriate measures so that employers of workers from any outside undertakings and/or establishments engaged in work in his undertaking and/or establishment receive, in accordance with national laws and/or practices, adequate information concerning the points referred to in paragraph 1(a) and (b) which is to be provided to the workers in question.

10(3) The employer shall take appropriate measures so that workers with specific functions in protecting the safety and health of workers, or workers' representatives with specific responsibility for the safety and health of workers shall have access, to carry out their functions and in accordance with national laws and/or practices, to:
- (a) the risk assessment and protective measures referred to in Article 9(1)(a) and (b);
- (b) the list and reports referred to in Article 9(1)(c) and (d);
- (c) the information yielded by protective and preventive measures, inspection agencies and bodies responsible for safety and health.

ART. 11 Consultation and participation of workers

11(1) Employers shall consult workers and/or their representatives and allow them to take part in discussions on all questions relating to safety and health at work.

This presupposes:
- the consultation of workers,
- the right of workers and/or their representatives to make proposals,
- balanced participation in accordance with national laws and/or practices.

11(2) Workers or workers' representatives with specific responsibility for the safety and health of workers shall take part in a balanced way, in accordance with national laws and/or good practices, or shall be consulted in advance and in good time by the employer with regard to:

(a) any measure which may substantially affect safety and health;

(b) the designation of workers referred to in Articles 7(1) and 8(2) and the activities referred to in Article 7(1);

(c) the information referred to in Articles 9(1) and 10;

(d) the enlistment, where appropriate, of the competent services or persons outside the undertaking and/or establishment, as referred to in Article 7(3);

(e) the planning and organisation of the training referred to in Article 12.

11(3) Workers' representatives with specific responsibility for the safety and health of workers shall have the right to ask the employer to take appropriate measures and to submit proposals to him to that end to mitigate hazards for workers and/or to remove sources of danger.

11(4) The workers referred to in paragraph 2 and the workers' representatives referred to in paragraph 2 and 3 may not be placed at a disadvantage because of their respective activities referred to in paragraphs 2 and 3.

11(5) Employers must allow workers' representatives with specific responsibility for the safety and health of workers adequate time off work, without loss of pay, and provide them with the necessary means to enable such representatives to exercise their rights and functions deriving from this directive.

11(6) Workers and/or their representatives are entitled to appeal, in accordance with national law and/or practice, to the authority responsible for safety and health protection at work if they consider that the measures taken and the means employed by the employer are inadequate for the purposes of ensuring safety and health at work.

Workers' representatives must be given the opportunity to submit their observations during inspection visits by the competent authority.

ART. 12 Training of workers

12(1) The employer shall ensure that each worker receives adequate safety and health training, in particular in the form of information and instructions specific to his workstation or job:
- on recruitment,
- in the event of a transfer or a change of job,
- in the event of the introduction of new work equipment or a change in equipment,
- in the event of the introduction of any new technology.

Dir. 89/391, Art. 11(1)

The training shall be:
- adapted to take account of new or changed risks, and
- repeated periodically if necessary.

12(2) The employer shall ensure that workers from outside undertakings and/or establishments engaged in work in his undertaking and/or establishment have in fact received appropriate instructions regarding health and safety risks during their activities in his undertaking and/or establishment.

12(3) Workers' representatives with a specific role in protecting the safety and health of workers shall be entitled to appropriate training.

12(4) The training referred to in paragraphs 1 and 3 may not be at the workers' expense or at that of the workers' representatives.

The training referred to in paragraph 1 must take place during working hours.

The training referred to in paragraph 3 must take place during working hours or in accordance with national practice either within or outside the undertaking and/or the establishment.

SECTION III – WORKERS' OBLIGATIONS

ART. 13 [Workers' obligations]

13(1) It shall be the responsibility of each worker to take care as far as possible of his own safety and health and that of other persons affected by his acts or Commissions at work in accordance with his training and the instructions given by his employer.

13(2) To this end, workers must in particular, in accordance with their training and the instructions given by their employer:

(a) make correct use of machinery, apparatus, tools, dangerous substances, transport equipment and other means of production;

(b) make correct use of the personal protective equipment supplied to them and, after use, return it to its proper place;

(c) refrain from disconnecting, changing or removing arbitrarily safety devices fitted, e.g. to machinery, apparatus, tools, plant and buildings, and use such safety devices correctly;

(d) immediately inform the employer and/or the workers with specific responsibility for the safety and health of workers of any work situation they have reasonable grounds for considering represents a serious and immediate danger to safety and health and of any shortcomings in the protection arrangements;

(e) cooperate, in accordance with national practice, with the employer and/or workers with specific responsibility for the safety and health of workers, for as long as may be necessary to enable any tasks or requirements imposed by the competent authority to protect the safety and health of workers at work to be carried out;

(f) cooperate, in accordance with national practice, with the employer and/or workers with specific responsibility for the safety and health of workers, for as long as may be necessary to enable the employer to ensure that the working environment and working conditions are safe and pose no risk to safety and health within their field of activity.

SECTION IV – MISCELLANEOUS PROVISIONS

ART. 14 Health surveillance

14(1) To ensure that workers receive health surveillance appropriate to the health and safety risks they incur at work, measures shall be introduced in accordance with national law and/or practices.

14(2) The measures referred to in paragraph 1 shall be such that each worker, if he so wishes, may receive health surveillance at regular intervals.

14(3) Health surveillance may be provided as part of a national health system.

ART. 15 Risk groups

15 Particularly sensitive risk groups must be protected against the dangers which specifically affect them.

ART. 16 Individual directives – Amendments – General scope of this directive

16(1) The Council, acting on a proposal from the Commission based on Article 118a of the Treaty, shall adopt individual directives, *inter alia*, in the areas listed in the Annex.

16(2) This directive and, without prejudice to the procedure referred to in Article 17 concerning technical adjustments, the individual directives may be amended in accordance with the procedure provided for in Article 118a of the Treaty.

16(3) The provisions of this directive shall apply in full to all the areas covered by the individual directives, without prejudice to more stringent and/or specific provisions contained in these individual directives.

ART. 17 Committee

17(1) For the purely technical adjustments to the individual directives provided for in Article 16(1) to take account of:

- the adoption of directives in the field of technical harmonisation and standardisation, and/or
- technical progress, changes in international regulations or specifications, and new findings,

the Commission shall be assisted by a committee composed of the representatives of the member states and chaired by the representative of the Commission.

17(2) The representative of the Commission shall submit to the committee a draft of the measures to be taken.

The committee shall deliver its opinion on the draft within a time limit which the chairman may lay down according to the urgency of the matter.

The opinion shall be delivered by the majority laid down in Article 148(2) of the Treaty in the case of decisions which the Council is required to adopt on a proposal from the Commission.

The votes of the representatives of the member states within the committee shall be weighted in the manner set out in that Article. The chairman shall not vote.

17(3) The Commission shall adopt the measures envisaged if they are in accordance with the opinion of the committee.

Dir. 89/391, Art. 14(1)

If the measures envisaged are not in accordance with the opinion of the committee, or if no opinion is delivered, the Commission shall, without delay, submit to the Council a proposal relating to the measures to be taken. The Council shall act by a qualified majority.

If, on the expiry of three months from the date of the referral to the Council, the Council has not acted, the proposed measures shall be adopted by the Commission.

ART. 18 Final provisions

18(1) Member states shall bring into force the laws, regulations and administrative provisions necessary to comply with this directive by 31 December 1992.

They shall forthwith inform the Commission thereof.

18(2) Member states shall communicate to the Commission the texts of the provisions of national law which they have already adopted or adopt in the field covered by this directive.

18(3) Member states shall report to the Commission every five years on the practical implementation of the provisions of this directive, indicating the points of view of employers and workers.

The Commission shall inform the European Parliament, the Council, the Economic and Social Committee and the Advisory Committee on Safety, Hygiene and Health Protection at Work.

18(4) The Commission shall submit periodically to the European Parliament, the Council and the Economic and Social Committee a report on the implementation of this directive, taking into account paragraphs 1 to 3.

ART. 19 [Application]

19 This directive is addressed to the member states.

ANNEX – LIST OF AREAS REFERRED TO IN ARTICLE 16(1)

- Work places
- Work equipment
- Personal protective equipment
- Work with visual display units
- Handling of heavy loads involving risk of back injury
- Temporary or mobile work sites
- Fisheries and agriculture

COUNCIL DIRECTIVE 89/656

On the minimum health and safety requirements for the use by workers of personal protective equipment at the workplace (third individual directive within the meaning of Article 16(1) of Directive 89/391/EEC)

(30 November 1989, OJ 1989 L393/18)

The Council of the European Communities,

Having regard to the Treaty establishing the European Economic Community and in particular Article 118a thereof,

Having regard to the Commission proposal, submitted after consultation with the Advisory Committee on Safety, Hygiene and Health Protection at Work,

In cooperation with the European Parliament,

Having regard to the opinion of the Economic and Social Committee,

[1] Whereas Article 118a of the Treaty provides that the Council shall adopt, by means of directives, minimum requirements designed to encourage improvements, especially in the working environment, to guarantee greater protection of the health and safety of workers;

[2] Whereas, under the said article, such directives shall avoid imposing administrative, financial and legal constraints in a way which would hold back the creation and development of small and medium-sized undertakings;

[3] Whereas the Commission communication on its programme concerning safety, hygiene and health at work provides for the adoption of a directive on the use of personal protective equipment at work;

[4] Whereas the Council, in its resolution of 21 December 1987 concerning safety, hygiene and health at work, noted the Commission's intention of submitting to it in the near future minimum requirements concerning the organisation of the safety and health of workers at work;

[5] Whereas compliance with the minimum requirements designed to guarantee greater health and safety for the user of personal protective equipment is essential to ensure the safety and health of workers;

[6] Whereas this directive is an individual directive within the meaning of Article 16(1) of Council Directive 89/391/EEC of 12 June 1989 on the introduction of measures to encourage improvements in the safety and health of workers at work; whereas, consequently, the provisions of the said directive apply fully to the use by workers of personal protective equipment at the workplace, without prejudice to more stringent and/or specific provisions contained in this directive;

[7] Whereas this directive constitutes a practical step towards the achievement of the social dimension of the internal market;

[8] Whereas collective means of protection shall be accorded priority over individual protective equipment; whereas the employer shall be required to provide safety equipment and take safety measures;

[9] Whereas the requirements laid down in this directive should not entail alterations to personal protective equipment whose design and manufacture complied with Community directives relating to safety and health at work;

[10] Whereas provision should be made for descriptions which member states may use when laying down general rules for the use of individual protective equipment;

[11] Whereas, pursuant to Decision 74/325/EEC, as last amended by the 1985 Act of Accession, the Advisory Committee on Safety, Hygiene and Health Protection at Work is consulted by the Commission with a view to drawing up proposals in this field,

has adopted this directive:

SECTION I – GENERAL PROVISIONS

ART. 1 Subject

1(1) This directive, which is the third individual directive within the meaning of Article 16(1) of Directive 89/391/EEC, lays down minimum requirements for personal protective equipment used by workers at work.

1(2) The provisions of Directive 89/391/EEC are fully applicable to the whole scope referred to in paragraph 1, without prejudice to more restrictive and/or specific provisions contained in this directive.

ART. 2 Definition

2(1) For the purposes of this directive, personal protective equipment shall mean all equipment designed to be worn or held by the worker to protect him against one or more hazards likely to endanger his safety and health at work, and any addition or accessory designed to meet this objective.

2(2) The definition in paragraph 1 excludes:
- (a) ordinary working clothes and uniforms not specifically designed to protect the safety and health of the worker;
- (b) equipment used by emergency and rescue services;
- (c) personal protective equipment worn or used by the military, the police and other public order agencies;
- (d) personal protective equipment for means of road transport;
- (e) sports equipment;
- (f) self-defence or deterrent equipment;
- (g) portable devices for detecting and signalling risks and nuisances.

ART. 3 General rule

3   Personal protective equipment shall be used when the risks cannot be avoided or sufficiently limited by technical means of collective protection or by measures, methods or procedures of work organisation.

SECTION II – EMPLOYERS' OBLIGATIONS

ART. 4 General provisions

4(1)   Personal protective equipment must comply with the relevant Community provisions on design and manufacture with respect to safety and health.

All personal protective equipment must:

   (a)   be appropriate for the risks involved, without itself leading to any increased risk;
   (b)   correspond to existing conditions at the workplace;
   (c)   take account of ergonomic requirements and the worker's state of health;
   (d)   fit the wearer correctly after any necessary adjustment.

4(2)   Where the presence of more than one risk makes it necessary for a worker to wear simultaneously more than one item of personal protective equipment, such equipment must be compatible and continue to be effective against the risk or risks in question.

4(3)   The conditions of use of personal protective equipment, in particular the period for which it is worn, shall be determined on the basis of the seriousness of the risk, the frequency of exposure to the risk, the characteristics of the workstation of each worker and the performance of the personal protective equipment.

4(4)   Personal protective equipment is, in principle, intended for personal use.

If the circumstances require personal protective equipment to be worn by more than one person, appropriate measures shall be taken to ensure that such use does not create any health or hygiene problem for the different users.

4(5)   Adequate information on each item of personal protective equipment, required under paragraphs 1 and 2, shall be provided and made available within the undertaking and/or establishment.

4(6)   Personal protective equipment shall be provided free of charge by the employer, who shall ensure its good working order and satisfactory hygienic condition by means of the necessary maintenance, repair and replacements.

However, member states may provide, in accordance with their national practice, that the worker be asked to contribute towards the cost of certain personal protective equipment in circumstances where use of the equipment is not exclusive to the workplace.

4(7)   The employer shall first inform the worker of the risks against which the wearing of the personal protective equipment protects him.

4(8)   The employer shall arrange for training and shall, if appropriate, organise demonstrations in the wearing of personal protective equipment.

4(9)   Personal protective equipment may be used only for the purposes specified, except in specific and exceptional circumstances.

It must be used in accordance with instructions.

Such instructions must be understandable to the workers.

Dir. 89/656, Art. 3

ART. 5 Assessment of personal protective equipment

5(1) Before choosing personal protective equipment, the employer is required to assess whether the personal protective equipment he intends to use satisfies the requirements of Article 4(1) and (2).

This assessment shall involve:

- (a) an analysis and assessment of risks which cannot be avoided by other means;
- (b) the definition of the characteristics which personal protective equipment must have in order to be effective against the risks referred to in (a), taking into account any risks which this equipment itself may create;
- (c) comparison of the characteristics of the personal protective equipment available with the characteristics referred to in (b).

5(2) The assessment provided for in paragraph 1 shall be reviewed if any changes are made to any of its elements.

ART. 6 Rules for use

6(1) Without prejudice to Articles 3, 4 and 5, member states shall ensure that general rules are established for the use of personal protective equipment and/or rules covering cases and situations where the employer must provide the personal protective equipment, taking account of Community legislation on the free movement of such equipment.

These rules shall indicate in particular the circumstances or the risk situations in which, without prejudice to the priority to be given to collective means of protection, the use of personal protective equipment is necessary.

Annexes I, II and III, which constitute a guide, contain useful information for establishing such rules.

6(2) When member states adapt the rules referred to in paragraph 1, they shall take account of any significant changes to the risk, collective means of protection and personal protective equipment brought about by technological developments.

6(3) Member states shall consult the employers' and workers' organisation on the rules referred to in paragraphs 1 and 2.

ART. 7 Information for workers

7 Without prejudice to Article 10 of Directive 89/391/EEC, workers and/or their representatives shall be informed of all measures to be taken with regard to the health and safety of workers when personal protective equipment is used by workers at work.

ART. 8 Consultation of workers and workers' participation

8 Consultation and participation of workers and/or of their representatives shall take place in accordance with Article 11 of Directive 89/391/EEC on the matters covered by this directive, including the Annexes thereto.

SECTION III – MISCELLANEOUS PROVISIONS

ART. 9 Adjustment of the Annexes

9   Alterations of a strictly technical nature to Annexes I, II and III resulting from:
- the adoption of technical harmonisation and standardisation directives relating to personal protective equipment, and/or
- technical progress and changes in international regulations and specifications or knowledge in the field of personal protective equipment,

shall be adopted in accordance with the procedure provided for in Article 17 of Directive 89/391/EEC.

ART. 10 Final provisions

10(1) Member states shall bring into force the laws, regulations and administrative provisions necessary to comply with this directive not later than 31 December 1992. They shall immediately inform the Commission thereof.

10(2) Member states shall communicate to the Commission the text of the provisions of national law which they adopt, as well as those already adopted, in the field covered by this directive.

10(3) Member states shall report to the Commission every five years on the practical implementation of the provisions of this directive, indicating the points of view of employers and workers.

The Commission shall inform the European Parliament, the Council, the Economic and Social Committee, and the Advisory Committee on Safety, Hygiene and Health Protection at Work.

10(4) The Commission shall report periodically to the European Parliament, the Council and the Economic and Social Committee on the implementation of the directive in the light of paragraphs 1, 2 and 3.

ART. 11 [Application]

11   This directive is addressed to the member states.

Dir. 89/656, Art. 9

ANNEX I – SPECIMEN RISK SURVEY TABLE FOR THE USE OF PERSONAL PROTECTIVE EQUIPMENT

		RISKS														
		PHYSICAL								CHEMICAL					BIOLOGICAL		
		MECHANICAL			THERMAL		ELEC-TRI-CAL	RADIATION		NOISE	AEROSOLS		LIQUIDS				
PARTS OF THE BODY		Falls from a height	Blows, cuts, impact, crushing	Stabs, cuts, grazes	Vibration	Slipping, falling over	Heat, fire	Cold		Non-ionizing	Ionizing		Dust, fibres	Fumes	Vapours	Immersion	Splashes, spurts	GASES, VAPOURS	Harmful bacteria	Harmful viruses	Mycotic fungi	Non-microbe biological antigens
HEAD	Cranium																					
	Ears																					
	Eyes																					
	Respiratory tract																					
	Face																					
	Whole head																					
UPPER LIMBS	Hands																					
	Arms (parts)																					
LOWER LIMBS	Foot																					
	Legs (parts)																					
VARIOUS	Skin																					
	Trunk/abdomen																					
	Parenteral passages																					
	Whole body																					

Dir. 89/656, Annex I

ANNEX II – NON-EXHAUSTIVE GUIDE LIST OF ITEMS OF PERSONAL PROTECTIVE EQUIPMENT

HEAD PROTECTION

- Protective helmets for use in industry (mines, building sites, other industrial uses).
- Scalp protection (caps, bonnets, hairnets – with or without eye shade).
- Protective headgear (bonnets, caps, sou'westers, etc. in fabric, fabric with proofing, etc.).

HEARING PROTECTION

- Earplugs and similar devices.
- Full acoustic helmets.
- Earmuffs which can be fitted to industrial helmets.
- Ear defenders with receiver for LF induction loop.
- Ear protection with intercom equipment.

EYE AND FACE PROTECTION

- Spectacles.
- Goggles.
- X-ray goggles, laser-beam goggles, ultra-violet, infra-red, visible radiation goggles.
- Face shields.
- Arc-welding masks and helmets (hand masks, headband masks or masks which can be fitted to protective helmets).

RESPIRATORY PROTECTION

- Dust filters, gas filters and radioactive dust filters.
- Insulating appliances with an air supply.
- Respiratory devices including a removable welding mask.
- Diving equipment.
- Diving suits.

HAND AND ARM PROTECTION

- Gloves to provide protection:
  - from machinery (piercing, cuts, vibrations, etc.),
  - from chemicals,
  - for electricians and from heat.
- Mittens.
- Finger stalls.
- Oversleeves.
- Wrist protection for heavy work.
- Fingerless gloves.
- Protective gloves.

FOOT AND LEG PROTECTION

- Low shoes, ankle boots, calf-length boots, safety boots.
- Shoes which can be unlaced or unhooked rapidly.
- Shoes with additional protective toe-cap.
- Shoes and overshoes with heat-resistant soles.

Dir. 89/656, Annex II

- Heat-resistant shoes, boots and overboots.
- Thermal shoes, boots and overboots.
- Vibration-resistant shoes, boots and overboots.
- Anti-static shoes, boots and overboots.
- Insulating shoes, boots and overboots.
- Protective boots for chain saw operators.
- Clogs.
- Kneepads.
- Removable instep protectors.
- Gaiters.
- Removable soles (heat-proof, pierce-proof or sweat-proof).
- Removable spikes for ice, snow or slippery flooring.

SKIN PROTECTION
- Barrier creams/ointments.

TRUNK AND ABDOMEN PROTECTION
- Protective waistcoats, jackets and aprons to provide protection from machinery (piercing, cutting, molten metal splashes, etc.).
- Protective waistcoats, jackets and aprons to provide protection from chemicals.
- Heated waistcoats.
- Life jackets.
- Protective X-ray aprons.
- Body belts.

WHOLE BODY PROTECTION
- **Equipment designed to prevent falls**
    - Fall-prevention equipment (full equipment with all necessary accessories).
    - Braking equipment to absorb kinetic energy (full equipment with all necessary accessories).
    - Body-holding devices (safety harness).
- **Protective clothing**
    - 'Safety' working clothing (two-piece and overalls).
    - Clothing to provide protection from machinery (piercing, cutting, etc.).
    - Clothing to provide protection from chemicals.
    - Clothing to provide protection from molten metal splashes and infra-red radiation.
    - Heat-resistant clothing.
    - Thermal clothing.
    - Clothing to provide protection from radioactive contamination.
    - Dust-proof clothing.
    - Gas-proof clothing.
    - Fluorescent signalling, retro-reflecting clothing and accessories (armbands, gloves, etc.).
    - Protective coverings.

Dir. 89/656, Annex II

ANNEX III – NON-EXHAUSTIVE GUIDE LIST OF ACTIVITIES AND SECTORS OF ACTIVITY WHICH MAY REQUIRE THE PROVISION OF PERSONAL PROTECTIVE EQUIPMENT

1. HEAD PROTECTION (SKULL PROTECTION)

   Protective helmets
   - Building work, particularly work on, underneath or in the vicinity of scaffolding and elevated workplaces, erection and stripping of formwork, assembly and installation work, work on scaffolding and demolition work.
   - Work on steel bridges, steel building construction, masts, towers, steel hydraulic structures, blast furnaces, steel works and rolling mills, large containers, large pipelines, boiler plants and power stations.
   - Work in pits, trenches, shafts and tunnels.
   - Earth and rock works.
   - Work in underground workings, quarries, open diggings, coal stock removal.
   - Work with bolt-driving tools.
   - Blasting work.
   - Work in the vicinity of lifts, lifting gear, cranes and conveyors.
   - Work with blast furnaces, direct reduction plants, steelworks, rolling mills, metalworks, forging, drop forging and casting.
   - Work with industrial furnaces, containers, machinery, silos, bunkers and pipelines.
   - Shipbuilding.
   - Railway shunting work.
   - Slaughterhouses.

2. FOOT PROTECTION

   Safety shoes with puncture-proof soles
   - Carcase work, foundation work and roadworks.
   - Scaffolding work.
   - The demolition of carcase work.
   - Work with concrete and prefabricated parts involving formwork erection and stripping.
   - Work in contractors' yards and warehouses.
   - Roof work.

   Safety shoes without pierce-proof soles
   - Work on steel bridges, steel building construction, masts, towers, lifts, steel hydraulic structures, blast furnaces, steelworks and rolling mills, large containers, large pipelines, cranes, boiler plants and power stations.
   - Furnace construction, heating and ventilation installation and metal assembly work.
   - Conversion and maintenance work.
   - Work with blast furnaces, direct reduction plants, steelworks, rolling mills, metalworks, forging, drop forging, hot pressing and drawing plants.
   - Work in quarries and open diggings, coal stock removal.
   - Working and processing of rock.
   - Flat glass products and container glassware manufacture, working and processing.
   - Work with moulds in the ceramics industry.

Dir. 89/656, Annex III

- Lining of kilns in the ceramics industry.
- Moulding work in the ceramic ware and building materials industry.
- Transport and storage.
- Work with frozen meat blocks and preserved foods packaging.
- Shipbuilding.
- Railway shunting work.

Safety shoes with heels or wedges and pierce-proof soles
- Roof work.

Protective shoes with insulated soles
- Work with and on very hot or very cold materials.

Safety shoes which can easily be removed
- Where there is a risk of penetration by molten substances.

3. EYE OR FACE PROTECTION

Protective goggles, face shields or screens
- Welding, grinding and separating work.
- Caulking and chiselling.
- Rock working and processing.
- Work with bolt-driving tools.
- Work on stock removing machines for small chippings.
- Drop forging.
- The removal and breaking up of fragments.
- Spraying of abrasive substances.
- Work with acids and caustic solutions, disinfectants and corrosive cleaning products.
- Work with liquid sprays.
- Work with and in the vicinity of molten substances.
- Work with radiant heat.
- Work with lasers.

4. RESPIRATORY PROTECTION

Respirators/breathing apparatus
- Work in containers, restricted areas and gas-fired industrial furnaces where there may be gas or insufficient oxygen.
- Work in the vicinity of the blast furnace charge.
- Work in the vicinity of gas converters and blast furnace gas pipes.
- Work in the vicinity of blast furnace taps where there may be heavy metal fumes.
- Work on the lining of furnaces and ladles where there may be dust.
- Spray painting where dedusting is inadequate.
- Work in shafts, sewers and other underground areas connected with sewage.
- Work in refrigeration plants where there is a danger that the refrigerant may escape.

5. HEARING PROTECTION

Ear protectors
- Work with metal presses.

Dir. 89/656, Annex III

- Work with pneumatic drills.
- The work of ground staff at airports.
- Pile-driving work.
- Wood and textile working.

6. BODY, ARM AND HAND PROTECTION

   Protective clothing
   - Work with acids and caustic solutions, disinfectants and corrosive cleaning substances.
   - Work with or in the vicinity of hot materials and where the effects of heat are felt.
   - Work on flat glass products.
   - Shot blasting.
   - Work in deep-freeze rooms.

   Fire-resistant protective clothing
   - Welding in restricted areas.

   Pierce-proof aprons
   - Boning and cutting work.
   - Work with hand knives involving drawing the knife towards the body.

   Leather aprons
   - Welding.
   - Forging.
   - Casting.

   Forearm protection
   - Boning and cutting.

   Gloves
   - Welding.
   - Handling of sharp-edged objects, other than machines where there is a danger of the glove's being caught.
   - Unprotected work with acids and caustic solutions.

   Metal mesh gloves
   - Boning and cutting.
   - Regular cutting using a hand knife for production and slaughtering.
   - Changing the knives of cutting machines.

7. WEATHERPROOF CLOTHING
   - Work in the open air in rain and cold weather.

8. REFLECTIVE CLOTHING
   - Work where the workers must be clearly visible.

9. SAFETY HARNESSES
   - Work on scaffolding.
   - Assembly of prefabricated parts.
   - Work on masts.

Dir. 89/656, Annex III

10. SAFETY ROPES
    - Work in high crane cabs.
    - Work in high cabs of warehouse stacking and retrieval equipment.
    - Work in high sections of drilling towers.
    - Work in shafts and sewers.

11. SKIN PROTECTION
    - Processing of coating materials.
    - Tanning.

Dir. 89/656, Annex III

COUNCIL DIRECTIVE 89/655

Concerning the minimum safety and health requirements for the use of work equipment by workers at work (second individual directive within the meaning of Article 16(1) of Directive 89/391/EEC)

(30 November 1989, OJ 1989 L393/13)

The Council of the European Communities,

Having regard to the Treaty establishing the European Economic Community, and in particular Article 118a thereof,

Having regard to the proposal from the Commission, submitted after consulting the Advisory Committee on Safety, Hygiene and Health Protection at Work,

In cooperation with the European Parliament,

Having regard to the opinion of the Economic and Social Committee,

[1] Whereas Article 118a of the Treaty provides that the Council shall adopt, by means of directives, minimum requirements for encouraging improvements, especially in the working environment, to guarantee a better level of protection of the safety and health of workers;

[2] Whereas, pursuant to the said article, such directives must avoid imposing administrative, financial and legal constraints in a way which would hold back the creation and development of small and medium-sized undertakings;

[3] Whereas the communication from the Commission on its programme concerning safety, hygiene and health at work provides for the adoption of a directive on the use of work equipment at work;

[4] Whereas, in its resolution of 21 December 1987 on safety, hygiene and health at work, the Council took note of the Commission's intention of submitting to the Council in the near future minimum requirements concerning the organisation of safety and health at work;

[5] Whereas compliance with the minimum requirements designed to guarantee a better standard of safety and health in the use of work equipment is essential to ensure the safety and health of workers;

[6] Whereas this directive is an individual directive within the meaning of Article 16(1) of Council Directive 89/391/EEC of 12 June 1989 on the introduction of measures to encourage improvements in the safety and health of workers at work; whereas, therefore, the provisions of the said directive are fully applicable to the scope of the use of work equipment by workers at work without prejudice to more restrictive and/or specific provisions contained in this directive;

Dir. 89/655

[7] Whereas this directive constitutes a practical aspect of the realisation of the social dimension of the internal market;

[8] Whereas, pursuant to Directive 83/189/EEC, member states are required to notify the Commission of any draft technical regulations relating to machines, equipment and installations;

[9] Whereas, pursuant to Decision 74/325/EEC, as last amended by the 1985 Act of Accession, the Advisory Committee on Safety, Hygiene and Health Protection at Work is consulted by the Commission on the drafting of proposals in this field,

has adopted this directive:

SECTION I – GENERAL PROVISIONS

ART. 1 Subject

1(1) This directive, which is the second individual directive within the meaning of Article 16(1) of Directive 89/391/EEC, lays down minimum safety and health requirements for the use of work equipment by workers at work, as defined in Article 2.

1(2) The provisions of Directive 89/391/EEC are fully applicable to the whole scope referred to in paragraph 1, without prejudice to more restrictive and/or specific provisions contained in this directive.

ART. 2 Definitions

2 For the purposes of this directive, the following terms shall have the following meanings:

    (a) **'work equipment'**: any machine, apparatus, tool or installation used at work;

    (b) **'use of work equipment'**: any activity involving work equipment such as starting or stopping the equipment, its use, transport, repair, modification, maintenance and servicing, including, in particular, cleaning;

    (c) **'danger'**: any zone within and/or around work equipment in which an exposed worker is subject to a risk to his health or safety;

    (d) **'exposed worker'**: any worker wholly or partially in a danger zone;

    (e) **'operator'**: the worker or workers given the task of using work equipment.

SECTION II – EMPLOYERS' OBLIGATIONS

ART. 3 General obligations

3(1) The employer shall take the measures necessary to ensure that the work equipment made available to workers in the undertaking and/or establishment is suitable for the work to be carried out or properly adapted for that purpose and may be used by workers without impairment to their safety or health.

In selecting the work equipment which he proposes to use, the employer shall pay attention to the specific working conditions and characteristics and to the hazards which exist in the undertaking and/or establishment, in particular at the workplace, for the safety and health of the workers, and/or any additional hazards posed by the use of work equipment in question.

Dir. 89/655, Art. 3(1)

3(2) Where it is not possible fully so to ensure that work equipment can be used by workers without risk to their safety or health, the employer shall take appropriate measures to minimise the risks.

ART. 4   Rules concerning work equipment

4(1) Without prejudice to Article 3, the employer must obtain and/or use:
- (a) work equipment which, if provided to workers in the undertaking and/or establishment for the first time after 31 December 1992, complies with:
    - (i) the provisions of any relevant Community directive which is applicable;
    - (ii) the minimum requirements laid down in the Annex, to the extent that no other Community directive is applicable or is so only partially;
- (b) work equipment which, if already provided to workers in the undertaking and/or establishment by 31 December 1992, complies with the minimum requirements laid down in the Annex no later than four years after that date.

4(2) The employer shall take the measures necessary to ensure that, throughout its working life, work equipment is kept, by means of adequate maintenance, at a level such that it complies with the provisions of paragraph 1(a) or (b) as applicable.

ART. 5   Work equipment involving specific risks

5 When the use of work equipment is likely to involve a specific risk to the safety or health of workers, the employer shall take the measures necessary to ensure that:
- the use of work equipment is restricted to those persons given the task of using it;
- in the case of repairs, modifications, maintenance or servicing, the workers concerned are specifically designated to carry out such work.

ART. 6   Informing workers

6(1) Without prejudice to Article 10 of Directive 89/391/EEC, the employer shall take the measures necessary to ensure that workers have at their disposal adequate information and, where appropriate, written instructions on the work equipment used at work.

6(2) The information and the written instructions must contain at least adequate safety and health information concerning:
- the conditions of use of work equipment,
- forseeable abnormal situations,
- the conclusions to be drawn from experience, where appropriate, in using work equipment.

6(3) The information and the written instructions must be comprehensible to the workers concerned.

ART. 7   Training of workers

7 Without prejudice to Article 12 of Directive 89/391/EEC, the employer shall take the measures necessary to ensure that:

Dir. 89/655, Art. 3(2)

- workers given the task of using work equipment receive adequate training, including training on any risks which such use may entail,
- workers referred to in the second indent of Article 5 receive adequate specific training.

ART. 8 Consultation of workers and workers' participation

8 Consultation and participation of workers and/or of their representatives shall take place in accordance with Article 11 of Directive 89/391/EEC on the matters covered by this Directive, including the Annexes thereto.

SECTION III – MISCELLANEOUS PROVISIONS

ART. 9 Amendment to the Annex

9(1) Addition to the Annex of the supplementary minimum requirements applicable to specific work equipment referred to in point 3 thereof shall be adopted by the Council in accordance with the procedure laid down in Article 118a of the Treaty.

9(2) Strictly technical adaptations of the Annex as a result of:
- the adoption of directives on technical harmonisation and standardisation of work equipment, and/or
- technical progress, changes in international regulations or specifications or knowledge in the field of work equipment

shall be adopted, in accordance with the procedure laid down in Article 17 of Directive 89/391/EEC.

ART. 10 Final provisions

10(1) Member states shall bring into force the laws, regulations and administrative provisions necessary to comply with this directive by 31 December 1992. They shall forthwith inform the Commission thereof.

10(2) Member states shall communicate to the Commission the texts of the provisions of national law which they have already adopted or adopt in the field governed by this directive.

10(3) Member states shall report to the Commission every five years on the practical implementation of the provisions of this directive, indicating the points of view of employers and workers.

The Commission shall accordingly inform the European Parliament, the Council, the Economic and Social Committee, and the Advisory Committee on Safety, Hygiene and Health Protection at Work.

10(4) The Commission shall submit periodically to the European Parliament, the Council and the Economic and Social Committee a report on the implementation of this directive, taking into account paragraphs 1 to 3.

ART. 11 [Application]

11 This directive is addressed to the member states.

ANNEX – MINIMUM REQUIREMENTS REFERRED TO IN ARTICLE 4(1)(a)(ii) and (b)

1. General comment

The obligations laid down in this Annex apply having regard to the provisions of the directive and where the corresponding risk exists for the work equipment in question.

2. General minimum requirements applicable to work equipment

2.1. Work equipment control devices which affect safety must be clearly visible and identifiable and appropriately marked where necessary.

Except where necessary for certain control devices, control devices must be located outside danger zones and in such a way that their operation cannot cause additional hazard. They must not give rise to any hazard as a result of any unintentional operation.

If necessary, from the main control position, the operator must be able to ensure that no person is present in the danger zones. If this is impossible, a safe system such as an audible and/or visible warning signal must be given automatically whenever the machinery is about to start. An exposed worker must have the time and/or the means quickly to avoid hazards caused by the starting and/or stopping of the work equipment.

Control systems must be safe. A breakdown in, or damage to, control systems must not result in a dangerous situation.

2.2. It must be possible to start work equipment only by deliberate action on a control provided for the purpose.

The same shall apply:
– to restart it after a stoppage for whatever reason,
– for the control of a significant change in the operating conditions (e.g. speed, pressure, etc.),

unless such a restart or change does not subject exposed workers to any hazard.

This requirement does not apply to restarting or a change in operating conditions as a result of the normal operating cycle of an automatic device.

2.3. All work equipment must be fitted with a control to stop it completely and safely.

Each work station must be fitted with a control to stop some or all of the work equipment, depending on the type of hazard, so that the equipment is in a safe state. The equipment's stop control must have priority over the start controls. When the work equipment or the dangerous parts of it have stopped, the energy supply of the actuators concerned must be switched off.

2.4. Where appropriate, and depending on the hazards the equipment presents and its normal stopping time, work equipment must be fitted with an emergency stop device.

2.5. Work equipment presenting risk due to falling objects or projections must be fitted with appropriate safety devices corresponding to the risk.

Work equipment presenting hazards due to emissions of gas, vapour, liquid or dust must be fitted with appropriate containment and/or extraction devices near the sources of the hazard.

2.6. Work equipment and parts of such equipment must, where necessary for the safety and health of workers, be stabilised by clamping or some other means.

Dir. 89/655, Annex

2.7. Where there is a risk of rupture or disintegration of parts of the work equipment, likely to pose significant danger to the safety and health of workers, appropriate protection measures must be taken.

2.8. Where there is a risk of mechanical contact with moving parts of work equipment which could lead to accidents, those parts must be provided with guards or devices to prevent access to danger zones or to halt movements of dangerous parts before the danger zones are reached.

The guards and protection devices must:

– be of robust construction,

– not give rise to any additional hazard,

– not be easily removed or rendered inoperative,

– be situated at sufficient distance from the danger zone,

– not restrict more than necessary the view of the operating cycle of the equipment,

– allow operations necessary to fit or replace parts and for maintenance work, restricting access only to the area where the work is to be carried out and, if possible, without removal of the guard or protection device.

2.9. Areas and points for working on, or maintenance of, work equipment must be suitably lit in line with the operation to be carried out.

2.10. Work equipment parts at high or very low temperature must, where appropriate, be protected to avoid the risk of workers coming into contact or coming too close.

2.11. Warning devices on work equipment must be unambiguous and easily perceived and understood.

2.12. Work equipment may be used only for operations and under conditions for which it is appropriate.

2.13. It must be possible to carry out maintenance operations when the equipment is shut down. If this is not possible, it must be possible to take appropriate protection measures for the carrying out of such operations or for such operations to be carried out outside the danger zones.

If any machine has a maintenance log, it must be kept up to date.

2.14. All work equipment must be fitted with clearly identifiable means to isolate it from all its energy sources.

Reconnection must be presumed to pose no risk to the workers concerned.

2.15. Work equipment must bear the warnings and markings essential to ensure the safety of workers.

2.16. Workers must have safe means of access to, and be able to remain safely in, all the areas necessary for production, adjustment and maintenance operations.

2.17. All work equipment must be appropriate for protecting workers against the risk of the work equipment catching fire or overheating, or of discharges of gas, dust, liquid, vapour or other substances produced, used or stored in the work equipment.

2.18. All work equipment must be appropriate for preventing the risk of explosion of the work equipment or of substances produced, used or stored in the work equipment.

Dir. 89/655, Annex

2.19. All work equipment must be appropriate for protecting exposed workers against the risk of direct or indirect contact with electricity.

3. Minimum additional requirements applicable to specific work equipment, as referred to in Article 9(1) of the directive.

Dir. 89/655, Annex

COUNCIL DIRECTIVE 90/270

On the minimum safety and health requirements for work with display screen equipment (fifth individual directive within the meaning of Article 16(1) of Directive 87/391/EEC)

(29 May 1990, OJ 1990 L156/14)

The Council of the European Communities,

Having regard to the Treaty establishing the European Economic Community, and in particular Article 118a thereof,

Having regard to the Commission proposal drawn up after consultation with the Advisory Committee on Safety, Hygiene and Health Protection at Work,

In cooperation with the European Parliament,

Having regard to the opinion of the Economic and Social Committee,

[1] Whereas Article 118a of the Treaty provides that the Council shall adopt, by means of directives, minimum requirements designed to encourage improvements, especially in the working environment, to ensure a better level of protection of workers' safety and health;

[2] Whereas, under the terms of that article, those directives shall avoid imposing administrative, financial and legal constraints, in a way which would hold back the creation and development of small and medium-sized undertakings;

[3] Whereas the communication from the Commission on its programme concerning safety, hygiene and health at work provides for the adoption of measures in respect of new technologies; whereas the Council has taken note thereof in its resolution of 21 December 1987 on safety, hygiene and health at work;

[4] Whereas compliance with the minimum requirements for ensuring a better level of safety at workstations with display screens is essential for ensuring the safety and health of workers;

[5] Whereas this directive is an individual directive within the meaning of Article 16(1) of Council Directive 89/391/EEC of 12 June 1989 on the introduction of measures to encourage improvements in the safety and health of workers at work; whereas the provisions of the latter are therefore fully applicable to the use by workers of display screen equipment, without prejudice to more stringent and/or specific provisions contained in the present directive;

[6] Whereas employers are obliged to keep themselves informed of the latest advances in technology and scientific findings concerning workstation design so that they can make any changes necessary so as to be able to guarantee a better level of protection of workers' safety and health;

[7] Whereas the ergonomic aspects are of particular importance for a workstation with display screen equipment;

[8] Whereas this directive is a practical contribution towards creating the social dimension of the internal market;

[9] Whereas, pursuant to Decision 74/325/EEC, the Advisory Committee on Safety, Hygiene and Health Protection at Work shall be consulted by the Commission on the drawing-up of proposals in this field,

has adopted this directive:

SECTION I – GENERAL PROVISIONS

ART. 1   Subject

1(1)   This directive, which is the fifth individual directive within the meaning of Article 16(1) of Directive 89/391/EEC, lays down minimum safety and health requirements for work with display screen equipment as defined in Article 2.

1(2)   The provisions of Directive 89/391/EEC are fully applicable to the whole field referred to in paragraph 1, without prejudice to more stringent and/or specific provisions contained in the present directive.

1(3)   This directive shall not apply to:

   (a) drivers' cabs or control cabs for vehicles or machinery;

   (b) computer systems on board a means of transport;

   (c) computer systems mainly intended for public use;

   (d) 'portable' systems not in prolonged use at a workstation;

   (e) calculators, cash registers and any equipment having a small data or measurement display required for direct use of the equipment;

   (f) typewriters of traditional design, of the type known as 'typewriter with window'.

ART. 2   Definitions

2   For the purpose of this directive, the following terms shall have the following meanings:

   (a) **display screen equipment:** an alphanumeric or graphic display screen, regardless of the display process employed;

   (b) **workstation:** an assembly comprising display screen equipment, which may be provided with a keyboard or input device and/or software determining the operator/machine interface, optional accessories, peripherals including the diskette drive, telephone, modem, printer, document holder, work chair and work desk or work surface, and the immediate work environment;

   (c) **worker:** any worker as defined in Article 3(a) of Directive 89/391/EEC who habitually uses display screen equipment as a significant part of his normal work.

Dir. 90/270, Art. 1(1)

SECTION II – EMPLOYERS' OBLIGATIONS

ART. 3   Analysis of workstations

3(1)   Employers shall be obliged to perform an analysis of workstations in order to evaluate the safety and health conditions to which they give rise for their workers, particularly as regards possible risks to eyesight, physical problems and problems of mental stress.

3(2)   Employers shall take appropriate measures to remedy the risks found, on the basis of the evaluation referred to in paragraph 1, taking account of the additional and/or combined effects of the risks so found.

ART. 4   Workstations put into service for the first time

4   Employers must take the appropriate steps to ensure that workstations first put into service after 31 December 1992 meet the minimum requirements laid down in the Annex.

ART. 5   Workstations already put into service

5   Employers must take the appropriate steps to ensure that workstations already put into service on or before 31 December 1992 are adapted to comply with the minimum requirements laid down in the Annex not later than four years after that date.

ART. 6   Information for, and training of, workers

6(1)   Without prejudice to Article 10 of Directive 89/391/EEC, workers shall receive information on all aspects of safety and health relating to their workstation, in particular information on such measures applicable to workstations as are implemented under Articles 3, 7 and 9.

In all cases, workers or their representatives shall be informed of any health and safety measure taken in compliance with this directive.

6(2)   Without prejudice to Article 12 of Directive 89/391/EEC, every worker shall also receive training in use of the workstation before commencing this type of work and whenever the organisation of the workstation is substantially modified.

ART. 7   Daily work routine

7   The employer must plan the worker's activities in such a way that daily work on a display screen is periodically interrupted by breaks or changes of activity reducing the workload at the display screen.

ART. 8   Worker consultation and participation

8   Consultation and participation of workers and/or their representatives shall take place in accordance with Article 11 of Directive 89/391/EEC on the matters covered by this directive, including its Annex.

ART. 9   Protection of workers' eyes and eyesight

9(1)   Workers shall be entitled to an appropriate eye and eyesight test carried out by a person with the necessary capabilities:
– before commencing display screen work,

- at regular intervals thereafter, and
- if they experience visual difficulties which may be due to display screen work.

9(2) Workers shall be entitled to an ophthalmological examination if the results of the test referred to in paragraph 1 show that this is necessary.

9(3) If the results of the test referred to in paragraph 1 or of the examination referred to in paragraph 2 show that it is necessary and if normal corrective appliances cannot be used, workers must be provided with special corrective appliances appropriate for the work concerned.

9(4) Measures taken pursuant to this article may in no circumstances involve workers in additional financial cost.

9(5) Protection of workers' eyes and eyesight may be provided as part of a national health system.

SECTION III – MISCELLANEOUS PROVISIONS

ART. 10   Adaptations to the Annex

10 The strictly technical adaptations to the Annex to take account of technical progress, developments in international regulations and specifications and knowledge in the field of display screen equipment shall be adopted in accordance with the procedure laid down in Article 17 of Directive 89/391/EEC.

ART. 11   Final provisions

11(1) Member states shall bring into force the laws, regulations and administrative provisions necessary to comply with this directive by 31 December 1992.

They shall forthwith inform the Commission thereof.

11(2) Member states shall communicate to the Commission the texts of the provisions of national law which they adopt, or have already adopted, in the field covered by this directive.

11(3) Member states shall report to the Commission every four years on the practical implementation of the provisions of this directive, indicating the points of view of employers and workers.

The Commission shall inform the European Parliament, the Council, the Economic and Social Committee and the Advisory Committee on Safety, Hygiene and Health Protection at Work.

11(4) The Commission shall submit a report on the implementation of this directive at regular intervals to the European Parliament, the Council and the Economic and Social Committee, taking into account paragraphs 1, 2 and 3.

ART. 12   [Application]

12 This directive is addressed to the member states.

ANNEX – MINIMUM REQUIREMENTS (ARTICLES 4 AND 5)

Preliminary remark

The obligations laid down in this Annex shall apply in order to achieve the objectives of this directive and to the extent that, firstly, the components concerned are present at the workstation, and secondly, the inherent requirements or characteristics of the task do not preclude it.

Dir. 90/270, Art. 9(2)

1. EQUIPMENT

    (a) **General comment**

    The use as such of the equipment must not be a source of risk for workers.

    (b) **Display screen**

    The characters on the screen shall be well-defined and clearly formed, of adequate size and with adequate spacing between the characters and lines.

    The image on the screen should be stable, with no flickering or other forms of instability.

    The brightness and/or the contrast between the characters and the background shall be easily adjustable by the operator, and also be easily adjustable to ambient conditions.

    The screen must swivel and tilt easily and freely to suit the needs of the operator. It shall be possible to use a separate base for the screen or an adjustable table.

    The screen shall be free of reflective glare and reflections liable to cause discomfort to the user.

    (c) **Keyboard**

    The keyboard shall be tiltable and separate from the screen so as to allow the worker to find a comfortable working position avoiding fatigue in the arms or hands.

    The space in front of the keyboard shall be sufficient to provide support for the hands and arms of the operator.

    The keyboard shall have a matt surface to avoid reflective glare.

    The arrangement of the keyboard and the characteristics of the keys shall be such as to facilitate the use of the keyboard.

    The symbols on the keys shall be adequately contrasted and legible from the design working position.

    (d) **Work desk or work surface**

    The work desk or work surface shall have a sufficiently large, low-reflectance surface and allow a flexible arrangement of the screen, keyboard, documents and related equipment.

    The document holder shall be stable and adjustable and shall be positioned so as to minimise the need for uncomfortable head and eye movements.

    There shall be adequate space for workers to find a comfortable position.

    (e) **Work chair**

    The work chair shall be stable and allow the operator easy freedom of movement and a comfortable position.

    The seat shall be adjustable in height.

    The seat back shall be adjustable in both height and tilt.

    A footrest shall be made available to any one who wishes for one.

2. ENVIRONMENT

    (a) **Space requirements**

    The workstation shall be dimensioned and designed so as to provide sufficient space for the user to change position and vary movements.

Dir. 90/270, Annex

(b) **Lighting**

Room lighting and/or spot lighting (work lamps) shall ensure satisfactory lighting conditions and an appropriate contrast between the screen and the background environment, taking into account the type of work and the user's vision requirements.

Possible disturbing glare and reflections on the screen or other equipment shall be prevented by coordinating workplace and workstation layout with the positioning and technical characteristics of the artificial light sources.

(c) **Reflections and glare**

Workstations shall be so designed that sources of light, such as windows and other openings, transparent or translucid walls, and brightly coloured fixtures or walls cause no direct glare and, as far as possible, no reflections on the screen.

Windows shall be fitted with a suitable system of adjustable covering to attenuate the daylight that falls on the workstation.

(d) **Noise**

Noise emitted by equipment belonging to workstation(s) shall be taken into account when a workstation is being equipped, in particular so as not to distract attention or disturb speech.

(e) **Heat**

Equipment belonging to workstation(s) shall not produce excess heat which could cause discomfort to workers.

(f) **Radiation**

All radiation with the exception of the visible part of the electromagnetic spectrum shall be reduced to negligible levels from the point of view of the protection of workers' safety and health.

(g) **Humidity**

An adequate level of humidity shall be established and maintained.

3. OPERATOR/COMPUTER INTERFACE

In designing, selecting, commissioning and modifying software, and in designing tasks using display screen equipment, the employer shall take into account the following principles:

(a) software must be suitable for the task;

(b) software must be easy to use and, where appropriate, adaptable to the operator's level of knowledge or experience; no quantitative or qualitative checking facility may be used without the knowledge of the workers;

(c) systems must provide feedback to workers on their performance;

(d) systems must display information in a format and at a pace which are adapted to operators;

(e) the principles of software ergonomics must be applied, in particular to human data processing.

Dir. 90/270, Annex

COUNCIL DIRECTIVE 90/269

On the minimum health and safety requirements for the manual handling of loads where there is a risk particularly of back injury to workers (fourth individual directive within the meaning of Article 16(1) of Directive 89/391/EEC)

(29 May 1990, OJ 1990 L156/9)

The Council of the European Communities,

Having regard to the Treaty establishing the European Economic Community, and in particular Article 118a thereof,

Having regard to the Commission proposal submitted after consultation with the Advisory Committee on Safety, Hygiene and Health Protection at Work,

In cooperation with the European Parliament,

Having regard to the opinion of the Economic and Social Committee,

[1] Whereas Article 118a of the Treaty provides that the Council shall adopt, by means of directives, minimum requirements for encouraging improvements, especially in the working environment, to guarantee a better level of protection of the health and safety of workers;

[2] Whereas, pursuant to that article, such directives must avoid imposing administrative, financial and legal constraints in a way which would hold back the creation and development of small and medium-sized undertakings;

[3] Whereas the Commission communication on its programme concerning safety, hygiene and health at work, provides for the adoption of directives designed to guarantee the health and safety of workers at the workplace;

[4] Whereas the Council, in its resolution of 21 December 1987 on safety, hygiene and health at work, took note of the Commission's intention of submitting to the Council in the near future a directive on protection against the risks resulting from the manual handling of heavy loads;

[5] Whereas compliance with the minimum requirements designed to guarantee a better standard of health and safety at the workplace is essential to ensure the health and safety of workers;

[6] Whereas this directive is an individual directive within the meaning of Article 16(1) of Council Directive 89/391/EEC of 12 June 1989 on the introduction of measures to encourage improvements in the health and safety of workers at work; whereas therefore the provisions of the said directive are fully applicable to the field of the manual handling of loads where there

is a risk particularly of back injury to workers, without prejudice to more stringent and/or specific provisions set out in this directive;

[7] Whereas this directive constitutes a practical step towards the achievement of the social dimension of the internal market;

[8] Whereas, pursuant to Decision 74/325/EEC, the Advisory Committee on Safety, Hygiene and Health Protection at Work shall be consulted by the Commission with a view to drawing up proposals in this field,

has adopted this directive:

SECTION I – GENERAL PROVISIONS

ART. 1   Subject

1(1) This directive, which is the fourth individual directive within the meaning of Article 16(1) of Directive 89/391/EEC, lays down minimum health and safety requirements for the manual handling of loads where there is a risk particularly of back injury to workers.

1(2) The provisions of Directive 89/391/EEC shall be fully applicable to the whole sphere referred to in paragraph 1, without prejudice to more restrictive and/or specific provisions contained in this directive.

ART. 2   Definition

2 For the purposes of this directives, 'manual handling of loads' means any transporting or supporting of a load, by one or more workers, including lifting, putting down, pushing, pulling, carrying or moving of a load, which, by reason of its characteristics or of unfavourable ergonomic conditions, involves a risk particularly of back injury to workers.

SECTION II – EMPLOYERS' OBLIGATIONS

ART. 3   General provision

3(1) The employer shall take appropriate organisational measures, or shall use the appropriate means, in particular mechanical equipment, in order to avoid the need for the manual handling of loads by workers.

3(2) Where the need for the manual handling of loads by workers cannot be avoided, the employer shall take the appropriate organisational measures, use the appropriate means or provide workers with such means in order to reduce the risk involved in the manual handling of such loads, having regard to Annex I.

ART. 4   Organisation of workstations

4 Wherever the need for manual handling of loads by workers cannot be avoided, the employer shall organise workstations in such a way as to make such handling as safe and healthy as possible and:

   (a) assess, in advance if possible, the health and safety conditions of the type of work involved, and in particular examine the characteristics of loads, taking account of Annex I;

Dir. 90/269, Art. 1(1)

(b) take care to avoid or reduce the risk particularly of back injury to workers, by taking appropriate measures, considering in particular the characteristics of the working environment and the requirements of the activity, taking account of Annex I.

ART. 5   Reference to Annex II

5   For the implementation of Article 6(3)(b) and Articles 14 and 15 of Directive 89/391/EEC, account should be taken of Annex II.

ART. 6   Information for, and training of, workers

6(1)   Without prejudice to Article 10 of Directive 89/391/EEC, workers and/or their representatives shall be informed of all measures to be implemented, pursuant to this directive, with regard to the protection of safety and of health.

Employers must ensure that workers and/or their representatives receive general indications and, where possible, precise information on:
- the weight of a load,
- the centre of gravity of the heaviest side when a package is eccentrically loaded.

6(2)   Without prejudice to Article 12 of Directive 83/391/EEC, employers must ensure that workers receive in addition proper training and information on how to handle loads correctly and the risks they might be open to particularly if these tasks are not performed correctly, having regard to Annexes I and II.

ART. 7   Consultation of workers and workers' participation

7   Consultation and participation of workers and/or of their representatives shall take place in accordance with Article 11 of Directive 89/391/EEC on matters covered by this directive, including the Annexes thereto.

SECTION III – MISCELLANEOUS PROVISIONS

ART. 8   Adjustment of the Annexes

8   Alterations of a strictly technical nature to Annexes I and II resulting from technical progress and changes in international regulations and specifications or knowledge in the field of the manual handling of loads shall be adopted in accordance with the procedure provided for in Article 17 of Directive 89/391/EEC.

ART. 9   Final provisions

9(1)   Member states shall bring into force the laws, regulations and administrative provisions needed to comply with this directive not later than 31 December 1992.

They shall forthwith inform the Commission thereof.

9(2)   Member states shall communicate to the Commission the text of the provisions of national law which they adopt, or have adopted, in the field covered by this directive.

9(3)   Member states shall report to the Commission every four years on the practical implementation of the provisions of this directive, indicating the points of view of employers and workers.

Dir. 90/269, Art. 9(3)

The Commission shall inform the European Parliament, the Council, the Economic and Social Committee and the Advisory Committee on Safety, Hygiene and Health Protection at Work thereof.

9(4) The Commission shall report periodically to the European Parliament, the Council and the Economic and Social Committee on the implementation of the directive in the light of paragraphs 1, 2 and 3.

ART. 10 [Application]

10 This directive is addressed to the member states.

ANNEX I – REFERENCE FACTORS (ARTICLE 3(2), ARTICLE 4(a) AND (b) AND ARTICLE 6(2))

1. **Characteristics of the load**

    The manual handling of a load may present a risk particularly of back injury if it is:
    - too heavy or too large,
    - unwieldy or difficult to grasp,
    - unstable or has contents likely to shift,
    - positioned in a manner requiring it to be held or manipulated at a distance from the trunk, or with a bending or twisting of the trunk,
    - likely, because of its contours and/or consistency, to result in injury to workers, particularly in the event of a collision.

2. **Physical effort required**

    A physical effort may present a risk particularly of back injury if it is:
    - too strenuous,
    - only achieved by a twisting movement of the trunk,
    - likely to result in a sudden movement of the load,
    - made with the body in an unstable posture.

3. **Characteristics of the working environment**

    The characteristics of the work environment may increase a risk particularly of back injury if:
    - there is not enough room, in particular vertically, to carry out the activity,
    - the floor is uneven, thus presenting tripping hazards, or is slippery in relation to the worker's footwear,
    - the place of work or the working environment prevents the handling of loads at a safe height or with good posture by the worker,
    - there are variations in the level of the floor or the working surface, requiring the load to be manipulated on different levels,
    - the floor or foot rest is unstable,
    - the temperature, humidity or ventilation is unsuitable.

Dir. 90/269, Art. 9(4)

4. **Requirements of the activity**

The activity may present a risk particularly of back injury if it entails one or more of the following requirements:
- over-frequent or over-prolonged physical effort involving in particular the spine,
- an insufficient bodily rest or recovery period,
- excessive lifting, lowering or carrying distances,
- a rate of work imposed by a process which cannot be altered by the worker.

ANNEX II – INDIVIDUAL RISK FACTORS (ARTICLES 5 AND 6(2))

The worker may be at risk if he/she:
- is physically unsuited to carry out the task in question,
- is wearing unsuitable clothing, footwear or other personal effects,
- does not have adequate or appropriate knowledge or training.

COUNCIL DIRECTIVE 89/654

Concerning the minimum safety and health requirements for the workplace (first individual directive within the meaning of Article 16(1) of Directive 89/391/EEC)

(30 November 1989, OJ 1989 L393/1)

The Council of the European Communities,

Having regard to the Treaty establishing the European Economic Community, and in particular Article 118a thereof,

Having regard to the proposal from the Commission, submitted after consulting the Advisory Committee on Safety, Hygiene and Health Protection at Work,

In cooperation with the European Parliament,

Having regard to the opinion of the Economic and Social Committee,

[1] Whereas Article 118a of the Treaty provides that the Council shall adopt, by means of directives, minimum requirements for encouraging improvements, especially in the working environment, to ensure a better level of protection of the safety and health of workers;

[2] Whereas, under the terms of that article, those directives are to avoid imposing administrative, financial and legal constraints in a way which would hold back the creation and development of small and medium-sized undertakings;

[3] Whereas the communication from the Commission on its programme concerning safety, hygiene and health at work provides for the adoption of a directive designed to guarantee the safety and health of workers at the workplace;

[4] Whereas, in its resolution of 21 December 1987 on safety, hygiene and health at work, the Council took note of the Commission's intention of submitting to the Council in the near future minimum requirements concerning the arrangement of the place of work;

[5] Whereas compliance with the minimum requirements designed to guarantee a better standard of safety and health at work is essential to ensure the safety and health of workers;

[6] Whereas this directive is an individual directive within the meaning of Article 16(1) of Council Directive 89/391/EEC of 12 June 1989 on the introduction of measures to encourage improvements in the safety and health of workers at work; whereas the provisions of the latter are therefore fully applicable to the workplace without prejudice to more stringent and/or specific provisions contained in the present directive;

[7] Whereas this directive is a practical contribution towards creating the social dimension of the internal market;

[8] Whereas, pursuant to Decision 74/325/EEC, as last amended by the 1985 Act of Accession, the Advisory Committee on Safety, Hygiene and Health Protection at Work is consulted by the Commission on the drafting of proposals in this field,

has adopted this directive:

SECTION I – GENERAL PROVISIONS

ART. 1 Subject

1(1) This directive, which is the first individual directive within the meaning of Article 16(1) of Directive 89/391/EEC, lays down minimum requirements for safety and health at the workplace, as defined in Article 2.

1(2) This directive shall not apply to:
  (a) means of transport used outside the undertaking and/or the establishment, or workplaces inside means of transport;
  (b) temporary or mobile work sites;
  (c) extractive industries;
  (d) fishing boats;
  (e) fields, woods and other land forming part of an agricultural or forestry undertaking but situated away from the undertaking's buildings.

1(3) The provisions of Directive 89/391/EEC are fully applicable to the whole scope referred to in paragraph 1, without prejudice to more restrictive and/or specific provisions contained in this directive.

ART. 2 Definition

2 For the purposes of this directive, '**workplace**' means the place intended to house workstations on the premises of the undertaking and/or establishment and any other place within the area of the undertaking and/or establishment to which the worker has access in the course of his employment.

SECTION II – EMPLOYERS' OBLIGATIONS

ART. 3 Workplaces used for the first time

3 Workplaces used for the first time after 31 December 1992 must satisfy the minimum safety and health requirements laid down in Annex I.

ART. 4 Workplaces already in use

4 Workplaces already in use before 1 January 1993 must satisfy the minimum safety and health requirements laid down in Annex II at the latest three years after that date.

However, as regards the Portuguese Republic, workplaces used before 1 January 1993 must satisfy, at the latest four years after that date, the minimum safety and health requirements appearing in Annex II.

ART. 5 Modifications to workplaces

5 When workplaces undergo modifications, extensions and/or conversions after 31 December 1992, the employer shall take the measures necessary to ensure that those modifications, extensions and/or conversions are in compliance with the corresponding minimum requirements laid down in Annex I.

ART. 6 General requirements

6 To safeguard the safety and health of workers, the employer shall see to it that:
- traffic routes to emergency exits and the exits themselves are kept clear at all times,
- technical maintenance of the workplace and of the equipment and devices, and in particular those referred to in Annexes I and II, is carried out and any faults found which are liable to affect the safety and health of workers are rectified as quickly as possible,
- the workplace and the equipment and devices, and in particular those referred to in Annex I, point 6, and Annex II, point 6, are regularly cleaned to an adequate level of hygiene,
- safety equipment and devices intended to prevent or eliminate hazards, and in particular those referred to in Annexes I and II, are regularly maintained and checked.

ART. 7 Information of workers

7 Without prejudice to Article 10 of Directive 89/391/EEC, workers and/or their representatives shall be informed of all measures to be taken concerning safety and health at the workplace.

ART. 8 Consultation of workers and workers' participation

Consultation and participation of workers and/or of their representatives shall take place in accordance with Article 11 of Directive 89/391/EEC on the matters covered by this directive, including the Annexes thereto.

SECTION III – MISCELLANEOUS PROVISIONS

ART. 9 Amendments to the Annexes

Strictly technical amendments to the Annexes as a result of:
- the adoption of directives on technical harmonisation and standardisation of the design, manufacture or construction of parts of workplaces, and/or
- technical progress, changes in international regulations or specifications and knowledge with regard to workplaces,

shall be adopted in accordance with the procedure laid down in Article 17 of Directive 89/391/EEC.

ART. 10 Final provisions

10(1) Member states shall bring into force the laws, regulations and administrative provisions necessary to comply with this directive by 31 December 1992. They shall forthwith inform the Commission thereof.

However, the date applicable for the Hellenic Republic shall be 31 December 1994.

Dir. 89/654, Art. 5

10(2) Member states shall communicate to the Commission the texts of the provisions of national law which they have already adopted or adopt in the field governed by this directive.

10(3) Member states shall report to the Commission every five years on the practical implementation of the provisions of this directive, indicating the points of view of employers and workers.

The Commission shall inform the European Parliament, the Council, the Economic and Social Committee and the Advisory Council on Safety, Hygiene and Health Protection at Work.

10(4) The Commission shall submit periodically to the European Parliament, the Council and the Economic and Social Committee a report on the implementation of this directive, taking into account paragraphs 1 to 3.

ART. 11 [Application]

11 This directive is addressed to the member states.

ANNEX I – MINIMUM SAFETY AND HEALTH REQUIREMENTS FOR WORKPLACES USED FOR THE FIRST TIME, AS REFERRED TO IN ARTICLE 3 OF THE DIRECTIVE

1. **Preliminary note**

    The obligations laid down in this Annex apply whenever required by the features of the workplace, the activity, the circumstances or a hazard.

2. **Stability and solidity**

    Buildings which house workplaces must have a structure and solidity appropriate to the nature of their use.

3. **Electrical installations**

    Electrical installations must be designed and constructed so as not to present a fire or explosion hazard; persons must be adequately protected against the risk of accidents caused by direct or indirect contact.

    The design, construction and choice of material and protection devices must be appropriate to the voltage, external conditions and the competence of persons with access to parts of the installation.

4. **Emergency routes and exits**

    4.1. Emergency routes and exits must remain clear and lead as directly as possible to the open air or to a safe area.

    4.2. In the event of danger, it must be possible for workers to evacuate all workstations quickly and as safely as possible.

    4.3. The number, distribution and dimensions of the emergency routes and exits depend on the use, equipment and dimensions of the workplaces and the maximum number of persons that may be present.

4.4. Emergency doors must open outwards.

Sliding or revolving doors are not permitted if they are specifically intended as emergency exits.

Emergency doors should not be so locked or fastened that they cannot be easily and immediately opened by any person who may require to use them in an emergency.

4.5. Specific emergency routes and exits must be indicated by signs in accordance with the national regulations transposing Directive 77/576/EEC into law.

Such signs must be placed at appropriate points and be made to last.

4.6. Emergency doors must not be locked.

The emergency routes and exits, and the traffic routes and doors giving access to them, must be free from obstruction so that they can be used at any time without hindrance.

4.7. Emergency routes and exits requiring illumination must be provided with emergency lighting of adequate intensity in case the lighting fails.

5. Fire detection and fire fighting

5.1. Depending on the dimensions and use of the buildings, the equipment they contain, the physical and chemical properties of the substances present and the maximum potential number of people present, workplaces must be equipped with appropriate fire-fighting equipment and, as necessary, with fire detectors and alarm systems.

5.2. Non-automatic fire-fighting equipment must be easily accessible and simple to use.

The equipment must be indicated by signs in accordance with the national regulations transposing Directive 77/576/EEC into law.

Such signs must be placed at appropriate points and be made to last.

6. Ventilation of enclosed workplaces

6.1. Steps shall be taken to see to it that there is sufficient fresh air in enclosed workplaces, having regard to the working methods used and the physical demands placed on the workers.

If a forced ventilation system is used, it shall be maintained in working order.

Any breakdown must be indicated by a control system where this is necessary for workers' health.

6.2. If air-conditioning or mechanical ventilation installations are used, they must operate in such a way that workers are not exposed to draughts which cause discomfort.

Any deposit or dirt likely to create an immediate danger to the health of workers by polluting the atmosphere must be removed without delay.

7. Room temperature

7.1. During working hours, the temperature in rooms containing workplaces must be adequate for human beings, having regard to the working methods being used and the physical demands placed on the workers.

7.2. The temperature in rest areas, rooms for duty staff, sanitary facilities, canteens and first aid rooms must be appropriate to the particular purpose of such areas.

7.3. Windows, skylights and glass partitions should allow excessive effects of sunlight in workplaces to be avoided, having regard to the nature of the work and of the workplace.

Dir. 89/654, Annex I

8. Natural and artificial room lighting

8.1. Workplaces must as far as possible receive sufficient natural light and be equipped with artificial lighting adequate for the protection of workers' safety and health.

8.2. Lighting installations in rooms containing workplaces and in passageways must be placed in such a way that there is no risk of accident to workers as a result of the type of lighting fitted.

8.3. Workplaces in which workers are especially exposed to risks in the event of failure of artificial lighting must be provided with emergency lighting of adequate intensity.

9. Floors, walls, ceilings and roofs of rooms

9.1. The floors of workplaces must have no dangerous bumps, holes or slopes and must be fixed, stable and not slippery.

Workplaces containing workstations must be adequately insulated, bearing in mind the type of undertaking involved and the physical activity of the workers.

9.2. The surfaces of floors, walls and ceilings in rooms must be such that they can be cleaned or refurbished to an appropriate standard of hygiene.

9.3. Transparent or translucent walls, in particular all-glass partitions, in rooms or in the vicinity of workplaces and traffic routes must be clearly indicated and made of safety material or be shielded from such places or traffic routes to prevent workers from coming into contact with walls or being injured should the walls shatter.

9.4. Access to roofs made of materials of insufficient strength must not be permitted unless equipment is provided to ensure that the work can be carried out in a safe manner.

10. Windows and skylights

10.1. It must be possible for workers to open, close, adjust or secure windows, skylights and ventilators in a safe manner. When open, they must not be positioned so as to constitute a hazard to workers.

10.2. Windows and skylights must be designed in conjunction with equipment or otherwise fitted with devices allowing them to be cleaned without risk to the workers carrying out this work or to workers present in and around the building.

11. Doors and gates

11.1. The position, number and dimensions of doors and gates, and the materials used in their construction, are determined by the nature and use of the rooms or areas.

11.2. Transparent doors must be appropriately marked at a conspicuous level.

11.3. Swing doors and gates must be transparent or have see-through panels.

11.4. If transparent or translucent surfaces in doors and gates are not made of safety material and if there is a danger that workers may be injured if a door or gate should shatter, the surfaces must be protected against breakage.

11.5. Sliding doors must be fitted with a safety device to prevent them from being derailed and falling over.

11.6. Doors and gates opening upwards must be fitted with a mechanism to secure them against falling back.

Dir. 89/654, Annex I

11.7. Doors along escape routes must be appropriately marked.

It must be possible to open them from the inside at any time without special assistance.

It must be possible to open the doors when the workplaces are occupied.

11.8. Doors for pedestrians must be provided in the immediate vicinity of any gates intended essentially for vehicle traffic, unless it is safe for pedestrians to pass through; such doors must be clearly marked and left permanently unobstructed.

11.9. Mechanical doors and gates must function in such a way that there is no risk of accident to workers.

They must be fitted with easily identifiable and accessible emergency shut-down devices and, unless they open automatically in the event of a power failure, it must also be possible to open them manually.

12. Traffic routes – danger areas

12.1. Traffic routes, including stairs, fixed ladders and loading bays and ramps, must be located and dimensioned to ensure easy, safe and appropriate access for pedestrians or vehicles in such a way as not to endanger workers employed in the vicinity of these traffic routes.

12.2. Routes used for pedestrian traffic and/or goods traffic must be dimensioned in accordance with the number of potential users and the type of undertaking.

If means of transport are used on traffic routes, a sufficient safety clearance must be provided for pedestrians.

12.3. Sufficient clearance must be allowed between vehicle traffic routes and doors, gates, passages for pedestrians, corridors and staircases.

12.4. Where the use and equipment of rooms so requires for the protection of workers, traffic routes must be clearly identified.

12.5. If the workplaces contain danger areas in which, owing to the nature of the work, there is a risk of the worker or objects falling, the places must be equipped, as far as possible, with devices preventing unauthorised workers from entering those areas.

Appropriate measures must be taken to protect workers authorised to enter danger areas.

Danger areas must be clearly indicated.

13. Specific measures for escalators and travelators

Escalators and travelators must function safely.

They must be equipped with any necessary safety devices.

They must be fitted with easily identifiable and accessible emergency shut-down devices.

14. Loading bays and ramps

14.1. Loading bays and ramps must be suitable for the dimensions of the loads to be transported.

14.2. Loading bays must have at least one exit point.

Where technically feasible, bays over a certain length must have an exit point at each end.

Dir. 89/654, Annex I

14.3. Loading ramps must as far as possible be safe enough to prevent workers from falling off.

15. Room dimensions and air space in rooms – freedom of movement at the workstation

15.1. Workrooms must have sufficient surface area, height and air space to allow workers to perform their work without risk to their safety, health or well-being.

15.2. The dimensions of the free unoccupied area at the workstation must be calculated to allow workers sufficient freedom of movement to perform their work.

If this is not possible for reasons specific to the workplace, the worker must be provided with sufficient freedom of movement near his workstation.

16. Rest rooms

16.1 Where the safety or health of workers, in particular because of the type of activity carried out or the presence of more than a certain number of employees, so require, workers must be provided with an easily accessible rest room.

This provision does not apply if the workers are employed in offices or similar workrooms providing equivalent relaxation during breaks.

16.2. Rest rooms must be large enough and equipped with an adequate number of tables and seats with backs for the number of workers.

16.3. In rest rooms appropriate measures must be introduced for the protection of non-smokers against discomfort caused by tobacco smoke.

16.4. If working hours are regularly and frequently interrupted and there is no rest room, other rooms must be provided in which workers can stay during such interruptions, wherever this is required for the safety or health of workers.

Appropriate measures should be taken for the protection of non-smokers against discomfort caused by tobacco smoke.

17. Pregnant women and nursing mothers

Pregnant women and nursing mothers must be able to lie down to rest in appropriate conditions.

18. Sanitary equipment

18.1. *Changing rooms and lockers*

18.1.1. Appropriate changing rooms must be provided for workers if they have to wear special work clothes and where, for reasons of health or propriety, they cannot be expected to change in another room.

Changing rooms must be easily accessible, be of sufficient capacity and be provided with seating.

18.1.2. Changing rooms must be sufficiently large and have facilities to enable each worker to lock away his clothes during working hours.

If circumstances so require (e.g. dangerous substances, humidity, dirt), lockers for work clothes must be separate from those for ordinary clothes.

18.1.3. Provision must be made for separate changing rooms or separate use of changing rooms for men and women.

Dir. 89/654, Annex I

18.1.4. If changing rooms are not required under 18.1.1, each worker must be provided with a place to store his clothes.

18.2. *Showers and washbasins*

18.2.1. Adequate and suitable showers must be provided for workers if required by the nature of the work or for health reasons.

Provision must be made for separate shower rooms or separate use of shower rooms for men and women.

18.2.2. The shower rooms must be sufficiently large to permit each worker to wash without hindrance in conditions of an appropriate standard of hygiene.

The showers must be equipped with hot and cold running water.

18.2.3. Where showers are not required under the first subparagraph of 18.2.1., adequate and suitable washbasins with running water (hot water if necessary) must be provided in the vicinity of the workstations and the changing rooms.

Such washbasins must be separate for, or used separately by, men and women when so required for reasons of propriety.

18.2.4. Where the rooms housing the showers or washbasins are separate from the changing rooms, there must be easy communication between the two.

18.3. *Lavatories and washbasins*

Separate facilities must be provided in the vicinity of workstations, rest rooms, changing rooms and rooms housing showers or washbasins, with an adequate number of lavatories and washbasins.

Provision must be made for separate lavatories or separate use of lavatories for men and women.

19. First aid rooms

19.1. One or more first aid rooms must be provided where the size of the premises, type of activity being carried out and frequency of accidents so dictate.

19.2. First aid rooms must be fitted with essential first aid installations and equipment and be easily accessible to stretchers.

They must be signposted in accordance with the national regulations transposing Directive 77/576/EEC into law.

19.3. In addition, first aid equipment must be available in all places where working conditions require it.

This equipment must be suitably marked and easily accessible.

20. Handicapped workers

Workplaces must be organised to take account of handicapped workers, if necessary.

This provision applies in particular to the doors, passageways, staircases, showers, washbasins, lavatories and workstations used or occupied directly by handicapped persons.

21. Outdoor workplaces (special provisions)

21.1. Workstations, traffic routes and other areas or installations outdoors which are used or

Dir. 89/654, Annex I

occupied by the workers in the course of their activity must be organised in such a way that pedestrians and vehicles can circulate safely.

Sections 12, 13 and 14 also apply to main traffic routes on the site of the undertaking (traffic routes leading to fixed workstations), to traffic routes used for the regular maintenance and supervision of the undertaking's installations and to loading bays.

Section 12 is also applicable to outdoor workplaces.

21.2. Workplaces outdoors must be adequately lit by artificial lighting if daylight is not adequate.

21.3. When workers are employed at workstations outdoors, such workstations must as far as possible be arranged so that workers:

(a) are protected against inclement weather conditions and if necessary against falling objects;

(b) are not exposed to harmful noise levels nor to harmful external influences such as gases, vapours or dust;

(c) are able to leave their workstations swiftly in the event of danger or are able to be rapidly assisted;

(d) cannot slip or fall.

ANNEX II – MINIMUM HEALTH AND SAFETY REQUIREMENTS FOR WORKPLACES ALREADY IN USE, AS REFERRED TO IN ARTICLE 4 OF THE DIRECTIVE

1. **Preliminary note**

    The obligations laid down in this Annex apply wherever required by the features of the workplace, the activity, the circumstances or a hazard.

2. **Stability and solidity**

    Buildings which have workplaces must have a structure and solidity appropriate to the nature of their use.

3. **Electrical installations**

    Electrical installations must be designed and constructed so as not to present a fire or explosion hazard; persons must be adequately protected against the risk of accidents caused by direct or indirect contact.

    Electrical installations and protection devices must be appropriate to the voltage, external conditions and the competence of persons with access to parts of the installation.

4. **Emergency routes and exits**

4.1. Emergency routes and exits must remain clear and lead as directly as possible to the open air or to a safe area.

4.2. In the event of danger, it must be possible for workers to evacuate all workstations quickly and as safely as possible.

Dir. 89/654, Annex II

4.3. There must be an adequate number of escape routes and emergency exits.

4.4. Emergency exit doors must open outwards.
Sliding or revolving doors are not permitted if they are specifically intended as emergency exits.
Emergency doors should not be so locked or fastened that they cannot be easily and immediately opened by any person who may require to use them in an emergency.

4.5. Specific emergency routes and exits must be indicated by signs in accordance with the national regulations transposing Directive 77/576/EEC into law.
Such signs must be placed at appropriate points and be made to last.

4.6. Emergency doors must not be locked.
The emergency routes and exits, and the traffic routes and doors giving access to them, must be free from obstruction so that they can be used at any time without hindrance.

4.7. Emergency routes and exits requiring illumination must be provided with emergency lighting of adequate intensity in case the lighting fails.

5. Fire detection and fire fighting

5.1. Depending on the dimensions and use of the buildings, the equipment they contain, the physical and chemical characteristics of the substances present and the maximum potential number of people present, workplaces must be equipped with appropriate fire-fighting equipment, and, as necessary, fire detectors and an alarm system.

5.2. Non-automatic fire-fighting equipment must be easily accessible and simple to use.
It must be indicated by signs in accordance with the national regulations transposing Directive 77/576/EEC into law.
Such signs must be placed at appropriate points and be made to last.

6. Ventilation of enclosed workplaces

Steps shall be taken to see to it that there is sufficient fresh air in enclosed workplaces, having regard to the working methods used and the physical demands placed on the workers.
If a forced ventilation system is used, it shall be maintained in working order.
Any breakdown must be indicated by a control system where this is necessary for the workers' health.

7. Room temperature

7.1. During working hours, the temperature in rooms containing workplaces must be adequate for human beings, having regard to the working methods being used and the physical demands placed on the workers.

7.2. The temperature in rest areas, rooms for duty staff, sanitary facilities, canteens and first aid rooms must be appropriate to the particular purpose of such areas.

8. Natural and artificial room lighting

8.1. Workplaces must as far as possible receive sufficient natural light and be equipped with artificial lighting adequate for workers' safety and health.

Dir. 89/654, Annex II

8.2. Workplaces in which workers are especially exposed to risks in the event of failure of artificial lighting must be provided with emergency lighting of adequate intensity.

9. Doors and gates

9.1. Transparent doors must be appropriately marked at a conspicuous level.

9.2. Swing doors and gates must be transparent or have see-through panels.

10. Danger areas

If the workplaces contain danger areas in which, owing to the nature of the work, there is a risk of the worker or objects falling, the places must be equipped, as far as possible, with devices preventing unauthorised workers from entering those areas.

Appropriate measures must be taken to protect workers authorised to enter danger areas. Danger areas must be clearly indicated.

11. Rest rooms and rest areas

11.1 Where the safety or health of workers, in particular because of the type of activity carried out or the presence of more than a certain number of employees, so require, workers must be provided with an easily accessible rest room or appropriate rest area.

This provision does not apply if the workers are employed in offices or similar workrooms providing equivalent relaxation during breaks.

11.2. Rest rooms and rest areas must be equipped with tables and seats with backs.

11.3. In rest rooms and rest areas appropriate measures must be introduced for the protection of non-smokers against discomfort caused by tobacco smoke.

12. Pregnant women and nursing mothers

Pregnant women and nursing mothers must be able to lie down to rest in appropriate conditions.

13. Sanitary equipment

13.1. *Changing rooms and lockers*

13.1.1. Appropriate changing rooms must be provided for workers if they have to wear special work clothes and where, for reasons of health or propriety, they cannot be expected to change in another room.

Changing rooms must be easily accessible and of sufficient capacity.

13.1.2. Changing rooms must have facilities to enable each worker to lock away his clothes during working hours.

If circumstances so require (e.g. dangerous substances, humidity, dirt), lockers for work clothes must be separate from those for ordinary clothes.

13.1.3. Provision must be made for separate changing rooms or separate use of changing rooms for men and women.

13.2. *Showers, lavatories and washbasins*

13.2.1. Workplaces must be fitted out in such a way that workers have in the vicinity:
- showers, if required by the nature of their work,
- special facilities equipped with an adequate number of lavatories and washbasins.

Dir. 89/654, Annex II

13.2.2. The showers and washbasins must be equipped with running water (hot water if necessary).

13.2.3. Provision must be made for separate showers or separate use of showers for men and women.

Provision must be made for separate lavatories or separate use of lavatories for men and women.

14. First aid equipment

Workplaces must be fitted with first aid equipment.
The equipment must be suitably marked and easily accessible.

15. Handicapped workers

Workplaces must be organised to take account of handicapped workers, if necessary.

This provision applies in particular to the doors, passageways, staircases, showers, washbasins, lavatories and workstations used or occupied directly by handicapped persons.

16. Movement of pedestrians and vehicles

Outdoor and indoor workplaces must be organised in such a way that pedestrians and vehicles can circulate in a safe manner.

17. Outdoor workplaces (special provisions)

When workers are employed at workstations outdoors, such workstations must as far as possible be organised so that workers:

(a) are protected against inclement weather conditions and if necessary against falling objects;

(b) are not exposed to harmful noise levels nor to harmful external influences such as gases, vapours or dust;

(c) are able to leave their workstations swiftly in the event of danger or are able to be rapidly assisted;

(d) cannot slip or fall.

Dir. 89/654, Annex II

Index

This index covers the commentary, regulations and EC directives and references are to paragraph numbers and provisions

Paragraph/Provision

A

Accidents – see also **Injury**
. falling objects 712;
    SI 1992/3004 reg. 13
. falls 712;
    SI 1992/3004 reg. 13
. manual handling operations – see
    Manual Handling Regulations
. occupational,
    record of . . . . Dir. 89/391 art. 9(1)
Approved code of practice 105

B

Back injuries
. manual handling operations – see
    Manual Handling Regulations

C

Ceilings
. cleanliness 708;
    SI 1992/3004 reg. 9(2);
    Dir. 89/654 Annex I(9.2)
Changing rooms 723;
    SI 1992/3004 reg. 24;
    Dir. 89/654
    Annex I(18.1), II(13.1)
Cleanliness
. toilets 719;
    SI 1992/3004 reg. 20
. washing facilities 720;
    SI 1992/3004 reg. 21
. workplace 708;
    SI 1992/3004 reg. 9;
    Dir. 89/654 art. 6
Clothing
. accommodation for 722;
    SI 1992/3004 reg. 23;
    Dir. 89/654
    Annex I(18.1), II(13.1)

Paragraph/Provision

. facilities for changing 723;
    SI 1992/3004 reg. 24;
    Dir. 89/654
    Annex I(18.1), II(13.1)
Competent persons
. appointment 206;
    SI 1992/2051 reg. 6;
    Dir. 89/391 art. 7
. evacuation of premises by . . . . 205(3);
    SI 1992/2051 reg. 7;
    Dir. 89/391 art. 8
Computers – see **VDU Regulations**
Construction sites
. proposed legislation 106
Control of Substances Hazardous to Health
    Regulations 1988 . . . . 102(2)
Controls and control systems
. work equipment . . . . 406(10)
. . controlling changes in operating
    conditions . . . . SI 1992/2932 reg. 14
. . controls . . . . SI 1992/2932 reg. 17
. . control systems . . . . . . SI 1992/2932 reg. 18
. . emergency stop controls . . . . . SI 1992/2932
    reg. 16
. . starting equipment . . . SI 1992/2932 reg. 14
. . stop controls . . . . SI 1992/2932 reg. 15

COSHH – see **Control of Substances**
    Hazardous to Health Regulations 1988

D

Dangerous substances
. persons falling into, preventative
    measures 712;
    SI 1992/3004 reg. 13
Definitions and meanings
. assessment . . . . SI 1992/2051 reg. 1(2)
. at work . . . . SI 1992/2051 reg. 16(2)

Definitions and meanings
– continued   **Paragraph/Provision**
. dangerous substance .... SI 1992/3004 reg. 13(7)
. danger zone....... SI 1992/2932 reg. 11(5); Dir. 89/655 art. 2(c)
. display screen equipment .... 503(1); SI 1992/2792 reg. 1(2); Dir. 90/270 art. 2(a)
. employer .... Dir. 89/391 art. 3
. employment business......... SI 1992/2051 reg. 1(2)
. exposed worker .... Dir. 89/655 art. 2(d)
. fixed-term contract of employment ...... SI 1992/2051 reg. 1(2)
. injury .... SI 1992/2793 reg. 2(1)
. load................ SI 1992/2793 reg. 2(1)
. manual handling of loads................ Dir. 90/269 art. 2
. manual handling operations... SI 1992/2793 reg. 2(1)
. new workplace ...... SI 1992/3004 reg. 2(1)
. operator........... SI 1992/2792 reg. 1(2); Dir. 89/655 art. 2(e)
. personal protective equipment.......... SI 1992/2966 reg. 2; Dir. 89/656 art. 2
. premises or undertakings .... 404(2)
. prevention .... Dir. 89/391 art. 3
. public road .... SI 1992/3004 reg. 2(1)
. stock-bar .... SI 1992/2932 reg. 11(5)
. suitable............. SI 1992/2932 reg. 5(4)
. traffic routes .... 711; SI 1992/3004 reg. 2(1)
. use .... SI 1992/2792 reg. 1(2); SI 1992/2932 reg. 2(1)
. use of work equipment..........Dir. 89/655 art. 2(b)
. user................ SI 1992/2792 reg. 1(2)
. work equipment................ 404(1); SI 1992/2932 reg. 2(1); Dir. 89/655 art. 2(a)
. worker ....Dir. 89/391 art. 3; Dir. 90/270 art. 2(c)
. workers' representative with specific responsibility for the health and safety of workers............ Dir. 89/391 art. 3
. workplace .... 702; SI 1992/3004 reg. 2(1); Dir. 89/654 art. 2
. workstation .... SI 1992/2792 reg. 1(2); Dir. 90/270 art. 2(b)

Disabled employees .... 701; Dir. 89/654 Annex I(20), II(15)

Paragraph/Provision
Display screen equipment – see **VDU Regulations**

Doors
. construction....................... 717; SI 1992/3004 reg. 18
. emergency.... Dir. 89/654 Annex 1(4), II(4)
. safety devices .... 717; SI 1992/3004 reg. 18; Dir. 89/654 Annex I(11)
. transparent/translucent
. . safety materials/protection from breakage .... 713; SI 1992/3004 reg. 14; Dir. 89/654 Annex I(11.4), II(9)
. . warning markings .... 713; SI 1992/3004 reg. 14; Dir. 89/654 Annex I(11.2)

Drinking water
. provision of....................... 721; SI 1992/3004 reg. 22

E

EC
. work equipment, compliance with requirements.................. 406(6); SI 1992/2932 reg. 10

Electrical installations
. accidents, protection against ... Dir. 89/654 Annex I(3), II(3)

Electricity
. protection of workers exposed to..... Dir. 89/655 Annex (2.19)

Emergency lighting systems 707

Emergency routes and exits ...... Dir. 89/654 Annex I(4), II(4)
. door markings... Dir. 89/654 Annex I(11.7)

Emergency stop controls
. escalators........................... 718; SI 1992/3004 reg. 19
. work equipment................ 406(10); SI 1992/2932 reg. 16; Dir. 89/655 Annex (2.4)

Employees
. information to – see Information
. obligations as to own health and safety .... 205(9); SI 1992/2051 reg. 12; Dir. 89/391 art. 13
. workstations, self-assessment....... 505(2)

Index 193

Paragraph/Provision

Employment agency workers
. information to.................. 205(7);
SI 1992/2051 art. 13

Energy sources
. electrical installations, protection
against accidents........... Dir. 89/654
Annex I(3), II(3)
. electricity, protection of workers
exposed to..... Dir. 89/655 Annex (2.19)
. isolation, work equipment....... 406(11);
SI 1992/2932 reg. 19

Equipment
. personal protective – see Personal
Protective Equipment
Regulations
. work – see Work Equipment
Regulations

Escalators 718;
SI 1992/3004 reg. 19;
Dir. 89/654 Annex I(13)

Evacuation of premises
. competent person to implement ... 205(3);
SI 1992/2051 reg. 7;
Dir. 89/391 art. 8
. emergency routes and exits .... Dir. 89/654
Annex I(4), II(4)

Exemption certificates
. exemption from regulations for
reasons of national security
.. management of health and safety
at work............SI 1992/2051 reg. 14
.. manual handling
operations ....SI 1992/2793 reg. 6
.. VDU ....SI 1992/2792 reg. 8
.. work equipment......SI 1992/2932 reg. 25
.. workplace ....SI 1992/3004 reg. 26

Explosions
. work equipment .. Dir. 89/655 Annex (2.18)

Eye and eyesight tests
. VDU users 508;
SI 1992/2792 reg. 5;
Dir. 90/270 art. 9
.. sample letter/forms for exchange
of information................. App. A

F

Factories Act 1961 .... 102(3)

Falling objects
. preventative measures............... 712;
SI 1992/3004 reg. 13

Paragraph/Provision

Falls
. personal injury..................... 712;
SI 1992/3004 reg. 13

Fire
. detection and fighting in the
workplace .. Dir. 89/654 Annex I(5), II(5)
.. equipment, provision ...Dir. 89/391 art. 8;
Dir. 89/654 Annex I(5), II(5)
.. training of employees... Dir. 89/391 art. 8

**First aid rooms and
equipment** ....Dir. 89/391 art. 8;
Dir. 89/654 Annex I(19), II(14)
. temperature................... Dir. 89/654
Annex I(7.2), II(7.2)
. training of designated
employees .... Dir. 89/391 art. 8

Fixed-term contracts
. employees on, information to ..... 205(7);
SI 1992/2051 reg. 13
. meaning .... SI 1992/2051 reg. 1(2)

Fixtures and fittings
. workplace cleanliness 708;
SI 1992/3004 reg. 9(1)

Floors
. drainage......................... 711;
SI 1992/3004 reg. 12(2)
. obstructions, removal 711;
SI 1992/3004 reg. 12(3)
. traffic routes, suitability 711;
SI 1992/3004 reg. 12
. workplace cleanliness 708;
SI 1992/3004 reg. 9(2);
Dir. 89/654 Annex I(9.2)

Framework Regulations – see **Management
of Health and Safety at Work
Regulations**

Furniture
. VDU use – see VDU Regulations
. workplace cleanliness 708;
SI 1992/3004 reg. 9(1)

G

Gates
. construction and safety devices 717;
SI 1992/3004 reg. 18;
Dir. 89/654 Annex I(11)
. transparent/translucent, safety
materials/protection from
breakage 713;
SI 1992/3004 reg. 14;
Dir. 89/654 Annex I(11.4)

Paragraph/Provision

Guidance notes 105

H

Handicapped employees 701;
    Dir. 89/654 Annex I(20), II(15)

Handrails and guards
. staircases 711;
    SI 1992/3004 reg. 12(5)

Health and Safety at Work Act 1974 ... 102(1)

Health and Safety Commission (HSC)
. approved code of practice 105

Health and Safety (Display Screen Equipment) Regulations 1992 – see **VDU Regulations**

Health and Safety Executive (HSE)
. guidance notes on regulations 105

Health and safety scheme
. employers' duty to provide .... 205(1);
    SI 1992/2051 reg. 4

Health surveillance
. provision where risks identifiable .. 205(2);
    SI 1992/2051 reg. 5;
    Dir. 89/391 art. 14

Hired equipment..................... 404(4)

HSC – see **Health and Safety Commission (HSC)**

HSE – see **Health and Safety Executive (HSE)**

I

Information
. 'any person at work' .... 205(3);
    SI 1992/2051 reg. 7;
    Dir. 89/391 art. 10
. EC Commission, implementation of directives
.. management of health and safety at work.............. Dir. 89/391 art. 18
.. manual handling operations .... Dir. 90/269 art. 9
.. personal protective equipment .... Dir. 89/656 art. 10
.. VDU .... Dir. 90/270 art. 11
.. work equipment....... Dir. 89/655 art. 10
.. workplace health and safety .. Dir. 89/654 art. 10

Paragraph/Provision

. employees
.. management of health and safety at work..................... 205(4);
    SI 1992/2051 reg. 8;
    Dir. 89/391 art. 10
.. manual handling operations ..... 603(5);
    SI 1992/2793 reg. 4;
    Dir. 90/269 art. 6
.. personal protective equipment ... 303(3);
    SI 1992/2966 reg. 9;
    Dir. 89/656 art. 4(5), 7
.. VDU users/operators 509;
    SI 1992/2792 reg. 6;
    Dir. 90/270 art. 6
.. work equipment................ 406(4);
    SI 1992/2932 reg. 8;
    Dir. 89/655 art. 6
.. workplace health and safety .... Dir. 89/654 art. 7

Injury
. back injuries, manual handling operations – see Manual Handling Regulations
. falls and falling objects 712

Inspectors
. enforcement powers 104

Instructions
. work equipment .... 406(4)

L

Leased equipment .... 404(4)

Legislation
. enforcement 104
. existing........................... 102
.. work equipment regulations, relationship with.................. 402
. non-compliance 104

Lighting
. equipment, use................ 406(12);
    SI 1992/2932 reg. 21;
    Dir. 89/655 Annex (2.9)
. workplace 707;
    SI 1992/3004 reg. 8;
    Dir. 89/654 Annex I(8), II(8)

Loading bays and ramps......... Dir. 89/654 Annex I(14)

Lockers 722;
    SI 1992/3004 reg. 23;
    Dir. 89/654 Annex I(18.1), II(13.1)

Index 195

Paragraph/Provision

M

Machinery – see also **Work Equipment Regulations**
. dangerous parts, hazards .... 406(7);
    SI 1992/2932 reg. 11
. protective devices................ 406(7)

Maintenance
. equipment.................. 406(2); 704;
    SI 1992/2932 reg. 6;
    SI 1992/3004 reg. 5;
    Dir. 89/654 art. 6;
    Dir. 89/655 art. 4(2),
    Annex (2.13)
. roofs............ Dir. 89/654 Annex I(9.4)
. workplace 704;
    SI 1992/3004 reg. 5;
    Dir. 89/654 art. 6

Management of Health and Safety at Work Regulations
. application........................ 202;
    Dir. 89/391 art. 2(1), 16, Annex
. assessment, meaning . SI 1992/2051 reg. 1(2)
. 'at work', meaning .. SI 1992/2051 reg. 16(2)
. capabilities of employees,
    assessment to reduce risks ...... 205(5);
    SI 1992/2051 reg. 11(1)
. citation............. SI 1992/2051 reg. 1(1)
. civil liability, exclusion .SI 1992/2051 reg. 15
. commencement..................... 201;
    SI 1992/2051 reg. 1(1);
    Dir. 89/391 art. 18(1)
. competent persons, appointment 206;
    SI 1992/2051 reg. 6
. consultation and participation of
    workers .... Dir. 89/391 art. 11
. disapplication .... SI 1992/2051 reg. 2;
    Dir. 89/391 art. 2(2)
. duties imposed by 202
. EC directives, committee for
    adjustments.......... Dir. 89/391 art. 17
. employees
. . obligations .... 205(9);
    SI 1992/2051 reg. 12;
    Dir. 89/391 art. 13
. . serious/imminent danger,
    avoidance............. Dir. 89/391 art. 8
. employers
. . general obligations .. Dir. 89/391 art. 5–12
. . meaning............... Dir. 89/391 art. 3
. employment business,
    meaning.......... SI 1992/2051 reg. 1(2)
. evacuation of employees. . Dir. 89/391 art. 8

Paragraph/Provision
. exemption certificates, interests of
    national security..... SI 1992/2051 reg. 14
. extension outside
    Great Britain .... SI 1992/2051 reg. 16(1)
. fire-fighting, equipment and
    training of designated
    employees .... Dir. 89/391 art. 8
. first aid, provision .... Dir. 89/391 art. 8
. fixed-term contract of
    employment, meaning...... SI 1992/2051
    reg. 1(2)
. health surveillance..... SI 1992/2051 reg. 5;
    Dir. 89/391 art. 14
. information
. . 'any person at work'............ 205(3);
    SI 1992/2051 reg. 7;
    Dir. 89/391 art. 10
. . EC Commission, implementation
    of directive .... Dir. 89/391 art. 18
. . employees..................... 205(4);
    SI 1992/2051 reg. 8;
    Dir. 89/391 art. 10(1)
. interpretation .... SI 1992/2051 reg. 1
. key areas covered by............. 203–206
. member states'
    obligations............ Dir. 89/391 art. 4
. necessity for 201
. occupational accidents,
    record of .... Dir. 89/391 art. 9(1)
. outside workers, information/
    procedures..................... 205(6);
    SI 1992/2051 reg. 10;
    Dir. 89/391 art. 10(2)
. prevention, meaning ..... Dir. 89/391 art. 3
. protective and preventative
    measures, identification and
    implementation.................... 205;
    SI 1992/2051 reg. 4
. . competent persons, appointment
    to assist 206;
    SI 1992/2051 reg. 6;
    Dir. 89/391 art. 7
. . meaning........... SI 1992/2051 reg. 1(2)
. purpose 201
. risk assessment..................... 204;
    SI 1992/2051 reg. 3;
    Dir. 89/391 art. 6, 9(1)
. . self-employed persons 204;
    SI 1992/2051 reg. 3(2)
. risk groups............. Dir. 89/391 art. 15
. Safety Representatives and Safety
    Committees Regulations 1977,
    modification ... SI 1992/2051 reg. 17, Sch.

Management of the Regulations
   – continued   **Paragraph/Provision**
. self-employed persons – see
    Self-employed persons
. serious and imminent danger,
    procedures for exposure to ..... 205(3);
                                  SI 1992/2051 reg. 7
. shared workplaces, co-ordination
    of measures/co-operation .... 205(8);
                                    SI 1992/2051 reg. 9
. temporary workers,
    information to................. 205(7);
                                    SI 1992/2051 reg. 13
. training in health and safety for
    employees .... 205(5);
                     SI 1992/2051 reg. 11(2), (3);
                                Dir. 89/391 art. 12
. worker, meaning .... Dir. 89/391 art. 3
. workers' representative with
    specific responsibility for the
    health and safety of workers,
    meaning .... Dir. 89/391 art. 3
. workers responsible for health and
    safety .... Dir. 89/391 art. 11
.. information for .....Dir. 89/391 art. 10(3)

Manual Handling Regulations
. application......................... 602;
                                      Dir. 90/269 art. 1
. citation................SI 1992/2793 reg. 1
. commencement........ SI 1992/2793 reg. 1;
                                    Dir. 90/269 art. 9(1)
. consultation and participation of
    workers .... Dir. 90/269 art. 7
. disapplication ....SI 1992/2793 reg. 3
. discontinuance of potentially
    hazardous activities .... 603(2);
                                SI 1992/2793 reg. 4(1);
                                Dir. 90/269 art. 3(1)
. employees' duties.......SI 1992/2793 reg. 5
. employers' duties................ 603(5);
                                  SI 1992/2793 reg. 4;
                                Dir. 90/269 art. 3–7
. 'ergonomic' approach to adopting
    safer practices.....................601
. exemption certificates, interests of
    national security......SI 1992/2793 reg. 6
. extension outside
    Great Britain ....SI 1992/2793 reg. 7
. identification of potentially
    hazardous activities .... 603(1)
. information, provision of
.. EC Commission on
    implementation of
    directive.............. Dir. 90/269 art. 9

                                Paragraph/Provision
.. employees...................... 603(5);
                                SI 1992/2793 reg. 4;
                                Dir. 90/269 art. 6
.. risk factors .... Dir. 90/269 art. 6(2),
                                              Annex II
. injury, meaning ..... SI 1992/2793 reg. 2(1)
. legislation
.. repealed by....... SI 1992/2793 reg. 8(1),
                                           Sch. 2, Pt. I
.. revoked by .... SI 1992/2793 reg. 8(2),
                                           Sch. 2, Pt. I
. load, meaning....... SI 1992/2793 reg. 2(1)
. manual handling of loads,
    meaning .... Dir. 90/269 art. 2
. manual handling operations,
    meaning.......... SI 1992/2793 reg. 2(1)
. necessity for 601
. organisation of
    workstations .... Dir. 90/269 art. 4
. purpose 601
. re-assessment of non-avoidable
    activities...................603(3), (4);
                                SI 1992/2793 reg. 4(2)
.. assessor .... 603(3)
.. factors to be considered......... 603(3);
                                SI 1992/2793 Sch. 1;
                              Dir. 90/269 Annex I
.. sample form .... 603(4)
.. written record .... 603(3)
. reduction/eradication of risk or
    hazard .... 603(4);
                                SI 1992/2793 reg. 4(1);
                                Dir. 90/269 art. 3(2)
. risk assessment 603;
                                  SI 1992/2793 reg. 4
. training..............Dir. 90/269 art. 6(2)

Meals
. facilities for eating 724;
                                SI 1992/3004 reg. 25(5)

Microfiche – see VDU Regulations

Moving walkways..................... 718;
                                SI 1992/3004 reg. 19;
                                Dir. 89/654 Annex I(13)

N

Noise at Work Regulations 1989 ...... 102(2)

Non-compliance with regulations
. consequences 104

Nursing mothers
. rest facilities 724;
                                SI 1992/3004 reg. 25(4);
                          Dir. 89/654 Annex I(17), II(12)

Index 197

Paragraph/Provision

O

Occupational accidents – see **Accidents**

Offences and penalties
. non-compliance with regulations 104
. personal protective equipment,
    misuse/failure to use . . . . 303(4)

Offices, Shops and Railway Premises Act 1963 . . . . .102(3)

Outdoor workstations 710;
    Dir. 89/654 Annex I(21), II(17)

'Outside workers'
. information/procedures . . . . 205(6);
    SI 1992/2051 reg. 10

Overalls – see **Clothing**

P

Penalties – see **Offences and penalties**

Personal Protective Equipment Regulations
. accommodation for
    equipment . . . . SI 1992/2966 reg. 8
. activities/sectors requiring,
    non-exhaustive list . . . . Dir. 89/656
        Annex III
. application 302;
    Dir. 89/656 art. 1
. citation . . . . SI 1992/2966 reg. 1
. commencement . . . . SI 1992/2966 reg. 1;
    Dir. 89/656 art. 10
. conditions for use. . Dir. 89/656 art. 3, 4(3), 6
. consultation and participation of
    employees . . . . Dir. 89/656 art. 8
. disapplication . . . . .SI 1992/2966 reg. 3
. employers' duties
. . assessment of tasks of at risk
    employees . . . . 303(2);
    SI 1992/2966 reg. 6;
    Dir. 89/656 art. 5
. . continuing obligations . . . . 303(4);
    SI 1992/2966 reg. 10
. . design and manufacture of
    equipment, compliance with EC
    provisions . . . . Dir. 89/656 art. 4(1)
. . employees' awareness of
    risks . . . . Dir. 89/656 art. 4(7)
. . free provision of
    equipment . . . . Dir. 89/656 art. 4(6)
. . information . . . . Dir. 89/656 art. 4(5), 7
. . instruction/training in use . . . . 303(3);
    SI 1992/2966 reg. 9

Paragraph/Provision

. . proper use . . . . 303(4);
    SI 1992/2966 reg. 10;
    Dir. 89/656 art. 4(9)
. . provision of equipment . . . . 303(1);
    SI 1992/2966 reg. 4;
    Dir. 89/656 art. 4(6)
. . training . . . . Dir. 89/656 art. 4(8)
. essential features .303
. exemption certificates, interests of
    national security . . . . . SI 1992/2966 reg. 12
. extension outside
    Great Britain . . . . SI 1992/2966 reg. 13
. information to EC Commission
    on implementation of
    directive . . . . Dir. 89/656 art. 10
. legislation
. . repealed by . . . . SI 1992/2966 reg. 14(2)
. . revoked by . . . . . . SI 1992/2966 reg. 14(3),
        Sch. 3
. list, non-exhaustive . . . Dir. 89/656 Annex II
. . activities/sectors requiring
    equipment . . . . Dir. 89/656 Annex III
. loss or defective equipment,
    employees obligations to report . 303(4);
    SI 1992/2966 reg. 11
. maintenance . . . . SI 1992/2966 reg. 7(1)
. modifications . . . . . . SI 1992/2966 reg. 14(1),
        Sch. 2
. more than one risk, compatibility
    of equipment . . . . 303(1);
    SI 1992/2966 reg. 5;
    Dir. 89/656 art. 4(2)
. more than one user . . . . Dir. 89/656 art. 4(4)
. necessity for 301
. personal protective equipment,
    meaning . . . . SI 1992/2966 reg. 2;
    Dir. 89/656 art. 2
. purpose 301
. relevant EC directives . . SI 1992/2966 Sch. 1
. replacement equipment . . . . SI 1992/2966
        reg. 7(1)
. risk assessment . . . . 303(2);
    SI 1992/2966 reg. 6;
    Dir. 89/656 art. 5
. . specimen survey table . . . . Dir. 89/656
        Annex I
. self-employed persons
. . accommodation for
    equipment . . . . .SI 1992/2966 reg. 8
. . maintenance . . . . SI 1992/2966 reg. 7(2)
. . more than one risk, compatibility
    of equipment . . . . 303(1);
    SI 1992/2966 reg. 5(2);
    Dir. 89/656 art. 4(2)

Personal Protective Equipment Regulations
 – continued   **Paragraph/Provision**
. . proper use . . . . SI 1992/2966 reg. 10
. . provision . . . . 303(1);
           SI 1992/2966 reg. 4(2)
. suitability . . . . 303(1);
           SI 1992/2966 reg. 4(3)
. use . . . . Dir. 89/656 art. 3

Pregnant women/nursing mothers
. rest facilities 724;
           SI 1992/3004 reg. 25(4);
           Dir. 89/654 Annex I(17), II(12)

Process control screens – see **VDU Regulations**

Protective and preventative measures 205;
           SI 1992/2051 reg. 4;
           Dir. 89/391 art. 6
. competent persons to assist
    implementation 206;
           SI 1992/2051 reg. 6;
           Dir. 89/391 art. 7
. meaning . . . . SI 1992/2051 reg. 1(2)

Protective devices
. machinery, dangerous parts . . . . 406(7);
           SI 1992/2932 reg. 11

Protective equipment
. personal – see Personal Protective
    Equipment Regulations

Provision and Use of Work Equipment Regulations 1992 – see **Work Equipment Regulations**

R

'Reasonably practicable'
. explanation of term 103
. manual handling operations,
    measures to reduce/eradicate
    risks . . . . 603(4)
. temporary work sites, provision of
    welfare benefits 702

Rest facilities 724;
           SI 1992/3004 reg. 25;
           Dir. 89/654 Annex I(16), II(11)

Risk assessment
. management of health and safety
    at work . . . . 204; 1992/2051 reg. 3;
           Dir. 89/391 art. 6, 9(1)
. manual handling operations – see
    Manual Handling Regulations

Paragraph/Provision
. personal protective equipment . . . . 303(2);
           SI 1992/2966 reg. 6;
           Dir. 89/656 art. 5
. . specimen survey table . . . . Dir. 89/656
           Annex I
. self-employed persons 204;
           SI 1992/2051 reg. 3(2)
. VDU workstations . . . . . . SI 1992/2792 reg. 2
. . person carrying out assessment . . . . 505(2)
. . risks identified . . . . 505(4)
. . self-assessment by employees . . . . . 505(2)
. . structural approach . . . . 505(1)
. . written record . . . . 505(3)

Risk groups
. protection . . . . Dir. 89/391 art. 15

Roofs
. access for maintenance . . Dir. 89/654 Annex
           I(9.4)

Room dimensions 709;
           SI 1992/3004 reg. 10,
           Sch. 1, Pt. I;
           Dir. 89/654 Annex I(15)

S

Safety devices
. doors and gates 717;
           SI 1992/3004 reg. 18
. escalators and moving walkways 718;
           SI 1992/3004 reg. 19

Safety Representatives and Safety Committees Regulations 1977
. modification . . . . . SI 1992/2051 reg. 17, Sch.

Sanitary conveniences 719;
           SI 1992/3004
           reg. 20, Sch. 1, Pt. II;
           Dir. 89/654
           Annex I(18.3),II(13.2)
. temperature . . . . Dir. 89/654
           Annex I(7.2), II(7.2)

Seating 710;
           SI 1992/3004 reg. 11(3), (4)

Second-hand equipment . . . . 404(3)

Self-employed persons
. Manual Handling Regulations,
    application 602
. outside workers, information/
    procedures . . . . 205(6);
           SI 1992/2051 reg. 10

Index 199

Paragraph/Provision

. personal protective equipment
.. accommodation for
   equipment . . . . SI 1992/2966 reg. 8
.. compatibility, more than
   one risk . . . . 303(1);
   SI 1992/2966 reg. 5(2)
.. maintenance . . . . SI 1992/2966 reg. 7(2)
.. proper use . . . . SI 1992/2966 reg. 10
.. provision . . . . 303(1);
   SI 1992/2966 reg. 4(2)
. risk assessment 204;
   SI 1992/2051 reg. 3(2)
. shared workplaces, co-operation
   and co-ordination . . . . 205(8);
   SI 1992/2051 reg. 9(2)
. temporary workers employed by,
   information . . . . 205(7);
   SI 1992/2051 reg. 13
. work equipment 405;
   SI 1992/2932 reg. 4(2)

Shared workplaces
. co-ordination of measures . . . . 205(8);
   SI 1992/2051 reg. 9

Ships
. master and crew, disapplication of
   regulations
.. management of health and safety
   at work 202;
   SI 1992/2051 reg. 2
.. manual handling operations . SI 1992/2793
   reg. 3
.. personal protective
   equipment . . . . SI 1992/2966 reg. 3(1)
.. work equipment . . . . SI 1992/2932 reg. 3
.. workplace health and
   safety . . . . SI 1992/3004 reg. 3(1)

Showers 720;
   SI 1992/3004 reg. 21;
   Dir. 89/654
   Annex I(18.2), II(13.2)

Skylights
. cleaning 715;
   SI 1992/3004 reg. 16
. opening, design/construction 714;
   SI 1992/3004 reg. 15

Smoking
. rest facilities, protection of
   non-smokers 724;
   SI 1992/3004 reg. 25(3);
   Dir. 89/654
   Annex I(16), II(11.3)

Paragraph/Provision

Staff agencies
. information provided for
  employers and employees . . . . 205(7);
  SI 1992/2051 reg. 13

Stairs
. handrails and guards 711;
   SI 1992/3004 reg. 12(5)

T

Temperature
. extremes of, protection of work
  equipment subject to . . . . 406(9);
  SI 1992/2932 reg. 13;
  Dir. 89/655 Annex (2.10)
. indoor workplaces 706;
   SI 1992/3004 reg. 7;
   Dir. 89/654 Annex I(7), II(7)

Temporary workers
. information to . . . . 205(7);
   SI 1992/2051 reg. 13

Temporary work sites
. provision of welfare benefits 702

Thermometers
. indoor workplaces, temperatures 706;
   SI 1992/3004 reg. 7(3)

Toilets 719;
   SI 1992/3004 reg. 20,
   Sch. 1, Pt. II;
   Dir. 89/654
   Annex I(18.3), II(13.2)
. temperature . . . . Dir. 89/654
   Annex I(7.2), II(7.2)

Traffic routes 711
. danger areas . . . . . . Dir. 89/654 Annex I(12)
. organisation 716;
   SI 1992/3004 reg. 17
. running over/across structure
  containing dangerous substances 712
. suitability 716;
   SI 1992/3004 reg. 17

Training
. employees training in health and
  safety . . . . 205(5);
  SI 1992/2051 reg. 11(2), (3);
  Dir. 89/391 art. 12
. manual handling operations . . . . Dir. 90/269
   art. 6(2)
. personal protective equipment,
  instruction in use . . . . 303(3);
  SI 1992/2966 reg. 9;
  Dir. 89/656 art. 4(8)

Training – continued   **Paragraph/Provision**
. VDU users/operators 509;
        SI 1992/2792 reg. 6;
        Dir. 90/270 art. 6
. work equipment, use and
   supervision .... 406(5);
        SI 1992/2932 reg. 9

Transparent/translucent doors and walls
   — see **Doors; Walls**

V

VDU Regulations
. application 502
. citation .... SI 1992/2792 reg. 1(1)
. commencement ..... SI 1992/2792 reg. 1(1);
        Dir. 90/270 art. 11(1)
. consultation and participation of
   employees .... Dir. 90/270 art. 8
. disapplication ...... SI 1992/2792 reg. 1(4);
        Dir. 90/270 art. 1
. display screen equipment,
   meaning .... 503(1);
        SI 1992/2792 reg. 1(2);
        Dir. 90/270 art. 2(a)
. exemption certificates for interests
   of national security ... SI 1992/2792 reg. 8
. extension outside
   Great Britain .... SI 1992/2792 reg. 9
. eye and eyesight tests 508;
        SI 1992/2792 reg. 5;
        Dir. 90/270 art. 9
.. sample letter/forms for exchange
   of information .... App. A
. information
.. EC Commission, implementation
   of directive .... Dir. 90/270 art. 11
.. users/operators 509;
        SI 1992/2792 reg. 7;
        Dir. 90/270 art. 6
. key areas 504–509
. necessity for 501
. operator, meaning ... SI 1992/2792 reg. 1(2)
. purpose 501
. risk assessment of workstations 505;
        SI 1992/2792 reg. 2
.. person carrying out .... 505(2)
.. risks identified .... 505(4)
.. self-assessment by employees ..... 505(2)
.. structured approach to
   assessment .... 505(1)
.. written record .... 505(3)
. scope 503

Paragraph/Provision
. training for users/operators 509;
        SI 1992/2792 reg. 6;
        Dir. 90/270 art. 6
. use, meaning .... SI 1992/2792 reg. 1(2)
. user, meaning .... SI 1992/2792 reg. 1(2)
. users and operators, classification ... 503(3)
. worker, meaning ...... Dir. 90/270 art. 2(c)
. work routines 507;
        SI 1992/2792 reg. 4;
        Dir. 90/270 art. 7
. workstations .... 503(2)
.. already in service 506;
        SI 1992/2792 reg. 3(2);
        Dir. 90/270 art. 5
.. analysis by employers ... Dir. 90/270 art. 3
.. into service for first time 506;
        SI 1992/2792 reg. 3(1);
        Dir. 90/270 art. 4
.. meaning .... SI 1992/2792 reg. 1(2);
        Dir. 90/270 art. 2(b)
.. minimum requirements 506;
        SI 1992/2792 reg. 3, Sch.;
        Dir. 90/270 Annex
.. risk assessment 505;
        SI 1992/2792 reg. 2

Ventilation of the workplace 705;
        SI 1992/3004 reg. 5, 6;
        Dir. 89/654 Annex I(6), II(6)
. ventilators, opening 714;
        SI 1992/3004 reg. 15;
        Dir. 89/654 Anex I(6)

Visitors
. information/procedures .... 205(3)

W

Walls
. cleanliness 708;
        SI 1992/3004 reg. 9(2);
        Dir. 89/654 Annex I(9.2)
. transparent/translucent, safety
   materials/protection from
   breakage 713;
        Dir. 89/654 Annex I(9.3)

Warning markings
. windows and transparent/
   translucent surfaces 713;
        SI 1992/3004 reg. 14;
        Dir. 89/654 Annex I(11.2)
. work equipment .... 406(14);
        SI 1992/2932 reg. 23, 24;
        Dir. 89/655 Annex (2.15)

Index

Paragraph/Provision

Washing facilities 720;
SI 1992/3004 reg. 21;
Dir. 89/654
Annex I(18.2), II(13.2)

Waste disposal 708;
SI 1992/3004 reg. 9(3)

Windows
. cleaning 715;
SI 1992/3004 reg. 16;
Dir. 89/654 Annex I(10.2)
. opening 714;
SI 1992/3004 reg. 15;
Dir. 89/654 Annex I(10.1)
. safety materials/protection against
 breakage 713;
SI 1992/3004 reg. 14
. warning markings................... 713;
SI 1992/3004 reg. 14

Work Equipment Regulations
. access, safe means of.......... Dir. 89/655
Annex (2.16)
. application..................... 404(5);
SI 1992/2932 reg. 4;
Dir. 89/655 art. 1
. citation............. SI 1992/2932 reg. 1(1)
. commencement....... SI 1992/2932 reg. 1;
Dir. 89/655 art. 10(1)
. consultation and participation of
 workers .... Dir. 89/655 art. 8
. controls and control systems ..... 406(10);
SI 1992/2932 reg. 14–18;
Dir. 89/655 Annex 2(2)
.. controlling changes in operating
 conditions .... SI 1992/2932 reg. 14;
Dir. 89/655 Annex (2.2)
.. controls .... SI 1992/2932 reg. 17
.. control systems ...... SI 1992/2932 reg. 18
.. emergency stop
 controls .... SI 1992/2932 reg. 16;
Dir. 89/655 Annex (2.4)
.. starting equipment .. SI 1992/2932 reg. 14;
Dir. 89/655 Annex (2.2)
.. stop controls........ SI 1992/2932 reg. 15;
Dir. 89/655 Annex
. danger zone,
 meaning........ SI 1992/2932 reg. 11(5);
Dir. 89/655 art. 2(c)
. disapplication .... SI 1992/2932 reg. 3
. EC requirements, compliance ..... 406(6);
SI 1992/2932 reg. 10
. electricity, protection of workers
 exposed to..... Dir. 89/655 Annex (2.19)

Paragraph/Provision

. emissions of gas/vapour/liquid
 dust, extraction devices...... Dir. 89/655
Annex (2.5), (2.17)
. equipment covered .... 404(2)
. exemption certificates, interests of
 national security..... SI 1992/2932 reg. 25
. existing equipment, coverage...... 404(2);
Dir. 89/655 art. 4(1), Annex
. existing health and safety
 legislation, relationship with 402
. explosions, prevention .... Dir. 89/655
Annex (2.18)
. exposed worker, meaning...... Dir. 89/655
art. 2(d)
. extension outside
 Great Britain .... SI 1992/2932 reg. 26
. falling objects, safety devices... Dir. 89/655
Annex (2.5)
. guards and protection devices .. Dir. 89/655
Annex (2.8)
. hired or leased equipment .... 404(4)
. identification of specific risks...... 406(3);
SI 1992/2932 reg. 7
. information
.. EC Commission, implementation
 of directive .... Dir. 89/655 art. 10
.. employees..................... 406(4);
SI 1992/2932 reg. 8;
Dir. 89/655 art. 6
. instructions, availability .... 406(4);
SI 1992/2932 reg. 8;
Dir. 89/655 art. 6
. isolation of energy sources....... 406(11);
SI 1992/2932 reg. 19;
Dir. 89/655 Annex (2.14)
. key factors......................... 404
. legislation
.. repealed by...... SI 1992/2932 reg. 27(1),
Sch. 2, Pt. II
.. revoked by ...... SI 1992/2932 reg. 27(3),
Sch. 2, Pt. II
. lighting........................ 406(12);
SI 1992/2932 reg. 21;
Dir. 89/655 Annex (2.9)
. machinery, dangerous parts .... 406(7);
SI 1992/2932 reg. 11
. maintenance of equipment.... 406(2), (13);
SI 1992/2932 reg. 6, 22;
Dir. 89/655 art. 4(2),
Annex (2.13)
. minimum requirements... Dir. 89/655 art. 4,
Annex
. necessity for 401

Work Equipment Regulations
 – continued   **Paragraph/Provision**

. new equipment, coverage......... 404(2);
    Dir. 89/655 art. 4(1), Annex
. new regulations, relationship with 403
. operator, meaning .....Dir. 89/655 art. 2(e)
. premises or undertakings, meaning . 404(2)
. purpose 401
. relevant EC directives.. SI 1992/2932 Sch. 1
. rupture/disintegration of
    equipment, protection
    measures .... Dir. 89/655 Annex (2.7)
. second-hand equipment .... 404(3)
. self-employed persons............... 405;
    SI 1992/2932 reg. 4(2)
. specific hazards.................. 406(8);
    SI 1992/2932 reg. 12;
    Dir. 89/655 art. 5
. stability of equipment .... 406(12);
    SI 1992/2932 reg. 20;
    Dir. 89/655 Annex (2.6)
. stock-bar, meaning.. SI 1992/2932 reg. 11(5)
. suitability of equipment and
    location of use .... 406(1);
    SI 1992/2932 reg. 5;
    Dir. 89/655 art. 3, Annex (2.12)
.. meaning........... SI 1992/2932 reg. 5(4)
. temperature extremes .... 406(9);
    SI 1992/2932 reg. 13;
    Dir. 89/655 Annex (2.10)
. training in use, supervision and
    management of equipment...... 406(5);
    SI 1992/2932 reg. 9;
    Dir. 89/655 art. 7
.. specific risks .... 406(3);
    SI 1992/2932 reg. 7(2);
    Dir. 89/655 art. 7
. use, meaning........ SI 1992/2932 reg. 2(1)
. use of work equipment,
    meaning............Dir. 89/655 art. 2(b)
. warning devices .. Dir. 89/655 Annex (2.11)
. warning markings............... 406(14);
    SI 1992/2932 reg. 23, 24;
    Dir. 89/655 Annex (2.15)
. work equipment, meaning .... 404(1);
    SI 1992/2932 reg. 2(1);
    Dir. 89/655 art. 2(a)

**Workplace (Health, Safety and Welfare)
    Regulations 1992** — see **Workplace
    Regulations**

Workplace Regulations
. application........................ 702;
    SI 1992/3004 reg. 3;
    Dir. 89/654 art. 1(2)

                                Paragraph/Provision

. ceilings, cleanliness 708;
    SI 1992/3004 reg. 9(2);
    Dir. 89/654 Annex I(9.2)
. citation............. SI 1992/3004 reg. 1(1)
. cleanliness 708;
    SI 1992/3004 reg. 9;
    Dir. 89/654 art. 6
. clothing
.. accommodation for................ 722;
    SI 1992/3004 reg. 23;
    Dir. 89/654
    Annex I(18.1), II(13.1)
.. facilities for changing 723;
    SI 1992/3004 reg. 24;
    Dir. 89/654
    Annex I(18.1), II(13.1)
. commencement..................... 701;
    SI 1992/3004 reg. 1(2), (3);
    Dir. 89/654 art. 10(1)
. consultation and participation of
    workers .... Dir. 89/654 art. 8
. danger areas .... Dir. 89/654
    Annex I(12), II(10)
. disabled employees 701;
    Dir. 89/654 Annex I(20), II(15)
. disapplication .... SI 1992/3004 reg. 3;
    Dir. 89/654 art. 1(2)
. doors
.. construction 717;
    SI 1992/3004 reg. 18;
    Dir. 89/654 Annex I(11.1)
.. safety devices..................... 717;
    SI 1992/3004 reg. 18;
    Dir. 89/654 Annex I(11)
.. transparent/translucent, safety
    materials and markings............ 713;
    SI 1992/3004 reg. 14;
    Dir. 89/654 Annex I(11), II(9)
. drinking water, provision 721;
    SI 1992/3004 reg. 22
. electrical installations .... Dir. 89/654
    Annex I(3), II(3)
. emergency routes and exits .... Dir. 89/654
    Annex I(4), II(4)
.. door markings . Dir. 89/654 Annex I(11.7)
. escalators and moving walkways...... 718;
    SI 1992/3004 reg. 19;
    Dir. 89/654 Annex I(13)
. exemption certificate, interests of
    national security.....SI 1992/3004 reg. 26
. falls/and falling objects 712;
    SI 1992/3004 reg. 13
. fire detection and fire fighting .. Dir. 89/654
    Annex I(5), II(5)

Paragraph/Provision

. first aid rooms and equipment.. Dir. 89/654 Annex I(19), II(14)
. fixtures and fittings, cleanliness .... 708; SI 1992/3004 reg. 9(1)
. floors
.. cleanliness .... 708; SI 1992/3004 reg. 9(2); Dir. 89/654 Annex I(9.2)
.. drainage .... 711; SI 1992/3004 reg. 12(2)
.. obstructions, removal .... 711; SI 1992/3004 reg. 12(3)
.. traffic routes .... 711; SI 1992/3004 reg. 12
. furniture, cleanliness .... 708; SI 1992/3004 reg. 9(1)
. handicapped employees .... 701; Dir. 89/654 Annex I(20), II(15)
. information
.. EC Commission, implementation of directive .... Dir. 89/654 art. 10
.. employees .... Dir. 89/654 art. 7
. interpretation .... SI 1992/3004 art. 2
. legislation
.. repealed by .... SI 1992/3004 reg. 27, Sch. 2, Pt. I
.. revoked by .... SI 1992/3004 reg. 27, Sch. 2, Pt. II
. lighting .... 707; SI 1992/3004 reg. 8; Dir. 89/654 Annex I(8), II(8)
. loading bays and ramps .... Dir. 89/654 Annex I(14)
. maintenance of workplace and equipment .... 704; SI 1992/3004 reg. 5; Dir. 89/654 art. 6
. meals, facilities for eating .... 724; SI 1992/3004 reg. 25(5)
. modifications to workplaces .... 701; Dir. 89/654 art. 5
. necessity for 701
. new workplace, meaning ..... SI 1992/3004 reg. 2(1)
. outdoor workplaces, special provisions Dir. 89/654 Annex I(21), II(17)
. pregnant women/nursing mothers, rest facilities .... 724; SI 1992/3004 reg. 25(4); Dir. 89/654 Annex I(17), II(12)
. public road, meaning. SI 1992/3004 reg. 2(1)
. purpose 701
. requirements .... SI 1992/3004 reg. 4

Paragraph/Provision

. rest facilities .... 724; SI 1992/3004 reg. 25; Dir. 89/654 Annex I(16), II(11)
.. temperature .... Dir. 89/654 Annex I(7.2), II(7.2)
. roofs, safe access to .... Dir. 89/654 Annex I(9.4)
. room dimensions and space .... 709; SI 1992/3004 reg. 10, Sch. 1, Pt. I; Dir. 89/654 Annex I(15)
. sanitary conveniences .... 719; SI 1992/3004 reg. 20, Sch. I, Pt. II; Dir. 89/654 Annex I(18.3), II(13.2)
.. temperature .... Dir. 89/654 Annex I(7.2), II(7.2)
. scope 702
. seating 710
. showers .... 720; SI 1992/3004 reg. 21; Dir. 89/654 Annex I(18.2), II(13.2)
. skylights
.. cleaning .... 715; SI 1992/3004 reg. 16
.. opening .... 714; SI 1992/3004 reg. 15
. stability of buildings .... Dir. 89/654 Annex I(2), II(2)
. temperature of indoor workplaces .... 706; SI 1992/3004 reg. 7; Dir. 89/654 Annex I(7), II(7)
.. thermometers, provision .... 706; SI 1992/3004 reg. 7(3)
. toilets .... 719; SI 1992/3004 reg. 20, Sch. 1, Pt. II; Dir. 89/654 Annex I(18.3), II(13.2)
.. temperature .... Dir. 89/654 Annex I(7.2), II(7.2)
. traffic routes .... 711; SI 1992/3004 reg. 12; Dir. 89/654 art. 6, Annex II(16)
.. danger areas ..... Dir. 89/654 Annex I(12)
.. meaning .... SI 1992/3004 reg. 2(1)
.. organisation .... 716; SI 1992/3004 reg. 17
.. running over/across structure containing dangerous substance 712
.. suitability .... 716; SI 1992/3004 reg. 17

Workplace Regulations
– continued   **Paragraph/Provision**

. transparent/translucent doors and walls
.. safety materials/protection from
    breakage 713;
         SI 1992/3004 reg. 14
.. warning markings 713;
         SI 1992/3004 reg. 14
. ventilation 705;
         SI 1992/3004 reg. 5, 6;
         Dir. 89/654 Annex II(6)
.. ventilators, opening 714;
         SI 1992/3004 reg. 15;
         Dir. 89/654 Annex I(6)
. walls
.. cleanliness...................... 708;
         SI 1992/3004 reg. 9(2);
         Dir. 89/654 Annex I(9.2)
.. transparent/translucent, safety materials/protection from
    breakage 713;
         Dir. 89/654 Annex I(9.3)
. washing facilities 720;
         SI 1992/3004 reg. 21;
         Dir. 89/654 Annex I(18.2)
. waste materials, disposal 708;
         SI 1992/3004 reg. 9(3)
. windows
.. cleaning........................ 715;
         SI 1992/3004 reg. 16;
         Dir. 89/654 Annex I(10.2)

                       Paragraph/Provision
.. opening 714;
         SI 1992/3004 reg. 15;
         Dir. 89/654 Annex I(10.1)
.. safety materials/protection from
    breakage 713;
         SI 1992/3004 reg. 14
.. warning markings 713;
         SI 1992/3004 reg. 14
. workplace, meaning................. 702;
         SI 1992/3004 reg. 2(1);
         Dir. 89/654 art. 2
. workplaces already in use........... 701;
         Dir. 89/654 art. 4, Annex II
. workplaces used for first time 701;
         Dir. 89/654 art. 3, Annex I
. workstations
.. suitability 710;
         SI 1992/3004 reg. 11

Work routines
. VDU users/operators 507;
         SI 1992/2792 reg. 4;
         Dir. 90/270 art. 7

Workstations
. organisation, manual handling
    operations .... Dir. 90/269 art. 4
. outdoor 710
. seating 710;
         SI 1992/3004 reg. 11(3), (4)
. suitability........................ 710;
         SI 1992/3004. reg. 11
. VDU users/operators – see VDU Regulations